"**As** Equine, Animal and Nature
Assisted Psychotherapists...We Live Deeply
Connected to the Ordinary Miracle of "
Nature and Relationship.

NOURISHED

Horses, Animals & Nature in Counselling, Psychotherapy & Mental Health

MEG KIRBY

Aware Publishing

NOURISHED

First published in Australia 2022 by Meg Kirby.

Copyright © 2022 Meg Kirby. All rights reserved.

The moral rights of the author have been asserted.

A catalogue record for this book is available from the National Library of Australia

ISBN: 978-0-6450621-4-4 (Paperback) & 978-0-6450621-5-1 (eBook)

Author: Meg Kirby

Title: Nourished: Horses, Animals & Nature in Counselling, Psychotherapy & Mental Health

Subject: Equine Assisted Therapy, Animal Assisted Therapy, Psychotherapy, Mental Health, Equine Assisted Psychotherapy, Nature Based Therapy, Wilderness Therapy

DISCLAIMER

Cover photography: Cailin Rose Photography

Inside photos: featuring Cailin Rose Photography and stock photos

DEDICATION

2021 was a hard year. I have lost some of my dearest friends
through old age, ill-health and storms.

This book is dedicated to Ali, Image and Lucy.

Ali, your gentleness and beauty is awe-inspiring to me. Image, you ground
me like no-one else with your pure masculine energy and calm way. Lucy, you
delighted me every-day with your open-hearted, trusting and playful being.

I am forever grateful and will remember you, Image, Ali and Lucy with the Deepest Love.

Meg Kirby

ABOUT THE EDITOR

MEG KIRBY

Meg Kirby is a Leading International Education Expert in Equine Assisted Psychotherapy and Animal Assisted Psychotherapy, Author, Founder, Director, Senior Trainer at The Equine Psychotherapy Institute and Animal Assisted Psychotherapy International, Mental Health Social Worker and Gestalt Therapist of over 25 years, Supervisor, Leadership Coach and Mentor.

Meg is passionate about supporting people from all walks of life to discover true freedom, to begin to deeply trust the wisdom of their body, feelings and whole-being, and to fall in love with Life, with the support and wisdom from horses, all animals and nature.

Meg began working in Child and Adolescent Psychiatry and Mental Health Inpatient and Outpatient Units, before moving to Adult Mental Health Therapeutic Community practice and working with Dual Diagnosis and Complex Needs, and finally settling into Private Practice as a Psychotherapist incorporating room-based, equine assisted, animal assisted, and nature assisted psychotherapy for children, adults, couples, families and organisations.

In 2011, Meg created and founded The Equine Psychotherapy Institute offering Australia's first comprehensive, private training pathway for students looking for robust education in equine assisted psychotherapy (for registered mental health professionals) and equine assisted learning (for teachers, animal-based professionals, coaches and disability workers).

The Institute is internationally renowned and nationally revered for delivering a humanistic, relationally-oriented and trauma-informed psychotherapy model, founded on an ethical inclusion of horses, and all animals. Meg developed her innovative I-Thou-Horse-Person-ship approach, to ensure horses' subjective experience was included in all EPI model sessions, to protect horse welfare and include an ethical foundation. Meg developed and teaches I-Thou Inter-species relating in the context of animal assisted psychotherapy and learning.

Meg published her first book in 2016, *An Introduction to Equine Assisted Psychotherapy: principles, theory and practice of the Equine Psychotherapy Institute Model*. She has since authored a second book, *Equine Therapy Exposed: Real Life Case Studies of Equine Assisted Psychotherapy and Equine Assisted Learning with Everyday People and Horses*: This book is an innovative behind the scenes look into what equine assisted therapy is, and how it works, with diverse clinical clients. This brand new, ground-breaking book has received praise and endorsement from academics and leading professionals in the field, across the nation and around the globe, for its engaging and in-depth look inside the inner workings of equine assisted therapy and equine assisted learning.

When Meg is not training students from all across the globe in equine, animal, and nature assisted psychotherapy, she spends her time caring for twelve family herd members, five kangaroo friends, five expressive cats, and dear dog, Bear, who is never far from her side. Not forgetting her loving husband, Noel, and two beautiful daughters, Rose and Jasmine. Meg lives and breathes the wisdom of animals and nature.

ACKNOWLEDGEMENTS

I want to share my heart-felt gratitude to each contributing author who so generously connected with me and shared their work in this book. It has been a challenge to bring together such a vibrant, passionate, and busy group of individuals...but absolutely worth every moment. We are each on a special mission, as you will read, and we share a common goal.

This type of international collaboration across the fields of equine, animal and nature assisted psychotherapy is a first, and one I am honoured to have played a role in creating. I am so thankful for the kindness of spirit of each of you.

I wish to give special thanks to Ayesha Hilton, Paula Jewell, and Stacey Andrew, who help me make things happen at the Institute. You are all amazing humans, and I couldn't have created this book without you all. I am also grateful to Cailin Rose who produced some beautiful photography featuring my dear inter-species friends for the front cover, back cover, and inside the book. The unique tone of Cailin's photography is very special and allowed me to add a very personal and Australian feel, to this internationally significant book.

I am eternally grateful to my daughters Jasmine and Rose, my husband Noel, and my beautiful extended family – my equine friends, Image, Ali, Stormy, River, Crystal, Star, Lily, Raj, Jensen, Amir, Ashaar, Exquisite, Mindy and Lexy; my feline friends Tilly, Edward and Pumpkin; my dear canine friend Bear; and my kangaroo friends Harry, Lucy, Luca, Dixie, Lottie and Lulu-Star. I love, live and share my life with you all, and you make Life incredibly beautiful. Thank you.

Meg Kirby

CONTENTS

Part 3: Nature - Nature Assisted Therapy

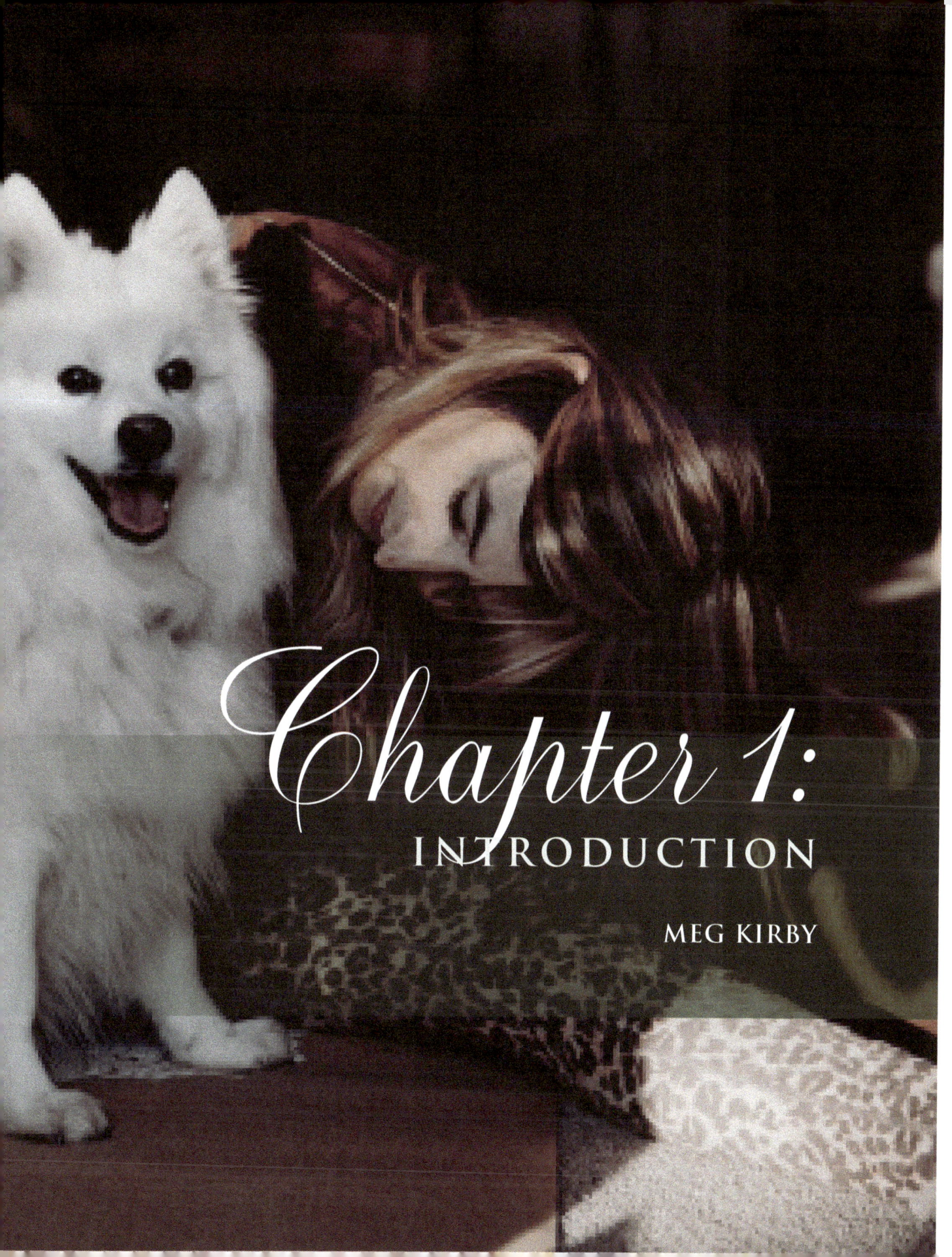

Chapter 1:
INTRODUCTION

MEG KIRBY

WHY NOURISHED?

L et us begin this book by tuning into the big picture.

Why Nourished?

Why this book?

It has become my personal passion and mission, and now The Equine Psychotherapy Institute's mission, to bring equine, animal and nature assisted psychotherapy and learning services, education and training to the world.

On some level, you the reader understand this is the nourishment needed, as it's partly what drew you to pick up and start reading this book! You know intuitively and perhaps personally or professionally, there is deep nourishment available in equine assisted therapy, animal assisted therapy, and nature assisted therapy, that is unlike any other form of therapy. There is a unique wisdom of horses, of animals, and of the forests, the bush, the ocean, and the natural environment, that is undeniable, and so very needed right now.

This book, will hopefully, help you understand exactly what that unique nourishment could look like across different practice approaches, and give you ideas, inspiration and networks to begin your journey into this emerging field of practice and new ways of thinking.

A big part of why, and why now, is directly related to the unique challenges inherent in this

I trust
you will enjoy
the journey,
reading and feeling
into the sessions, and
reflecting on the theory
and practice, the
key ingredients that
support client change.

particular time in history. We are all currently managing the COVID-19 pandemic and the reality of climate change is no longer something to debate or ignore. This is impacting us all in various shared, and uniquely personal, ways. I believe that now, more than ever, the world really needs different kinds of support, education, advocacy, services, and therapeutic practices, that meet the unique stressors and suffering that people are experiencing. It could be argued, the world, all people, and our environments, really need equine, animal, and nature assisted work right now.

THE PROBLEM

The current context and our so-called *modern* ways of living present people with unique challenges and stressors. These are calling for *different responses, radical shifts in thinking, practice and different service-provision.* As a species, we have largely become an indoor species. Around the world, many people now spend a majority of their time indoors. Just pause to consider that. As social mammals, humans now spend most of their time indoors – not connected to the ground, the earth, the natural elements, the light, the changing weather, and the natural systems. Many are largely disconnected (to varying degrees) from the soil, the seasons, trees, forests, lakes and oceans, flora and fauna, and the various species of animals who co-inhabit this wonderful planet of earth. Consider the impact of this *modern* shift, this dis-connect, on our physiology, psychology, and overall well-being, and on our shared human existence and our shared human struggles. Consider the impact of this on the current climate change crisis.

We have become a technologically-based species. Technology dominates how we spend our time. We are spending a lot of time looking at screens. That has not only increased our existing disconnection to nature and the natural world, but it has also created a degree of techno-stress. Children and adults are constantly checking their phones, working on tablets, laptops, and computer games, compulsively photographing, sharing, updating and feeling the need to be continually connected on social media, and maintaining a public profile or facade. Pause to consider how this could contribute to dysregulation of the nervous system, psychological distress, social dis-connection, mental health conditions and a deeper disconnect from oneself, and from social intimacy and community living (including a slower or more mindful way of living in connection with the natural world). Consider the degree of disconnect from the earth's natural cycles and the needs of a healthy planet, that has become the norm for the human species on the whole.

Mental health practitioners are hearing how indoor and city-based living, coupled with technologically-based stressors, are being further exacerbated by the fear, unpredictability, distress and loss associated with adapting to the COVID-19 virus and the ever-changing personal, social, political and scientific goalposts associated with the pandemic. Lockdowns are creating financial and business-related loss that is irreparable, psychological distress, all leading to mental health deterioration that is sometimes permanent, with increased rates of suicide. Many people are struggling with disconnection, disembodiment, stress, and anxiety as the new norm. Humans, on the whole, are experiencing levels of high stress, anxiety, depression and suicidality. Somatic health-related illnesses are through the roof, including headaches, migraines, fatigue, insomnia, diabetes, and heart disease.

Workaholism has also become the norm. We have largely become an urban species and many people and businesses gravitate around cities. City life is inherently stressful and inherently disconnected from the natural world, no matter how hard we try to develop green pockets, parks, and design. Our modern life is overwhelming for many. High levels of sickness or un-wellness are the new norm, including high rates of heart attack, stroke, cancer, and addictions. We cannot think clearly, or behave or orient to what is needed, when we are un-well and disconnected.

Previous to the climate change awareness and the current COVID-19 pandemic, the World Health Organization had already identified stress as the health epidemic of the 21st century. Now stress and suffering is significantly further magnified. Remember, these current conditions and stressors exist on top of all the *complexities and difficulties that we all face in just being human.* It is incredibly hard to be a healthy human in today's age. Blessed (or cursed) with our unique brain structure (including our frontal lobes, and capacity to reflect continually on ourselves, others, and the world), physiology, body, heart, and mind — it is arguably an enormous challenge to be a healthy human social mammal, in these so-called modern times.

Clearly, we, as a human species, *need ways* to manage stress, to think clearly, manage our mental health and physical health, and manage current crises on a global scale. We need new ways to manage all these complexities and all these difficulties, and, we need a different way to live. We need a different *guidance* to step towards a new paradigm of health and wellbeing (for ourselves, our natural world, and the planet). A guidance that helps us to transcend the modern disadvantages, restrictions, and constraints, that we have mostly (ironically and unfortunately) developed for ourselves. Part of the solution needs to come from *outside of ourselves.* Outside of our modernised, logical, human ways of perceiving, relating, thinking, and organising our experience.

THE SOLUTION

Now is the time for a different kind of guidance, support, care, connection, awareness, and knowing. A new guidance to ultimately ensure not just the survival and wellness of our species, but the survival and wellness of all species, the natural environment, and the planet as a whole.

I believe that the answer partly lies (of course only partly) in what has brought you to this book! The answer partly lies in expanding, extending and re-thinking how we support ourselves, each-other, and the environment with personal and professional development, education, therapy, design and action that incorporates and is guided by the wisdom of animals and the natural environment.

When we begin to understand the truth that our existence, our survival and capacity to thrive, is inextricably linked and inter-dependent on our co-existence and good relationship with all species and the natural world, then we start to understand that good health for ourselves is good health for all. Health for all, or shared-health, requires humans, animals, and nature to relate and co-inhabit in completely new ways.

To heal the dis-connect and move towards this shared-health, naturally, we look towards connection, inter-connection, relating, and relationship. Psychotherapy, therapy and counselling are founded on the premise that, *fundamentally, it is the medium of and experience of relating and relationship, that holds the capacity to heal*. In psychotherapy, (regardless of the different theoretical and practice approaches or biases) we understand that it is the container of *safe, supportive, challenging, relating and relationship* that sits as the fertile ground for growth, learning, change, and healing. When we consider the modern challenges humans and the planet face, with an understanding of shared-health, and the sensibilities and wisdom of psychotherapy, naturally, we start to look toward a new solution. I believe, this solution must include our animal friends, nature, and our natural environment, to support, teach, and guide us *back home* towards a deeper connection and potential for growth and re-generation. We are, of course, nature.

THE NEEDED NOURISHMENT
EQUINE, ANIMAL AND NATURE ASSISTED THERAPY

Equine assisted therapy, animal assisted therapy and nature-based therapy essentially incorporates horses, domestic animals, wildlife, and elements of nature, the natural world and our eco-system into therapeutic practice. In this way, counselling, psychotherapy, clinical practice, or mental health work transcends the traditional container, limitations, safety or constraints of room-based practice. *Therapy becomes enlivened by the multi-layered relationships and natural, spontaneous intelligence of horses, other animals, and the natural world.* It offers clients the potential richness of relationship and meaningful exchange, a re-connection to one's senses, a rainbow of seasonal gifts, and an opportunity to tap into the wisdom of animals and the natural world. This acts as an incredible support for people to start to breathe, ground, regulate, connect, attach safely, work through ruptures and trauma, express, feel enlivened, learn about the world, and so much more. It can offer nourishment that goes well beyond the confines of traditional psychotherapy, inspiring a deeper change, care, kindness and want to give back and protect the natural eco-systems that we are all dependent on and a part of. Care, protection, and a *sustainability sensibility* is inspired through this most important work. This work has the potential to develop a deeper, more profound understanding of our shared-health. This work has the potential, at its greatest impact, to save our species and the planet, through connection.

A PERSONAL NOTE

I have heard and shared in many people's journeys, witnessing how distressing this time has been for many — the loss, the fear, the panic, and the unknown has been devastating and created much suffering. Personally, during this COVID-19 context, I have managed to stay sane, to be present, to be connected deeply to my family, my animal friends (including my herd of 12 horses, my mob of 6 kangaroos, cats and my dog Bear), and the natural environment that I live in. The reason I remain so well in this difficult time, the reason I am so readily able to regulate and maintain connection to the beauty and the good in life, is due to *how and where I live*. I have developed *a way of life* that relies on and includes not just safe and nourishing practices with people, but most essentially, nourishing practices with animals and nature. It is this way of life, this way of living, that keeps me really well in times of stress and times of peace, equally. Animal and nature-based wisdom supports and guides me in my daily quest for wellness.

My equine, animal and nature assisted therapy practice and teachings, nourish, ground, connect, and support my regulation, resilience, creativity, and my ability to continually grow, potentialise, and contribute to others' wellbeing. This does not mean I do not experience intense feelings, stress, disturbance or traumatic experiences, but it does mean I know how to live well with the disturbance in the difficult times. Resilience is born of this work.

OUR INTERNATIONAL COLLABORATION OF KINDNESS AND DEEP APPRECIATION FOR DIVERSITY

Together, the following chapters offer you the reader an incredible smorgasbord of juicy, nourishing, creative, and diverse approaches in equine, animal, and nature assisted therapy from educational experts and leaders around the globe. It is because of our diversity, that this book is so nourishing. We all come together to share our deep allegiance and passion for horses, all animals, and the natural world, as a source for healing, growth, and learning. And we all think about and do this work differently.

I wanted to showcase our diversity, as a model for how to be different, and not necessarily agree, but absolutely co-exist with integrity, kindness and a trust that there is room for everyone. I invite you to whole-heartedly taste each author's work. Dip your toes into their world, perspectives, theories, and practices, and feel the nourishment that is available from within these diverse approaches.

Trust your heart and follow your interest and passion. Bringing animals and nature into therapy is truly rewarding and potentially healing for our clients, ourselves, the animals, the natural world, and the planet as a whole.

Meg Kirby

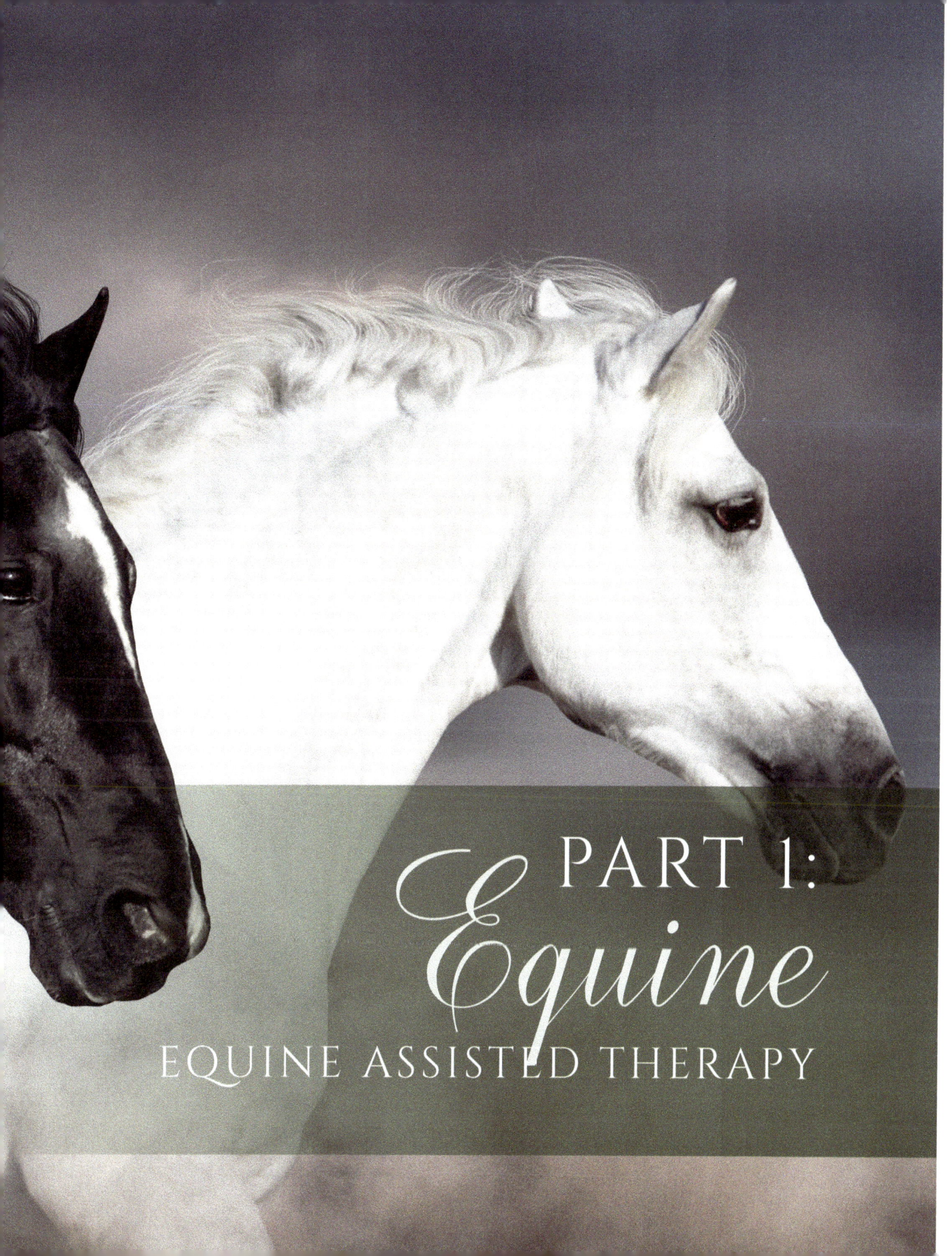

PART 1:
Equine
EQUINE ASSISTED THERAPY

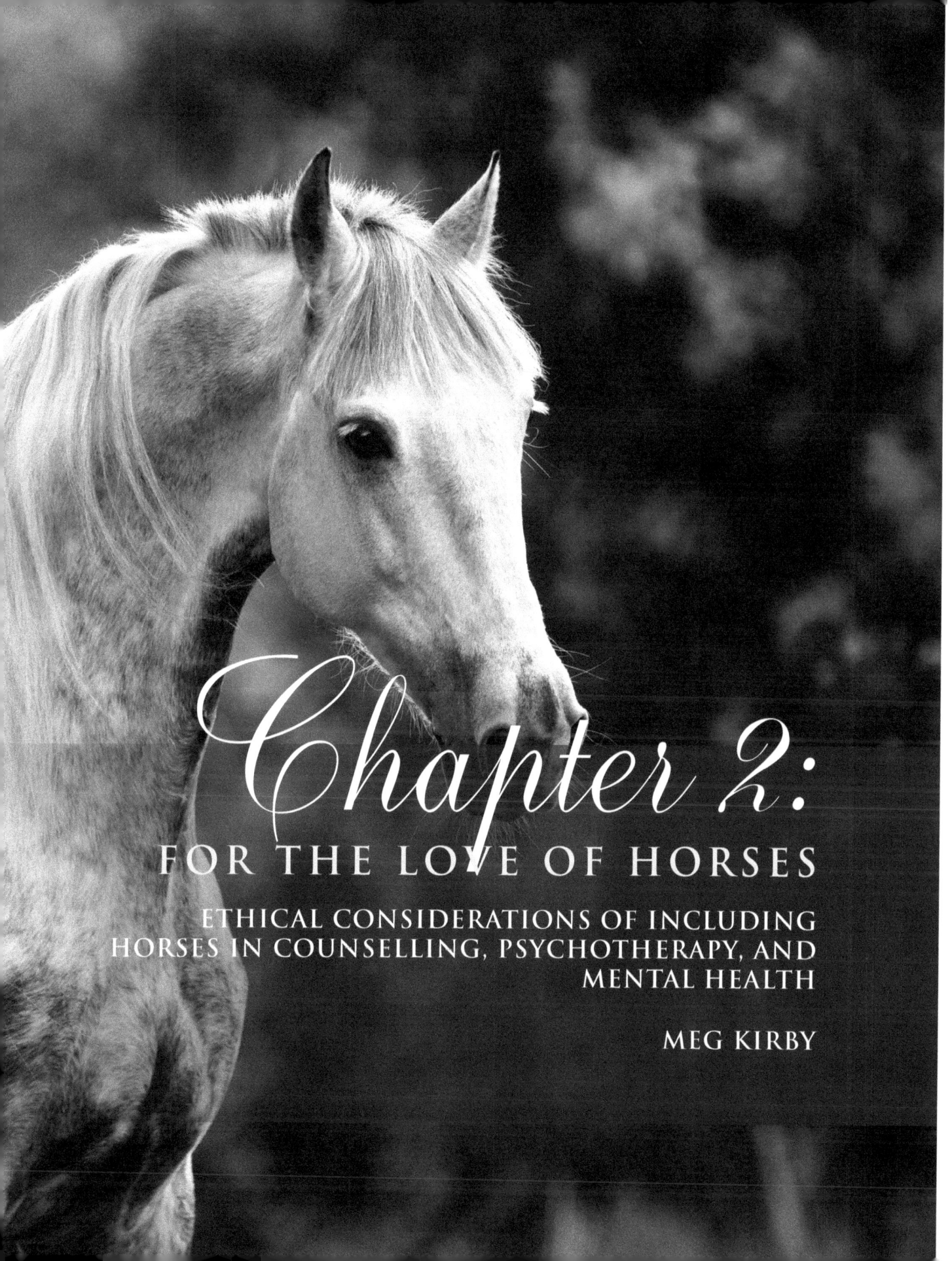

Chapter 2:

FOR THE LOVE OF HORSES

ETHICAL CONSIDERATIONS OF INCLUDING HORSES IN COUNSELLING, PSYCHOTHERAPY, AND MENTAL HEALTH

MEG KIRBY

ABOUT MEG

Degree Psychology / Sociology, Masters Social Work, Diploma Gestalt Therapy, Mental Health Social Worker, Psychotherapist of 25 years, Founder, Director, Head of Learning at The Equine Psychotherapy Institute & Animal Assisted Psychotherapy International

Meg Kirby is an international leader in the growing field of Equine Assisted Psychotherapy and is passionate about the ethical considerations of working with horses in a therapeutic environment. Meg heads The Equine Psychotherapy Institute, Australia's leading educational and training organisation for equine assisted psychotherapy and equine assisted learning, delivering live, online and postgraduate equivalent training to Australian and international students.

INTRODUCTION

Equine Assisted Psychotherapy (EAP) is growing in popularity throughout Australia, the United States, Europe, and all across the globe. Clients are drawn to psychotherapy, counselling, trauma practice and mental health services that incorporate horses into their practice, because in many ways clients feel emotionally safer with horses than with people. Many clients feel more engaged, interested and motivated to do their personal work and address trauma and challenges in their life, if horses are supporting, facilitating, assisting and engaged alongside them. Horses can be very effective change agents and supports for therapeutic growth and learning when included by knowledgeable and well-trained practitioners facilitating equine assisted psychotherapy.

I have been educating, training and supervising allied health practitioners, counsellors and psychotherapists in equine assisted psychotherapy at The Equine Psychotherapy Institute since 2011. Over the last decade, I have noticed a steady increase in demand for this sophisticated work from the public and varied client cohorts, as described in my book, *Equine Therapy Exposed: Real Life Case Studies of Equine Assisted Psychotherapy and Equine Assisted Learning with Everyday People and Horses*. Our PACFA Accredited (Psychotherapy and Counselling Federation of Australia) *Postgraduate equivalent in Equine Assisted Psychotherapy* offers an internationally competitive level of training and education, being one of only a few educational experiences worldwide, offered at this postgraduate equivalent standard. This is wonderful and potentially very rewarding work for many clients. It appears to increase psychotherapeutic outcomes for some client groups. Robust research is yet to provide a platform for a solid evidence-based practice, but I feel confident that this will happen in good time, with good research.

One of the big ethical questions that must be asked in the context of equine assisted psychotherapy then is, how do we incorporate horses in a way that serves the horses well? Additionally, how do we ensure horses are not used for client outcomes? How do we ensure the horses have consent, are engaged in dialogue (non-verbal inter-species dialogue), and are empowered in the process? In a nutshell, how do we ensure the horses' safety, welfare and wellbeing is centre-stage in the practice of equine assisted psychotherapy and the ever-increasing demand for these services? How can we ensure our services are ethical?

IT'S IN THE HOW

I believe, the answers to the above questions are found in *the how*. How horses are included in psychotherapy and experiential learning services is dictated by how *the individual practitioner includes the horses*, and, how the *model of EAP* that the practitioner is applying in their practice, conceptualises, theorises, and literally includes the horses in the therapeutic process. This includes the *initial invitation and consent*, the *ongoing consent*, the ongoing *role of the horse* during the session, as well as, the *care, support, education and management of the horse or herd* after the session.

The practitioner brings their own personal tendencies, including their temperament, patterns, values, experience of trauma, personal history, and understanding and practice of being with horses, into the equine assisted psychotherapy context. What is their knowledge and understanding of equine behaviour, herd behaviour, equine communication, and the unique needs of the equine species? What are their horsemanship skills, their understanding of equitation science and their horse management skills? How do they meet their horses' basic needs for clean water, nutrition, shelter, herd living and socialisation, movement, grazing, and meet their unique species tendencies around prey, play and herd instincts and behaviours?

The practitioner brings all of this, including the way they relate, handle, train, ride (potentially) and care for horses, into both the equine assisted psychotherapy session and broader context. The model of equine assisted psychotherapy that the practitioner is trained in and applies, determines the role of the horse, and, therefore how horses are included into the equine assisted psychotherapy context. These factors profoundly shape the *experience of the horse* in equine assisted psychotherapy, the experience the client receives, and the overall ethics of the practice.

PRACTICE

In Australia and around the world, there are many models of equine assisted psychotherapy, and we teach a unique model of equine assisted psychotherapy at The Equine Psychotherapy Institute that integrates the AWARE Therapy™ Approach – a humanistic psychotherapy synthesis of relational gestalt therapy, mindfulness psychotherapy, somatic experiencing trauma approaches, cognitive-behavioural therapy, and neuroscience. The ten overarching theoretical and practice principles include — **A**wareness; **W**isdom **A**pproach (horse wisdom); **R**elationship; regulation; resourcing; **E**xperiential; experiments and experimenting; **E**mbodiment; ethical orientation; and enrichment.

ETHICS

At its simplest, ethics is a system of moral principles. Ethics is concerned with what is good, right, and moral. So ethically, equine assisted psychotherapy practitioners must consider *is this good for the horse?* This is different to *is this tolerable for the horse? Is this safe for the horse?* For example, the horse will not be physically harmed or is this okay for the horse?

This question would be answered by different horse-people in very different ways, given their principles, theories, practice, skills, and education. Is this good for the horse to be a part of your services with clients? How is it good for the horse? Physically, emotionally, mechanically (bio-mechanics lens), psychologically and from the perspective of protecting and honouring the horses' species-specific needs for herd-life, prey and play tendencies?

These are important questions for equine assisted practitioners, that I believe, we must consider and fundamentally integrate into our code of ethics and ethical conduct in practice. It is the practitioner's ethical responsibility to be continually reflecting on these questions in an ongoing way.

DEVELOPMENT OF THE EQUINE PSYCHOTHERAPY INSTITUTE MODEL

Historically, when I first created our Practitioner Training model 10 years ago in 2011, I was looking for ways to bring equine studies and horsemanship into the training, so I could not only bring consistency and standardise the equine assisted psychotherapy and equine assisted learning (a non-therapeutic approach) practitioner model that I was teaching in Australia, but, most importantly, so I could address head-on, the ethical issues, horse welfare and wellbeing issues that inevitably arise, when we bring horses into psychotherapy, human development and education services.

Horse consent, safety and welfare was the single most important area of interest and concern when developing my new model of equine assisted psychotherapy and equine assisted learning. The Equine Psychotherapy Institute model of equine assisted psychotherapy and equine assisted learning had to, at its very core, serve the horses' well, benefit the horses, and potentially even heal the horses (with trauma) alongside the great and varied benefits for the human clients. That was my mission. And remains my mission today.

Being a Gestalt Psychotherapist since 1997 (over 25 years!), my focus and practice has always been *relationally oriented*, focusing on the clients' subjective experience in relationship, and, utilising the practitioner-client relationship per se, as the experiential learning mechanism. So, I was looking for a way to include *the horses' subjective experience and relational experience* into our model of practice, alongside, foundational education that would provide equine knowledge and skills.

I considered a lot of equine education avenues and horsemanship models, but fundamentally could not find what I was looking for. There was nothing I found that focused on both the equine knowledge and training skill, and importantly, included in the theory and methodology, *the horses' experience*. Different horsemanship, riding coaching and equine studies appeared to all have so much diversity in the knowledge and skills utilised, and there were no unifying values, interest, and methodology to *include the horses' subjective experience, communications, needs and wants into the horse-human interaction*. Even some of the Australian safety protocols that were being taught unfortunately, appeared to, at best, miss the horses' feelings, behaviours, activation and stress responses, and at worst, trigger activation and stress responses in the horse. The opposite, of what I was looking to include in our model

of relational psychotherapy practice. Essentially, I was looking for a relational template that included consent, mutuality, mutual benefit, deep care, safety and welfare of both horse and human parties. I could not find one such template!

So, in 2011, I developed "*I-Thou Horsemanship*", which I described and published in my book, An Introduction to Equine Assisted Psychotherapy: Principles, Theory and Practice of the Equine Psychotherapy Institute Model" in 2016. I have since re-named this as *I-Thou Horse-person-ship*, addressing the important issue of gender neutrality.

This addressed at least the latter part of what I felt was essential to teach new practitioners in equine assisted practice, to ensure the horses' subjective experience, wellbeing, safety and welfare was centre stage in the practice. It does not, however, replace the essential equine knowledge and horse education knowledge and skill, which sits underneath and alongside *I-Thou Horse-person-ship* approach, to together, provide the equine training components of our EPI (The Equine Psychotherapy Institute) Foundation Training in Equine Assisted Psychotherapy and Equine Assisted Learning Practitioner.

I-THOU HORSE-PERSON-SHIP AS AN ETHICAL STANCE

I-Thou was first coined by Martin Buber (1878-1965). When I learnt about his work 28 years ago as a Gestalt therapy and psychotherapy student and beginning therapist, it marked the beginning of a change in my interest and capacity to practice as a relationally based psychotherapist. Buber's focus was on relating to the "whole person" and exploring "dialogic intersubjectivity". His I-Thou relating concept included, in a nutshell, an understanding that there was essentially no I that stands alone, rather an I and Thou, or an I and It.

I and Thou relating can very generally be understood as presence based relating, where each *being* relates to the being-ness of the other, without any need to change the other but rather feel into the other's experience so there could be an experience of the other's subjectivity and potentially a shared experience of inter-subjectivity. I and It relating is essentially strategic relating, where one orients to the other in an attempt to influence, change, direct, use or achieve something requiring a degree of objectification and using the "relating with other", as a means to get to a greater goal or end, for example, to change their behaviour or influence the other to do something for them.

This inter-subjectivity between the horse-client and practitioner is essentially what I wished to teach equine assisted psychotherapy and equine assisted learning students about, to ensure the focus of the practice was relationally-based and furthermore, served to ensure the horses' experience, feelings, needs, behaviours and consent was not missed, used or mis-used in the service of the *so-called* greater goal of client change, growth and development. Horse knowledge and horse training skills were not enough, on their own, to invite horses into a relationally oriented encounter (and service), where the "live" relationship included consent, invitation and an exploration of the subjective experience of the client whilst including the subjective experience of the horse (to varying degrees dependent on the therapeutic goals of the client).

I -Thou Horse-person-ship has as its primary focus *regard for the horse, his or her feelings, wants and needs*, as the most important intention in the relating, relationship and /or training (in the context of broader horse education and training).

I-Thou relating is both an intention and practice. It is an intimate form of contact that includes an intimate "felt sense", a deep attention and openness to connect with the horse, with no need or want for the horse to be any different than who she or he is. It is a deep reverence for the unique being that is the horse before you, and no need or want to change him or her, in their essence. It is an attunement and curiosity about the horse's inner world, an awareness of our shared 'being' (human and equine as "beings" meeting) and an opportunity for an authentic and expressive connecting that can only occur, of this moment, and of this unique encounter.

It requires then that the practitioner conducting the equine assisted practice develops four capacities. These include:

1. Presence
2. Inclusion
3. Confirmation
4. Commitment to "Dialogue"

1. PRESENCE

Presence includes developing capacities around being authentically open, vulnerable, and available. Not "seeming", pretending, or being attached to how you may appear or want the 'other' to view you. You are not the "trainer" or "horseperson", rather the other being "showing up" in your experiential truth to meet the horse. This requires being present with your horse. This is often quite difficult, at first, for many horse-people entrenched in a paradigm of thinking, behaving and valuing horses', related to their behaviour, performance, or appearance. This skill of becoming present to the horse, as another being with their own individuality and needs, develops over time, with lots of training and support, to peel back the layers of previous orienting and training, and, to develop a lot of foundational skills in awareness and phenomenological practice including open curiosity.

2. INCLUSION

Inclusion is deeply attuning to the unique phenomenological experience and world of the horse. Feeling into, getting curious about, imagining into the experience of the other, whilst also remaining in contact with your own sense of self (so you are not projecting onto the horse, your feelings, needs, tendencies, and patterns). Stepping into what would it feel like to be this horse, in this moment, what is this horse experiencing, feeling in their body, wanting, and communicating to me right now? Putting yourself inside your horse's experience, life, relationships, and species-perspective, and wanting to deeply feel into and know him/her.

Again, this skill develops over time and practice, once practitioners have developed a lot of awareness skill, phenomenological skill including bracketing and processing their own feelings, unconscious patterns, and tendencies. One cannot stay grounded and present to their own experience, whilst observing and feeling into the experience of the other, without being skilful in, first, knowing their own experience, feelings, and patterned ways of thinking, believing, and behaving in relationship. Without this essential personal awareness work, the human simply projects... which is the opposite of inclusion!

3. CONFIRMATION

Confirmation is offered to our horses as a pervasive attitude of offering *unconditional positive regard*, accepting, and loving the being that is before you, in all his/her uniqueness, inherent value, and potential. "I see your uniqueness, I accept you as you are, I value you, I honour your potential to grow...with the right field conditions." This is especially important when in moments of challenge, confusion, or difficulty in relating with the horse, when the human feels frustrated and pressured, wanting the horse to be different than they are in the moment.

Utilising confirmation skills when training or educating horses is essential (which many equine assisted psychotherapy and equine assisted learning practitioners do outside of their sessions or practice), as this attitude and skill sits alongside our skilful capacity to track the horses' activation and deactivation levels and behaviours, body language and overall window of tolerance for exposure to novelty, cues or environmental shifts.

When training, we value the horse as they ARE, and, for their potential, as operationalised or demonstrated in the moment of the horses' responses. Without confirmation skills, horses can easily become tools for human service or activities, in the context of equine assisted psychotherapy and equine assisted learning, and in the context of horse education and training, they can easily drift too far into the human's needs and goals, and loose mutuality and true relationship.

4. COMMITMENT TO "DIALOGUE"

This dialogic (non-verbal relating) attitude is expressed by holding an intention to "hang in there" when the connection becomes difficult or uncomfortable, not giving up on the other, judging, blaming and withdrawing from the relationship with the horse. Stepping into the real work of relationship — working through differences, conflict, rupture and repair and commitment to the relationship and mutual understanding across species.

This principle is expressed in practice by not "giving up" on the horse, blaming them, turning away from the relationship, and seeing difference and difficulty as an inherent part of inter-species relationship. "*I am here for you. I am here to grow with you and from our relationship together. I understand you are different from me, as a species, as an individual, and I am committed to finding safe ways to communicate and be together, in a way that serves us both well.*"

Your Horses are not your Therapist – Horses are Whole, Complete Equine Beings.

With the development of these four attitudes and skills comes the possibility for profound connection with horses, and natural opportunities for growth and change. You cannot go unchanged in a connection with another, such as this. It is life changing for both the human and the horse.

Then, when we add these attitudes and skills into the arena with clients, we set up a safe relational container for clients to witness and experience this intimate form of relationship that is essentially attuned, present, accepting, hopeful and committed. All the ingredients of an emotionally safe, healthy relationship that is the ground for both or all parties to the relationship to feel safe, seen, heard, valued, and co-creating the shared experience.

THE SAFE RELATIONAL CONTAINER IS THE CORNERSTONE OF PSYCHOTHERAPY AND EQUINE ASSISTED PSYCHOTHERAPY

Practitioners bring in these skills and attitudes into the session with the client-horse/herd-practitioner relationship, and this supports the three-way relating of presence, deep acceptance, differentiation, valuing uniqueness and leaning into any relational challenges with an attitude of open curiosity and commitment. Practitioners are trained to develop these skills independently with human clients and with horses, so that they can combine these skills in the context of the practitioner-client-horse/herd relational system.

The depth of this healing relationship is a core component in The Equine Psychotherapy model theory of change — where change happens in the context of a very particular relationship being developed that deepens therapeutic growth and acts as a developmentally corrective experience and supports trauma-informed practice. A corrective experience is broadly speaking, a powerful process where the client experiences a core attachment need (such as attunement, mirroring, touch, holding or movement that is regulating and soothing) being met in the here and now. The client has a chance to update their experience of self, other or life, supporting a healthy life trajectory. These experiences will often help re-condition an old memory with a new memory or association of healing, or, development of mastery, expression, or empowerment, supporting long-term change.

Within the context of the I-Thou triad of relating between practitioner-horse-client, the qualities of presence, inclusion, confirmation, and commitment to dialogue serve to foster and operationalise,

opportunities for attachment based corrective experiences. For example, a client who has a history of being parented by a typically avoidantly-attached parent may share (verbally or non-verbally) with their practitioner and horse, unmet needs for being seen, held, touched, and attuned to. Whilst the horse (miraculously) approaches with a softness, intimacy and approach towards the client, that they have (reportedly) never experienced before. The I-Thou relating container sets up the potential for the being-ness of the horse to be experienced, the being to being of the client-horse experience, and the present, inclusion of the human practitioner holding space for and supporting both the horse and client to meet together in a safe and organically authentic, emergent way.

TRAUMA INFORMED PRACTICE

Trauma informed practice is supported via the *safety of the relating that I-Thou provides*. The I-Thou approach with horses supports the ground for emotionally and psychologically safe ways of interacting, where there is no (unintentional) violation, pressure or force between the practitioner and horse (e.g. where the horse is not required or made to meet or move without consent, carry a rider without consent, do a lap of an arena due to pressure, perform a behaviour due to an "aide" or "cued" or trained command). These are all examples of *I-It relating*, where the objective of the relating or interaction is to produce a desired outcome or result, rather than meeting *being to being*, and tracking the emergent relating or emergent experience.

When working with clients with trauma, for example, the *relational environment* that the practitioner-horse/herd relationship provides is fundamental to the client's experience and healing from traumatic history. If the client has themselves experienced having no voice, no consent, feeling pressured, having their personal space or touch boundaries violated or abused by others, having events happen that were overwhelming or unwanted, witnessing this happening between the practitioner-horse interaction, along with words or an intention that implies the horse is *willing, enjoying, choosing, wanting this experience*, can be confusing at best. At worst, it is replaying the exact experience of the trauma survivor – feeling they had no voice, no consent, no control, dis-empowerment, violation and endured harm, *for their own good*. This is potentially re-traumatising for the client.

These ethical issues and this ethical orientation towards the horses' experience becomes vital in the specific context of working with clients with trauma histories, and the broader context of including horses in the therapeutic process. Consider this question, "How much no consent, no control, violation of personal space boundaries and touch boundaries and one-way relating or demanding of another is good for the horse? For the client? For the therapeutic process and healthy relationship?"

I believe once we openly consider these questions and ethical issues, the answer becomes clear. I believe relationally oriented equine assisted psychotherapy practitioners therefore must make this paradigm shift, from more common I-It practices with horses (from an equitation lens) to I-Thou practices with horses, such as I-Thou Horse-person-ship and I-Thou Inter-species relating.

CONCLUSION

I-Thou Horse-person-ship sits, then, as an ethical intervention as well as a corrective relationship, in the EPI model of equine assisted psychotherapy. I-Thou Horse-person-ship is a part of the whole experience of the client, and the whole client-horse-practitioner-field system of relating, that supports *safe relationship*. Safe relationship must include a therapeutic process where *each being* has a voice, has consent, is being attuned to, and where each beings' feelings and needs are included, negotiated and an active part of the relational conversation and interaction.

Just for clarification purposes, I-Thou Horse-person-ship as an ethical foundation for EAP does not mean there is no I-It or strategic relating moment with horses, in session or outside of session (where the human does something that the horse does not choose to do or want to do). There are of course times when, for safety reasons, medical reasons, horse care, and self-centred or client-centred reasons we become I-It in our relating with horses. However, the big difference is we are aware, intentional, clear and choiceful about this behaviour. We (as human practitioners) have perhaps acknowledged and negotiated this with the horse in some way.

For example, "How can we do this together, knowing that you (horse) don't want to? How can I make this okay enough for you, or enjoyable enough for you right now?" We do this via appropriate use of communication, non-verbal dialogue, touch, praise, food, environment enrichment or some other value-laden exchange that suits the individual horse and situation. This kind of aware relationship and conversation with the horses is direct, honest and relational, and this changes the situation and experience for the horse, to whatever degree.

What I-Thou Horse-person-ship does mean, is that the I-Thou relating, is the *primary and fundamental way of relating with horses*, the more dominant approach, where there are also, of course, moments of swinging into I-It encounters and moments, in particular contexts, and with ensuring the safety of the human clients. However, *safety and training biases*, are not used as an excuse for predominant I-It relating in the context of equine assisted psychotherapy. The I-Thou relational system, then, provides the safe place, the corrective space, the rich "live relationship" material for the client to explore, to learn about themselves, and about how they "do relationship" and where they can practice healthy, mutually beneficial relationship, to transition back to their broader lives. The horses benefit from and enjoy the equine assisted sessions, having their experience, feelings, communications and wants included in the time together. They have an opportunity to be horse, to have inter-species relationships that are not just safe, tolerable, or okay, but are enriching for them.

I trust you are now considering some of the ethical issues related to including horses into counselling and psychotherapy practice. I am hoping to inspire further open curiosity and reflection into many challenging areas, and to do so we must bring in a lot of self-compassion as we reflect upon the following:

> *"What is the experience of my horses and ponies in session? What is the experience of my horses living and being with me, outside of sessions? Am I bringing in the richness of what is*

possible in the relational encounter with horses? Am I unintentionally providing services where clients witness pressure of one being by another being, or where clients experience and participate in the use of the horse as a tool or learning opportunity, or unintentionally violate the horses' consent? Is my practice, essentially good for my horses, does it enrich their quality of life?"

Utilising I-Thou Horse-person-ship, alongside a solid equine education and understanding of equine training (where the horses' basic needs for herd living, nutritional food, water, shelter, movement, grazing and enrichment are centre stage, alongside relaxation-based training, positive reinforcement training techniques, and choiceful negative reinforcement approaches that minimise stress), is one way to address the ethical considerations and increase the relational potency of equine assisted psychotherapy. It is one way to ensure that equine assisted psychotherapy fundamentally looks to benefit the horse and prioritise their feelings, instincts, needs and wants in the inter-species relationship, alongside, the rich and varied benefits for the client, and practitioner.

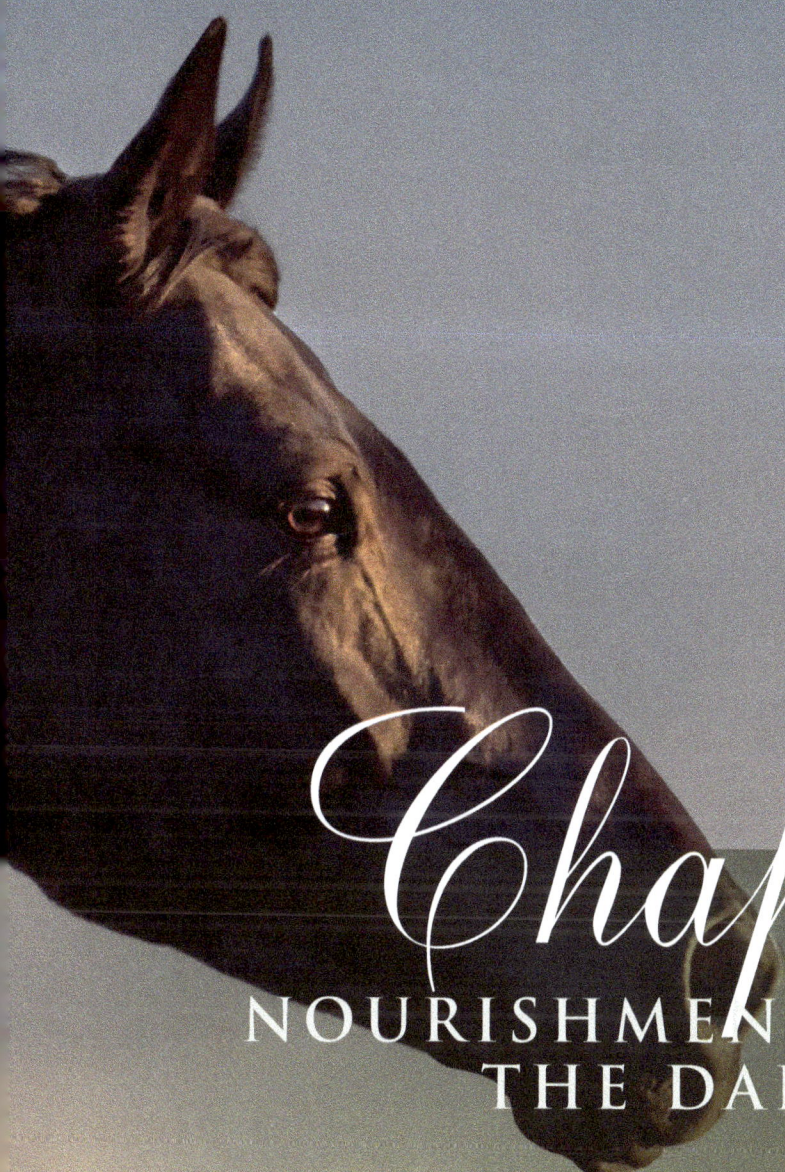

Chapter 3:
NOURISHMENT THROUGH THE DARING HERD®

DR VERONICA LAC

ABOUT DR VERONICA LAC

PhD Psychology, Masters Gestalt Therapy, Masters, Training & Performance Management, Founder and Executive Director of The HERD Institute®, Florida USA

Dr Veronica Lac is the Founder & Executive Director of The HERD Institute® and has 20 years of experience as a corporate trainer and mental health professional, as well as a certified therapeutic riding instructor, providing her with an integrated perspective to Equine Facilitated Work. She has a passion for social justice work and incorporates this into her work with horses. Her academic background includes a Masters in Training and Performance Management, a Masters in Gestalt Psychotherapy, and a PhD in Psychology.

The HERD Institute® offers training and certifications in Equine Facilitated Psychotherapy and Learning. Veronica specialises in working with eating disorders, trauma, and attachment, and has developed equine and canine assisted programs for at-risk adolescents in collaboration with residential treatment centres and eating disorder clinics. Veronica is committed to research in the field of equine facilitated psychotherapy and has multiple publications internationally in peer-reviewed journals and is the author of two best-selling books in the field of equine-facilitated work.

NOURISHMENT THROUGH THE DARING HERD®

I n February 2021, The HERD Institute® held the first ever global gathering of equine facilitated psychotherapy and learning practitioners, led and hosted by Black, Indigenous, and People of Colour (BIPOC) within the industry. The motivation for this "Diversifying the HERD Virtual Summit" came from a desire to highlight practitioners of colour in the field who are doing some incredible work in their communities. Our hope is that by increasing representation, we can encourage a new generation of BIPOC practitioners to enter into the field. We also wanted to support people in

the equine industry who want to increase equity and inclusion in their barns and programs to find creative strategies to move forward. Most importantly, we wanted to help challenge, change, and create organisations to be more welcoming of diversity. Our hope is that by offering a space where people could come together to listen with curiosity about each other's experiences, we can begin to dismantle systems of oppression and build a more diverse and equitable industry.

The civil unrest that followed the murder of George Floyd in the USA in 2020 prompted many organisations globally to release statements that declared their commitment to anti-racism. While many of these statements were motivated by a genuine desire to cultivate change, very few took action to implement policies for systemic change. Many leaders were also faced with resistance from their communities and organisational members, believing that engaging in conversations about

> *I know of many well-meaning folks who believe that change is needed but are unaware of their own biases as they attempt to make a difference.*

racism, white privilege, and social justice only served to increase divisiveness. This prompted several conversations I had with various leaders within our field about how to make "More than a Statement" when faced with resistance to change. I know of many well-meaning folks who believe that change is needed but are unaware of their own biases as they attempt to make a difference. I also know many people who have worked hard to uncover their implicit biases but struggle to know how to take the next steps towards challenging the systems and organisations in which they belong. These efforts are difficult but appreciated. It requires vulnerability to become an ally, to take a stand and declare your hand, and I want to invite you to embrace this journey courageously, knowing that it is a hill that we need to climb together in order for systems to change. As the poet Amanda Gorman so beautifully says:

> When day comes we step out of the shade,
> aflame and unafraid
> The new dawn blooms as we free it
> For there is always light,
> if only we're brave enough to see it
> If only we're brave enough to be it

It's not only racial diversity that has historically been lacking in our field. The Diversifying the HERD summit was successful in engaging people in conversations about racial inequalities, systemic oppression, and white privilege, and how these show up in our industry. I came out of the experience feeling encouraged that our community within the larger equine industry is doing a small part to address these issues. However, I also felt that there was so much more that needed to be done to address the wider topic of diversity, equity, and inclusion for all.

We continued the conversations through our PRIDE in The HERD event, the first ever virtual summit led and hosted by Lesbian, Gay, Bi-sexual, Transgender, Queer, Intersex and Asexual (LGBTQIA) practitioners within the equine facilitated space in June 2021. As part of PRIDE month, we wanted to highlight the achievements and contributions of LGBTQIA members of our community while also addressing their lack of visibility. While I know that there are many LGBTQIA members in our industry, I also know that not everyone is comfortable coming out to clients and colleagues. It might not be safe. Jobs may be at risk. People want to maintain their privacy.

Bringing all these concepts into the context of this Nourished book chapter, I am grateful for the invitation from Meg Kirby to share how working with horses can help us to address some of the difficulties of navigating issues of diversity, equity, and inclusion in our field. Whether we are talking about differences in age, race, ethnicity, gender, sexual orientation, neurodiversity, or physical abilities, our equine partners have led the way in showing us what compassion and connection looks and feels like.

The HERD Institute® approach to equine facilitated psychotherapy and learning is based on existential-humanistic and Gestalt principles. We engage with our clients in the present moment, allowing them to make meaning of the experience themselves, and focus on bringing awareness to how they are interacting with us and our equine partners in the actual emerging relationships. In other words, we work not only with metaphors within the therapy and learning process, but also with deepening the relationships themselves.

This case study offers an example of how we can organically attend to issues of diversity, equity, and inclusion in our work with horses through working within the HERD approach. Details of the client have been changed to protect confidentiality. This example is not intended as a step-by-step process for practitioners to bring up issues of diversity, equity, and inclusion. It is offered as an example of what can emerge if we are open to exploring these issues with our clients.

Riley was referred to me through a local non-profit that works with LGBTQIA youth. Riley identified as male and used the pronouns he/him/his and was quick to let me know that this was his chosen name. His "dead name", or the name that his parents had given him, was Helen. Riley had been using his chosen name for over a year outside of the family home, but his parents were still using his dead name.

At 15 years old, Riley was a keen soccer player, stood around 5' 8" tall with a stocky build. He lived in what he described as a very white neighbourhood and felt that his presence as a 15-year-old African American boy was beginning to "freak people out". He was suffering from depression and anxiety; aside from being in the soccer team, Riley didn't engage in any social activities outside of school. Riley had also been experiencing some bullying at school since transitioning his gender identity which had led him to isolate himself even more.

With this information, I knew that Riley was at a high risk for suicide. According to the Trevor Project survey in 2020 of LGBTQIA youth in the United States, 52% of transgender and non-binary youth have seriously considered suicide. Fifty-two percent. While Riley had not revealed any suicidal ideation yet, this statistic was certainly in my awareness.

In our first session, Riley arrived at the barn with his mum. It was a cold, crisp morning in Ohio and the overnight frost was still glistening in the early light. As Riley got out of the car, I noticed that he was wearing a plain black t-shirt with black jeans, black boots, and a grey beanie hat. I heard his mum pleading with Riley to take his jacket with him, which he responded by slamming the car door and walking away. Mum got out of the car and ran after him with the black, puffy, down jacket.

Mum: Helen! Stop being ridiculous. It's cold. Put this on!

Riley: (Sigh) I'm fine. I don't need it.

Mum: Just take the damn thing. Just in case.

Riley: (Sigh) I. Don't. Need. It.

His mum looked at me and threw up her hands, indicating that she'd leave the jacket hanging on the fence. I nodded and turned to Riley to welcome him into the space. Riley stuck his hands in his pockets and looked down at the ground as I introduced myself and went through my usual safety instructions in preparation to go into the barn. The horses were already turned out for the day in the back paddock, so I invited Riley to walk through the barn with me towards the herd.

As we walked past his jacket on the fence post, Riley reached over, picked it up, and put it on. I smiled and told him that I was glad that he was taking care of himself. "I would've just put it on if she'd called me by my name," he said, and so, our work began.

We made our way through the barn and out towards the back paddock where my horses were munching on hay. Arrow, my gelding, lifted his head up and turned to watch us as we walked up to the fence line. Slowly, he began to meander his way towards us. The two mares, Reba and Cheyenne, continued to graze. Riley stepped forward as Arrow approached the gate and stretched his neck out. After sniffing Riley's shoulder, Arrow shook his head and blew out a big breath, startling himself and the boy. Riley laughed and reached his hand out to stroke Arrow's neck.

Riley (laughing): Did I make you sneeze? You're a silly...

Riley paused. Turning to me, Riley asked, "Is he a boy or a girl?

Me: Well, he's a gelding. Which means he's been neutered.

Riley: So, you still refer to him as "he"?

Me: I do. I guess that's traditional in the horse world to refer to geldings as "he".

Riley: So, he's a...different...kind of boy. Kind of like me, then?

Riley smiled and continued petting Arrow on his neck. I asked him how he felt about Arrow approaching him as a fellow "different kind of boy". Riley paused his petting momentarily as he considered my question.

Riley: I guess I feel like we can be friends. But I think Arrow would like to use the pronoun "they" instead of "he".

Me: I can see how important that is to you.

Riley: It is. It's not that difficult to make the effort and you get used to it pretty quickly. I don't know why it's so hard for people.

Me: Well...I'd like to honour that request and I know I might slip up because I'm so used to using referring to Arrow as "he". So, I'm going to do my best to transition and please feel free to correct me when I slip up. Is that ok?

Riley nodded. I asked him how he would like to get to know his new friend and Riley suggested going into the paddock to be closer to Arrow. Once inside the paddock, I asked Riley to look around to take in his surroundings and notice where he wanted to position himself.

Riley: I'd like to go and sit under the tree over there, but I also want to be close to Arrow.

Me: How might you invite them to walk with you to the tree?

Riley: Well, I could just throw a rope around their neck and make them come with me, but I don't want to do that. I don't know how else to make a horse do something they don't want to.

Me: What makes you say they don't want to?

Riley: I guess I don't know that. Do you think if I start walking over there, they'd follow me?

Me: I don't know. How would you feel about giving it a go?

Meanwhile, Arrow had stayed by Riley's side, with a low head and eyes half closed. Riley shook his head at my question.

Me: What's happening for you right now?

Riley: I just know that they won't want to come with me.

Me: I notice that they haven't moved away from you since we came into the paddock. What's that like for you?

Riley: I suppose they're happy enough to stay so that makes me feel they're with me.

Me: What does being "with" you mean?

Riley: I'm usually all alone, like I'm either the odd one out, or just invisible. Arrow's here with me, so, I'm not alone.

I paused and allowed him to feel into that, encouraging him to reach out and feel Arrow's physical presence, and to notice how Arrow responded to his touch. After a few moments of gently stroking Arrow's neck, Riley leaned in and buried his head and began to weep quietly into Arrow's mane.

Me: I want you to really take in what it's like to be here with Arrow. To not be alone. I see your tears and I see he's turned his head towards you. How do you feel?

Riley: They.

Me: Yes, thank you for the correction. They've turned their head towards you. What's that like for you?

Riley: It's like they're really looking at me.

Me: I noticed that you took a step backwards when you said that, and Arrow's now turned their head away. What do you make of that?

Riley: Ugh....story of my life!

With that, Riley turned and started walking towards the willow tree in the middle of the paddock. I allowed him to lead the way, staying a few paces behind him, and watched as Arrow slowly turned and followed him. Our little procession made its way across the field; Riley, then Arrow, then me. As he approached the tree, my two mares lifted their heads, watching the procession from their vantage point on the other side of the field. They whinnied, snorted, and then dropped their heads to continue grazing. Arrow remained focused on Riley.

Riley: They followed me!

Me: They did. Did you hear the girls whinnying?

Riley: Yes. But I don't think they want to join us here. They're just doing their own thing. But Arrow's here. (Turning to Arrow) I can't believe you followed me. I walked away because I thought you were done with hanging out. (Turning to me) I don't like it when people look at me. I feel like everyone's always looking at me or talking about me behind my back. Like, "look at that freak". And now, they're talking about how I might not be allowed to play soccer with the girls, but I'm also not allowed to try out for the boys' team. My parents don't get it either. My dad keeps asking me why I'd want to "choose" to be a black man in this world when it's hard enough to be a black woman. Like he thinks this is optional and I'm doing it for attention. They do what the other horses are doing – tell me they care but then turn their backs. (Turning back to Arrow.) But you get it though, don't you? I mean, you didn't choose to transition yourself, it was kinda forced on you, but you know what I mean.

Riley let out a big sigh. Arrow let out a big breath. I exhaled deeply. I found myself caught up momentarily on the parallel between human and non-human animal oppression; that through the process of neutering and spaying our animals we were inflicting our will over their natural way of being, and how this was so relevant for all the minoritised clients that I work with.

I was aware that Riley's experiences of discrimination were at the intersection of being both Black and transgender. I felt the heaviness of this burden upon his young shoulders and my heart ached for him. I wanted to empower him to show up and be visible in his life, but I also felt hugely protective of him, knowing that to do so meant taking enormous risks. I was in awe of the courage he showed with me in this session, revealing his loneliness and isolation of not being seen, the simultaneous desire and fear of being seen, and the resulting consequences of being seen.

I could hear in his statements about Arrow how important it was for him to find others like him; the importance of representation for young LGBTQIA and BIPOC folks; the need for mentors in our society, who have gone through their own battles to help guide those behind them. Most of all, in that moment, I wanted Riley to sink into the support he was feeling from Arrow, through this strange kinship of gender reassignment.

In subsequent sessions with Riley, we returned again and again to his experiences of being seen and not seen. The choices that emerged in each session allowed him to connect to his embodied experiences of belonging and not belonging in different arenas of his life. Riley's gender identity and transitional journey was supported by his relationship with Arrow, empowering him to speak his truth while also assessing the impact of that, within relationships with his parents and peers. He advocated for his rights to play on the boys' soccer team and while he wasn't successful in that endeavour, the process helped him to find his voice.

For me, this case study demonstrates the power of connection with our equine partners. Particularly when working at liberty where the horses have the choice to engage or not, clients experience profound insights into their inner lives and are able to increase their awareness of how they enter into relationships with others. This way of working in the present moment, attending to the meaning that clients make for themselves, without inserting our own interpretations of their experience, and allowing the relationship between client and horse to emerge is foundational to The HERD Institute® approach.

This example also highlights the importance of cultural competency when working with at-risk youth. Our ability to honour their reality, their truth, and their choices about themselves, while staying educated on the cultural context that forms the background of their lives is critical to the process. In this way, practitioners can become part of the solution for our at-risk communities and help to challenge, change, and create a brave new world where everyone can belong.

REFERENCES

Lac, V. (2020). *It's not about the activity: Thinking outside the toolbox of equine facilitated psychotherapy & learning.* CO: University Professors Press, Colorado Springs.

Lac, V. (2019). Human-equine relational development (HERD) approach to working with clients suffering from bulimia nervosa, in Trotter, K.S. and Baggerley, J.N. (eds) *Equine- assisted mental health interventions: Harnessing solutions to common problems.* Routledge, New York, NY.

Lac, V. (2017). *Equine-facilitated psychotherapy and learning: The Human-Equine Relational Development (HERD) approach.* Elsevier/Academic Press, Cambridge, MA.

Lac, V. (2015) Hopes and dreams: Impact of therapeutic riding for families with ASD children, *Scientific and Educational Journal of Therapeutic Riding,* 20, 32-43.

Lac, V. (2015) Amy's story: An existential-integrative equine facilitated psychotherapy approach to anorexia nervosa, *Journal of Humanistic Psychology,* DOI:10.1177/0022167815627900.

Lac, V. (2014) Horsing around: Gestalt equine psychotherapy as Humanistic play therapy, *Journal of Humanistic Psychology,* DOI: 10.1177/0022167814562424.

Lac, V., Marble, E., & Boie, I. (2013) Equine Assisted Psychotherapy as a Creative Relational Approach to Treating Clients with Eating Disorders. *Journal of Creativity in Mental Health,* 8:4, 483-498.

Chapter 4:
WORKING WITH HORSES TO DEVELOP SECURE ATTACHMENT

BETTINA SHULTZ-JOBE & KATE NAYLOR

ABOUT BETTINA SHULTZ-JOBE

Co-Founder/CEO of Natural Lifemanship

Bettina Shultz-Jobe is a licensed professional counsellor. Ten years ago, she and her husband, Tim Jobe, founded The Natural Lifemanship Institute. Natural Lifemanship joins with mental health professionals, equine professionals, coaches, and others in the healing professions on a journey of personal and professional healing, growth, and transformation through education and certification. This journey's foundations are found in the horse-human relationship and the neurobiology of attachment and trauma. Their vision is a world where connection and the value of healthy relationships is seen and felt in everything we do. Nowadays, Bettina spends a lot of time "helping the helpers" as over 250 professionals move through Natural Lifemanship certification. She also continues to carry a part-time client load. She has worked in this field for over 20 years and is passionate about helping people and animals form trusting relationships to overcome toxic stress and trauma.

ABOUT KATE NAYLOR

Director of Trainer Development and Coumminity Engagement at Natural Lifemanship

Kate Naylor is a masters level therapist specialising in marriage and family therapy; a certified Natural Lifemanship clinician, equine professional, and trainer; and the Director of Trainer Development and Community Engagement at Natural Lifemanship. As a mother, wife, nature-based therapist, and horsewoman, Kate believes strongly in the interconnectedness of our own mind/body/soul as well our connection with others and the larger web of life. In her work with families, mothers, and other professionals in the mental health field Kate draws from her education in the relational sciences, family systems, trauma-conscious yoga, and psychodrama to create fully experiential learning and therapy that honours one's unique place in the world. She lives and loves in Austin, Texas.

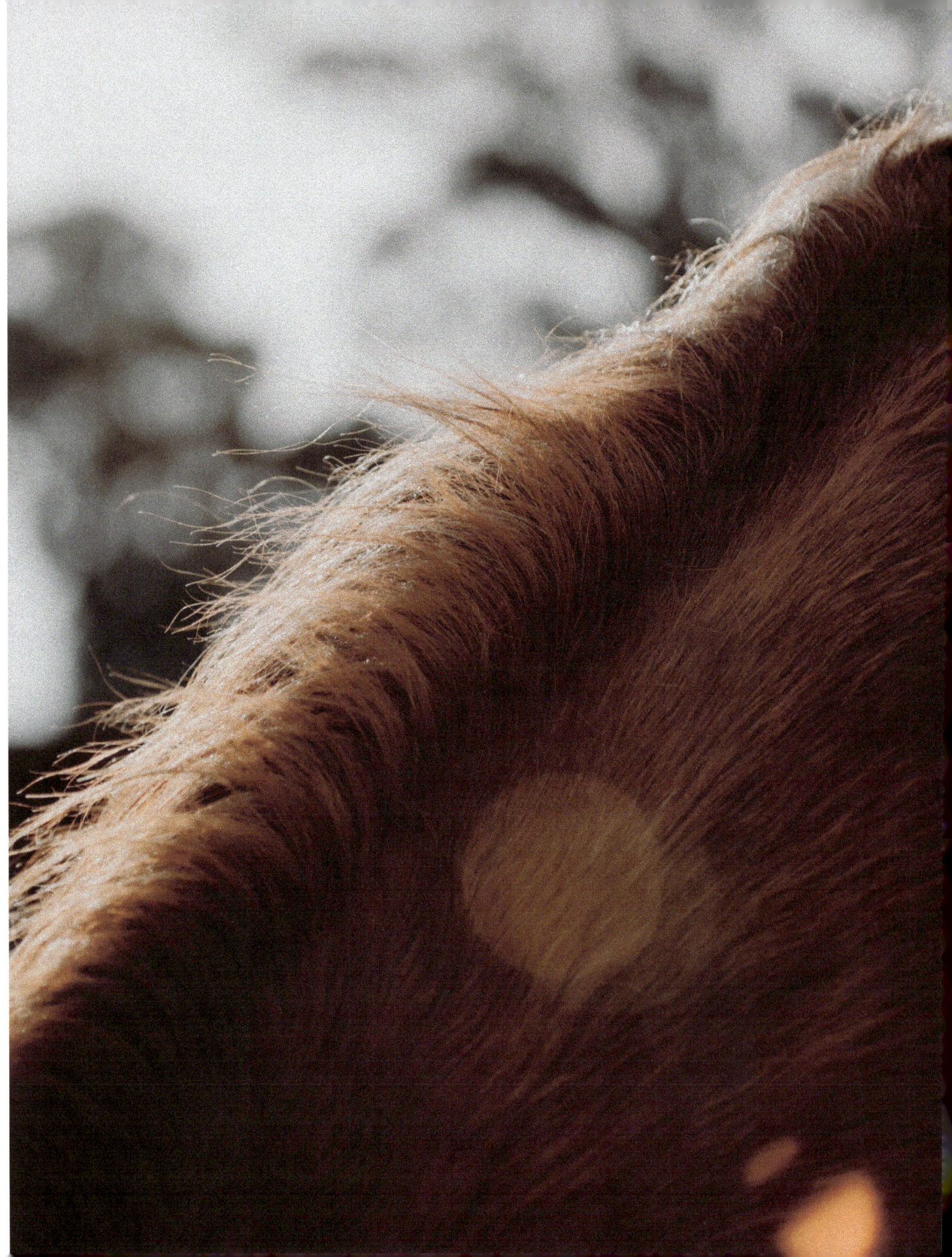

INTRODUCTION

There are many ways to include horses into a personal growth process, and people grow, heal, and transform in response to all sorts of moments in life. What we present here is our perspective on exploring long-held relational patterns and practicing new ways of being in relationship — made possible while in a warm and supportive therapeutic environment. Throughout this chapter there are prompts to reflect on your experience of what you are reading. It could be helpful to have a journal, sketch pad, or other means of processing your reactions.

WHAT IS OUR APPROACH?

Our approach to working with horses is called Natural Lifemanship — and our educational organisation is The Natural Lifemanship Institute — which we often refer to as "NL". The Natural Lifemanship Institute is a teaching, mentoring, and certifying organisation specialising in a trauma-informed approach to helping and healing humans, horses, and other animals.

Our foundational principle is that healing happens in the context of a relationship, and how that relationship is formed makes all the difference. Our approach is informed by the ever-growing field of Interpersonal Neurobiology and Attachment Theory and Sciences (often referred to by the umbrella term of the Relational Sciences).

We strive to support therapists, coaches, educators, and other helping/healing professionals to develop a holistic mind-body-spirit approach to their equine assisted services that is based on an understanding of how stress shows up in the brain and body, both in the moment and over time, and how a healthy relationship with self and others can heal both the long and short term effects. It is also our belief that equine and animal assisted services should be mutually beneficial, healing the animals involved as well as the humans. These are our guiding principles.

Attachment science has been an anchoring force in our work because it is universal, every human being experiences the attachment process in both beneficial and detrimental ways, and every human being builds a life based on their experiences of this process. Attachment science also offers guidance on how to move forward with healing - providing real, tangible goals for secure (healthy) relationships. Much of this translates to all other mammals as well. For this reason, it makes for a powerful framework for offering transformative equine assisted services.

WHAT IS ATTACHMENT?

The concept of attachment is built on an understanding of how our first relationships in infancy and childhood lay the groundwork for our patterns for relating later in life. Developed from a field of science dating back nearly 100 years, we understand that each one of us builds a map in our brains of how to navigate relationships in a way that keeps us safe and meets our needs in the best way possible. This map is built through repeated interactions throughout infancy and childhood — it tells us how to behave and what to expect from others (this is called the basic attachment cycle, which we explain in the next section).

Because our maps are built so early in life, they are deeply embedded and often pre-verbal — we follow these maps with our bodies as well as our minds. Our beliefs, expectations, and behaviours therefore are often automatic and occur beneath our conscious awareness — making it very easy to play out a preconceived map in our friendships, work places, intimate relationships, communities and in our parenting. Attachment also creates a map, or set of deeply embedded expectations and beliefs, about ourselves. How we feel about who we are as people is a result of our attachments in early life. Attachment, fundamentally, is the framework through which we see everything else.

Importantly, this understanding of attachment also tells us that in order to heal deeply held patterns of being in the world doing purely cognitive (thought-based) therapy work can only impact so much. In order to affect the deepest, oldest maps in our brains and bodies, we must approach attachment healing as reparative full-body experiences — that include the physical, mental, and interpersonal (or interspecies in our case!). We will explore the facets of attachment in more detail in the following sections, as well as treatment from a Natural Lifemanship perspective.

WHAT IS THE BASIC ATTACHMENT CYCLE?

The basic attachment cycle is the bare-bones interaction that occurs repeatedly between two individuals over and over again throughout the course of a relationship. It is most significantly impactful in the relationship between an infant and their primary caregiver because of the rapid development that is occurring for infants and young children. An infant is building pathways in the brain at an astonishing rate, and the interactions the infant has with their environment and caregiver tells the infant's brain what kind of pathways to build. A person learns how to keep themselves safe, and ultimately, how to engage with the world, through these interactions.

Very simply, the cycle begins when a request is made for a need to be met, and then the need is either met or not and the need can be met in a variety of ways. How the need is met creates the building blocks for attachment. Let's consider a common request made from infants — crying. Imagine a baby crying from their crib, to communicate a need for comfort. Depending on the well-being, resources, and history of the caregiver, they may respond in a variety of ways. A caregiver may leave the baby lying in their crib but call out to them angrily to "Be quiet". Another caregiver may approach the baby, but in their own distress be unable to soothe the baby's crying alternating between trying to soothe and becoming overwhelmed and giving up. And yet another caregiver may approach the baby calmly, cooing soft words, lift the baby, and carry them in a rocking motion around the home until the crying is complete. All three are different responses to the attachment cycle, and all three will communicate different messages to the baby. Repeated with enough frequency, these communications develop patterns for the child. These patterns result from pathways that have been built in the brain and provide the structure for how the child will engage with the world around them, and with their internal life.

Over time one begins to develop both an unconscious and conscious belief system about the "rules" of relationships, how one feels about relationships in general, how one feels about their own needs, and how one behaves in relationships. This feedback loop teaches us how to make future requests in order to best survive and feel safe in our childhoods, which, while adaptable for surviving the vulnerability and dependency of childhood, isn't always a successful approach as we grow into adulthood and form new relationships. Importantly, this cycle also impacts how one feels about making requests in the first place. In equine assisted services there are frequent (almost constant) opportunities to observe the attachment cycle playing out for your clients, and support them in building new pathways, new patterns, that better serve them in their lives outside of sessions.

Throughout this chapter we will ask you to pause and notice Sensations, Images, Feelings and Thoughts that arise for you. This is the beginning to a practice of self-awareness that allows you to see yourself and those around you more clearly. As you read about the concept of attachment, what arises for you? Jot some notes, sketch, or speak aloud what you are noticing.

WHAT IS SECURE ATTACHMENT?

Secure attachment is the attachment tendency most associated with happy, successful adulthood. Research tells us that adults who are securely attached experience more physical and mental well-being in their lives on the whole. Typically, secure attachment is reflected in an individual's openness to relationships, an ability to maintain a flexible internal and external life, and a balance between their own needs and the needs of others. Securely attached adults exhibit a comfort with interdependence — the ability to connect and become close with others while also maintaining a connection with self.

When we think about the extremes of hyperarousal (high sympathetic nervous system activation that can look like agitation) and hypoarousal (under activation of the nervous system that often looks like apathy or inattention) in the nervous system, security exists in the balance between the two. When this balance and flexibility exists, connection, intimacy, and vulnerability can co-exist with boundaries, individuality, self-worth, and personal space.

Secure attachment is a both/and approach to relationships, ideas, and the inner world of the self. And ultimately, secure attachment means a general worldview that supports a person in health and wellness. Securely attached individuals see that relationships are good, meaningful, and worth the effort, including the relationship one has with oneself and the larger web of life.

WHAT IS INSECURE ATTACHMENT?

When the attachment cycle repeatedly ends with a response that feels unpredictable, rejecting, or scary, a different series of patterns emerge that have been called Insecure Attachment. Within insecure attachment tendencies, there is less balance, less flexibility both in one's internal life and in one's relationships with others. The insecure styles fall on more extreme ends of the spectrum of relating and of nervous system functioning. There are three forms of insecure attachment generally called anxious, avoidant, and fearful in children or entangled, dismissive, and disorganised in adulthood. The following diagram can help us understand attachment tendencies as a nervous system response as well.

FIGURE 1: AROUSAL AND RELATING CONTINUUM

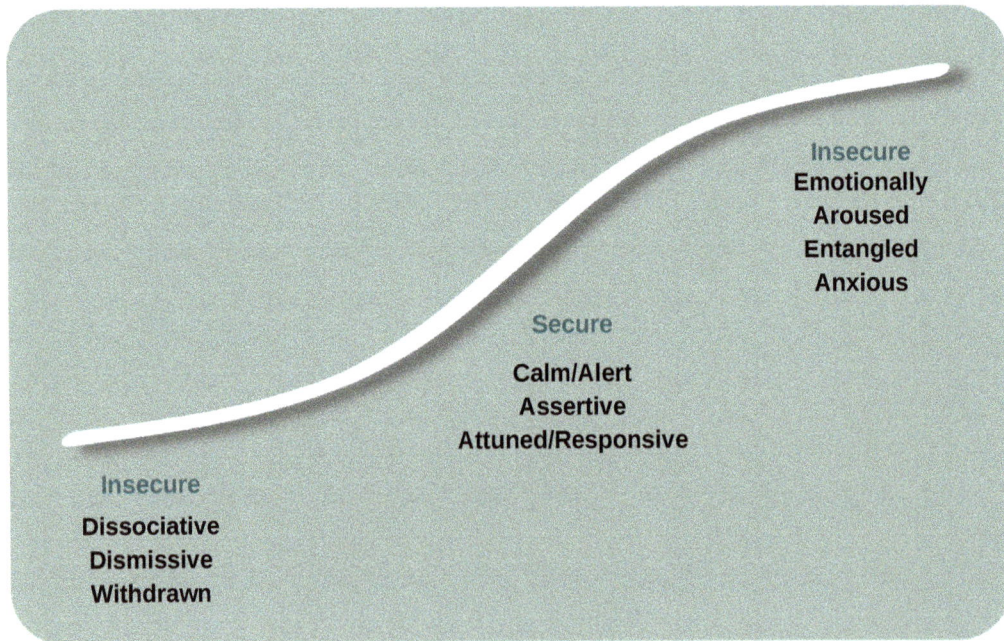

Insecure
Emotionally
Aroused
Entangled
Anxious

Secure
Calm/Alert
Assertive
Attuned/Responsive

Insecure
Dissociative
Dismissive
Withdrawn

ENTANGLED

An entangled tendency is often characterised by hyperarousal in relationships (high sympathetic nervous system activation — agitation), as well as presenting with an over emphasis on closeness and intimacy with an under emphasis on independence and self-reliance. This tendency is often the result of unpredictable, anxious, controlling, and erratic caregiving behaviours during early development.

For example, a caregiver in this pattern may have trouble attuning to their child's needs and requests and so can find themselves responding inconsistently in the moment, perhaps trying to soothe a crying child at first but becoming overwhelmed and giving up before the crying child is soothed. These caregivers can be overly anxious themselves, tend toward "hovering" or interfering with a child's freedom to explore, and may respond to a child's distress with distress of their own.

In adulthood, individuals with an entangled tendency exhibit a lot of preoccupation and worry about their relationships; they can spend a lot of time and energy in trying to maintain some control in a relationship. Like the infant, the adult is trying to get their needs met by making sure the other individual pays attention and stays focused on them. Any kind of separation can feel dangerous because of the lack of predictability expected in the reunion.

DISMISSIVE

A dismissive tendency is often characterised by a hypoarousal in relationships (low energy in the nervous system) often presenting with an over emphasis on independence and an apathy toward or avoidance of intimacy and vulnerability. This tendency is often a result of consistently rejecting, neglectful, or disconnected caregiving behaviours during early development.

For example, when a child is crying, they may be punished or shamed/scolded in some way for their crying, or ignored altogether. Caregivers in this pattern can sometimes be physically present, but are unable to offer emotional connection to their child. Closeness is undervalued, and children may be allowed too much freedom to explore. As the child grows, dismissive tendencies might look like an adult who seems uninterested in intimacy or avoidant of closeness.

Dismissive adults may enter into relationships but give up when challenges arise and can be characterised as adults who avoid or even reject vulnerable feelings. Separation can feel more comfortable than closeness.

FEARFUL/DISORGANISED

A fearful or disorganised attachment tendency often swings back and forth from the two extremes of entangled and dismissive which can present as a disorganisation of approaches to relationships. This tendency is often the result of frightening or abusive caregiving behaviours from caregivers who struggle with their own trauma.

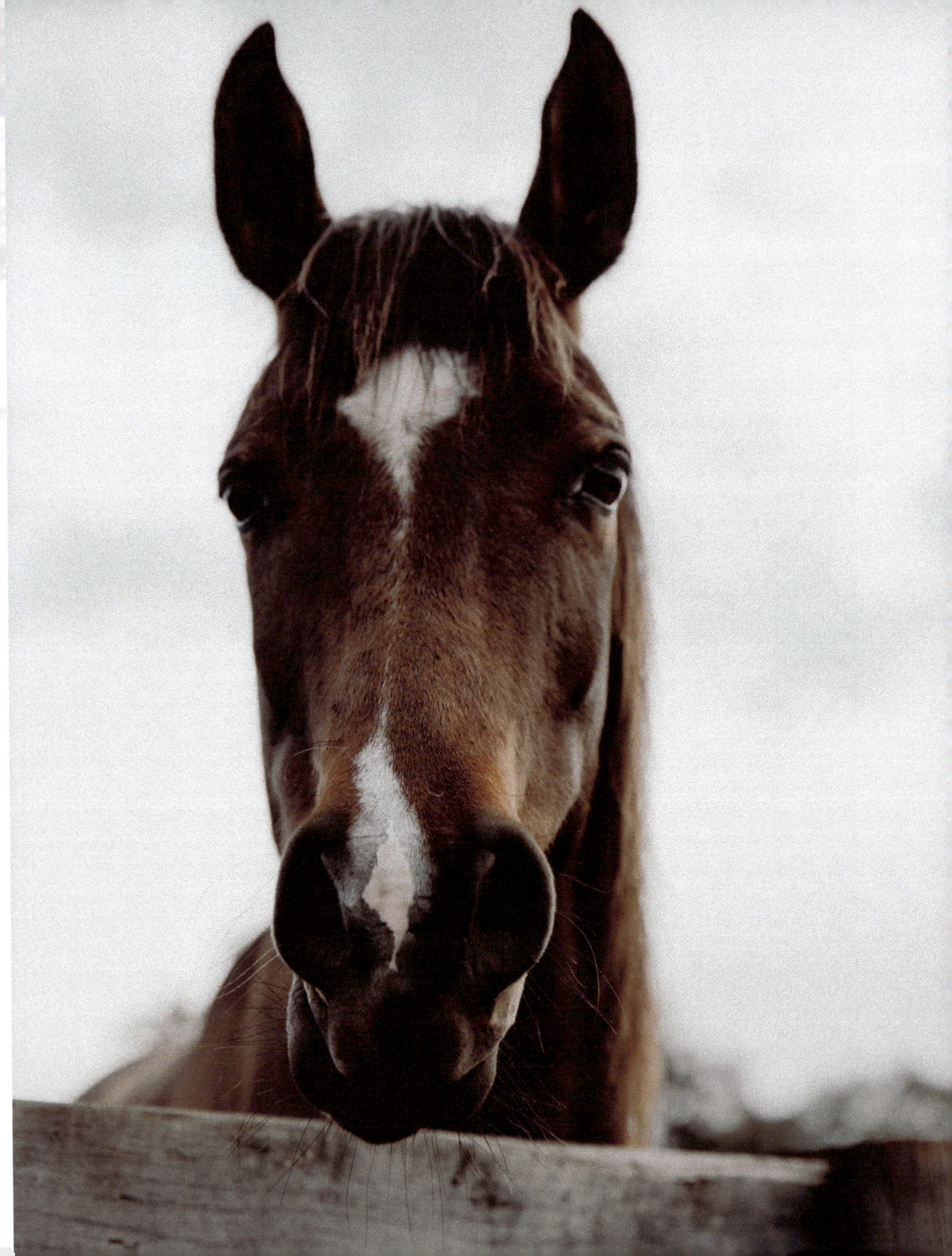

Typically, a child seeks out a caregiver for safety and protection (this is a primal drive), however, when the caregiver is the source of the danger, the child experiences chaos both internally and in the relationship. There is an internal conflict present that is extremely distressing — move toward the caregiver for safety, or move away for safety? Repeated with frequency the infant/child develops disorganisation in their pathways around "what to do" to be safe and get needs met in relationships.

In adulthood, individuals with a disorganised approach to relationships may desire closeness, but become fearful of intimacy and push away, yet could also feel entangled with others, then abandoned, and become agitated when a partner or friend exhibits a desire for independence. This sense of push-pull in relationships can be disorienting and overwhelming for all involved.

While these approaches to attachment were developed from a highly sophisticated attunement to caregivers such that an infant/child could survive their early environments as best as possible, oftentimes these approaches in adulthood can result in relational and general life challenges, bringing clients to our door. Surviving is not thriving. However, it is important to note that an individual's approach is likely to have served them well at least early in life, if not also in adulthood, depending on the culture and communities they find themselves in.

It is not our job to disregard relational approaches that serve a client well in their lives, but to seek out and support clients in change they desire for themselves. Remember that the hallmark of secure functioning is balance and flexibility. This means that it can be beneficial to anyone to work toward it, once resources and support are in place. Moving toward secure attachment is a process involving all aspects of life and is gained in moment to moment reparative experiences with others.

> *As you finish this section, pause and notice your own body and mind in this moment. How is your body reacting to what you have read? What is the quality of your breath? What are the thoughts and feelings that are arising? Jot notes, sketch, or speak aloud what you are noticing.*

HOW CAN WE BEGIN TO HEAL ATTACHMENT?

It is all about relationships. Attachment patterns are laid down in the interplay of two individuals, and the healing of attachment patterns is done the same way. Therefore, attachment work is all about repeated, predictable, and reparative experiences in safe relationships. It is the ultimate "do-over". We help our clients experience what they did not get when they were an infant, a baby, and a young child. Therapy is then all about the relationship offered, and the relationship built. Because our patterns are so strongly, and frequently unconsciously, held — the **how** of the relationship building makes all the difference.

It is therefore imperative that as the facilitator, we have a clear understanding of our own lens through which we view relationships. So, attachment healing for our clients, begins with understanding our own attachment tendencies. The more closely we ourselves move toward secure functioning, the more likely we are to help our clients with this. We cannot take clients where we have not yet gone. As a facilitator, our personal healing and movement toward a secure attachment style is paramount to doing impactful, ethical attachment work in others.

Pause and notice any sensations, thoughts or feelings that come up for you as you consider that your own personal development will influence how impactful you can be as a facilitator. You cannot have one without the other. Write, sketch, or speak aloud what you notice as you sit with this information.

So, as we look at ourselves, and as we enter a therapeutic relationship, the question becomes, what do we actually do to support attachment healing?

A SAMPLE CASE STUDY

In order to better illustrate the ways in which different relational tendencies show up in both one's thoughts and behaviours, and how practicing a secure connection with horses can help - we present a case study of an individual seeking therapy. The individual presented here is an amalgam of several clients, with names and details adjusted to protect the privacy of those with whom we work.

Serena is a woman in her 30s who has come to therapy to explore her difficulties in finding and maintaining relationships. Serena has been married and divorced three times, all three marriages involved abusive interactions with her husbands, and ended explosively.

When Serena first arrives to therapy, her body posture is hunched, as though she is closing in on herself, her voice is quiet, halting, and demonstrates timidity and perhaps fear. She is a kind and sweet woman who feels confused by her previous relationships.

In order to build a thoughtful treatment plan, we explore aspects of Serena's history, particularly her family of origin (her nuclear family as a baby and child growing up). Serena describes her mother as unpredictable — alternating between being checked out and ignoring, to being punitive and demanding — at times, Serena was afraid of her mother and experienced abuse.

Based on her experiences and a thorough history taking, it becomes evident that Serena likely demonstrates a disorganised approach to relationships. At times she expends enormous amounts of energy to elicit connection and please others, and at other times feels safer withdrawing from connection or avoiding connection altogether. This shows up for Serena in her description of her marriages within which she doted on her partners, asking little to nothing of them for years, until she was fed up and burnt out and the marriage imploded with Serena in a rage, causing immediate and complete cut-off.

A disorganised pattern in relationships feels chaotic. Individuals shift abruptly from entanglement to withdrawal and back again in an effort to maintain any level of connection, healthy or otherwise. This chaos mirrors the chaos the individual experienced from primary caregivers in the first months and years of life.

As we continue in this chapter, we will bring in Serena's story to help illustrate the concepts presented.

Pause here to notice any reactions you are having to Serena's story. Can you relate to pieces of it? Take a moment to note any thoughts/emotions/sensations you may be having and allow yourself to pause for a few breaths if needed, before moving on. If your body feels particularly unsettled, feel free to take a break and move around before continuing.

THE POWER OF REQUESTS

As we have described previously, the most basic and foundational interaction in any relationship is the request for a need to be met, and the response given to that request. It is the beginning of all communication between infant and caregiver, and the cycle of request and response is the building block for brain structure, for relational expectations, and for fundamental beliefs about our own value and worthiness. Is it any surprise then, that making a request is an incredibly vulnerable experience?

I invite you to take a moment to let your mind drift to a time of being a young child and for now, notice the physical experience of it — everyone and everything around you is bigger, taller, and often foreign and out of reach. This physical experience often parallels the emotional experience — everything seems big, foreign, and what one wants and needs is often out of reach. Imagine the vulnerability of requesting someone else's attention, or a drink of water you cannot get for yourself, or help with using the bathroom, or help falling asleep.

While we are all adults now, (take a moment to look around the room, breathe, and remind yourself!) the vulnerability of requests never truly fades; and for many who had less than ideal responses to their requests in childhood, requests can be more than just a little vulnerable, they can be downright terrifying. For some, making a request of someone else is as vulnerable as it was when one's very survival depended on the response — there can be chaotic physical sensation, emotional feeling, and a flurry of thoughts all at once. The flow of energy between two individuals in the moment of a request can be quite charged. This is why it is so crucial to have this opportunity for making and responding to requests a focal point in therapeutic work. *Moments with energetic charge are opportunities for transformation.*

The ability to attune to self, make a request based on that introspection, attune to the response made by another, and make a decision about what to do next (based in worthiness of self and one's own needs) is an integral aspect of secure functioning. Therefore, we cannot gloss over this attachment cycle of request and response in our sessions, even though focusing on it will likely cause our clients some discomfort.

Stress (within one's window of tolerance) is necessary for growth — some discomfort is important. Imagine if an individual with dismissive tendencies were never encouraged to make a clear request and stick with it until a connection was made. Imagine an individual with entangled tendencies who never had to ask for space and learn to regulate and rest in that separation. If we allow clients to come to session and simply repeat their attachment patterns they have always followed, we miss powerful opportunities for healing. Experiential work, like that of equine assisted services, is meant to be a safe and brave container for transformation.

At The Natural Lifemanship Institute, we have cultivated (with the help of our partners, the horses) a somewhat operationalised approach to the attachment cycle that is emblematic of secure functioning, *and also promotes secure functioning when practiced*. Our principles of connection offer a beginning to transforming patterns of insecure functioning to more secure ways of being in relationship, both with oneself and with others.

> *Take a moment here to pause and tune inward. How does it feel to consider making clear requests of your horses, your clients, or individuals in your personal life? How does it feel to know this might make your clients appropriately uncomfortable? How does it feel to know your ability to do these things yourself will impact how effective you are with your clients?*

SERENA'S EXPERIENCE OF MAKING REQUESTS

When Serena first begins to interact with her horse, she sets the pace with little interference from us. Serena chooses to spend time sharing space with her horse, Flower, and then moves in closer to stroke Flower on her face and down her neck. Serena passes time in her session petting Flower, grooming Flower, and practicing energy work on Flower. She asks little of Flower, and Flower seems, at times, to enjoy the attention — her ears flop to the sides, her eyes close, she rests a hoof. The equine professional does notice some signs that Flower may be dissociating from the touch that Serena is offering. These signs are nuanced and subtle. (These are perfect examples of an entangled approach to relationships — doting on another, meeting another's needs, without any expectations in return, and without true consent from the other.) Serena also seems to be content to stay in this place, in this dynamic with Flower.

What would it be like for the therapy team to leave Serena and Flower in this way, over and over again, each session? One can assume they both might remain fairly content, though Serena's pattern of relating would suggest she would eventually tire of doting on Flower with very little reciprocation. Serena has also stated that her goal for therapy is to improve her relationships and move from a disorganised pattern to a more secure way of relating. Therefore, the therapy team knows this interaction may be pleasant and comfortable, but it is not enough for change. Indeed, the greatest risk is that it is reinforcing the attachment pattern that Serena seeks to change in her relationships.

The therapist encourages Serena to try making a request for Flower to pay attention to her and to be alert and present during their interactions — perhaps even walk with her in the pen, doing so in a way that allows Flower to choose how she will respond. Serena's previous interactions, while low energy and doting, did not allow Flower an option to give consent. When Serena is encouraged to make a clear request and allow Flower to make up her own mind on how to respond, Serena begins to feel vulnerable. *Vulnerability arises when the question of responsiveness enters — it is in these moments that our attachment wounding is triggered.*

Serena steps back from Flower to allow her some room and attempts to request that Flower turn and look at her using body language and calling to her, but without stepping into Flower's space and demanding attention. At this point, after all the doting attention Flower has received, she is asleep, relatively checked out from Serena, and Serena's requests go unnoticed. Despite Serena's sense that they were experiencing a loving connection earlier, she is ignored when she asks Flower to notice her, respond to her, and connect with her on some level.

Therapist: "*What is it like for you to be right here - giving Flower choice while also asking for the attention and connection you need?*"

Serena, who has become angry by this interaction of making a request and being ignored, says with a raised and somewhat panicky voice: "*You want to know what it is like?! WHAT IS THE POINT?! Why would Flower want to come be with me, of course she is ignoring me! Why would she want to come over here!?!*" (dismissive)

Therapist (with a soft, quiet voice): "*It seems that you're angry and feeling quite vulnerable right now. Is that right? (Serena nods) That is absolutely understandable given your attachment history. As a little girl your needs were frequently ignored or punished. Remember, we are here with you, and together we will get through this. You've been doing so many lovely things for Flower, but when you ask for what you need, she does not seem to notice. . .*" (a tendency common with entanglement)

Serena: "*This is why I don't ask for anything, it isn't worth it! She did just what I thought she would do. This is ridiculous.*" (dismissive)

Equine Professional: "*Is it hard to believe that simply connecting with you, engaging with you and being in your presence, is enough for Flower? That she might enjoy it? You don't have to do things to earn a connection - you are worthy of connection right now. You do need to ask...*" (a secure belief)

Serena: "*Yeah, and when I ask, she ignores me! At least before, she was letting me pet her. At least I felt connected.*" (entangled)

Therapist: "*Did you notice if she said 'yes' to being petted before? Remember, the absence of a no is not a yes.*"

Serena (softens a bit): "*Okay, so she just stood there - I have no idea if she wanted me to do any of that. Well, what am I supposed to do, just stand here too? If I go up to her and touch her or lead her, I take away her ability to choose.*"

Equine Professional: "*What if you were to stay right where you are, giving her room to make her own decision, but increased the energy behind your request?*"

Therapist: "*What if you committed to doing what it takes to build a relationship with Flower where you get to practice asking for your most basic need for connection - without controlling Flower or trying to force her to give it to you?*" (secure attachment)

Tears fill Serena's eyes.

Therapist (takes a deep breath and breathes out slowly): "*It certainly isn't easy. There is so much vulnerability in this, but we are in this with you. This pattern started when you were so little, so vulnerable, and so desperately in need of a regulated and loving Mama. AND with practice and support this pattern can shift.*"

Serena's having a powerful emotional response to being ignored and realises her efforts to dote on Flower did not, in fact, create mutual connection. This is of course understandable, and it also gives Serena an opportunity (with the facilitator's guidance) to notice her pattern. During these interactions, the therapist encourages Serena to confront and perhaps shift her pattern, but with lots of support. There are many breaks for regulation (calming the body with rhythm, movement, and connection) both between the therapy team and Serena, and Serena on her own. Soon, we will describe what happens when someone feels supported and regulated enough to confront their pattern and make a shift. This is how one can develop secure relating from an insecure history — through ongoing support as changes are slowly made.

THE PRINCIPLE OF CONNECTION

The Natural Lifemanship approach is built out of a collection of principles — concepts that apply to any relationship whether it is with a human animal, non-human animal, with the self, or with our concept of something larger than ourselves. These principles guide our decision making as we engage in building healthy relationships. One such principle is the principle of connection.

The principle of connection is simply this — in order for a relationship to exist two beings must connect and engage with each other, or else they are simply "ships passing in the night", and this sort of engaged connection needs to be mutually beneficial. Connection and engagement are the result of a request for attention, at the very least, and then the relationship can continue to build on that engagement and find levels of trust and intimacy. A request for connection made in a healthy relationship comes from the security of knowing one's own inherent worthiness and value, and the confidence that connection in the relationship is reward enough for both of us. *While tasks are an inevitable aspect of a relationship, they come second to connection, always.* This means there are a variety of possible responses to one's request.

IGNORE, RESIST, CONNECT

In any exchange between two individuals, there is, like in the attachment cycle, a request made and then a response to that request. Then, there is a response to the response, and the response to the response of the response...and so on. This is the basic structure of communication. What we at NL have found is that responses to requests fall into three categories: ignoring the request, resisting the request, and connecting or cooperating with the request. We chose the word "cooperate" intentionally reflecting the autonomy of choice that occurs when we choose to cooperate, as opposed to the appeasement that can occur when we "comply". Cooperation conveys collaboration. Note that we don't necessarily mean cooperation as in cooperation in behaviour — more importantly, we focus on cooperation in connection.

Actually, at times, connection may mean not cooperating if we are attempting to move from a place of robotic compliance into a place of real connection. Sometimes "no" is the beginning of connection. *A desire and effort to connect and respond to a request in a healthy way is considered cooperation from our perspective.* Behaviour and tasks are a by-product. To avoid confusion, we will use the word 'connection' from here on out.

Ignoring we define as "not engaged" with the request, for whatever reason — perhaps as a choice, perhaps due to dissociation, distraction, etc.

Resistance we define as "engaged" with the request but not in a productive/healthy manner —this can look like evading a request, negotiating with a request, stalling, etc. Neither ignoring, resistance, nor appeasement/compliance (a form of resistance, in our eyes) are seen as malicious or "bad", but simply as responses to requests that do not build the relationship in a positive, healthy way.

Connection is considered the "right" answer for building healthy relationships — it is the response that promotes engagement, builds trust, and deepens intimacy. There are myriad ways to connect with a request. It will depend entirely on the context of that particular relationship. Sometimes it will involve cooperation in behaviour, but not always. The nuances of this are difficult to convey in writing. Attunement to self and other, and a judgement made in the moment based on a desire for healthy, mutually beneficial relationship help us decide what is connection and what is not.

WHAT WE PRACTICE BECOMES A PATTERN

In our early years, our requests were met with patterns of ignoring, resisting and connection. As small children, with our safety and well-being resting solely on the good will of our caregivers, the responses to the requests we made were life-alteringly important. If we were routinely ignored, for example, we received and internalised messages that the value of our needs and requests, the value of our own feelings and internal lives were unimportant, and the strategies we employed to survive result in a dismissive approach to life and relationships.

As vulnerable children, we had to employ a strategy that served us in that time, and this strategy became our map for the future. Among other things, the routinely ignored child becomes an adult who likely ignores their own needs, places little value on the act of requesting, and expects, perceives, (and is re-wounded by) ignoring responses everywhere he/she goes. This practice throughout childhood is often repeated in adulthood, and becomes a deeply held pattern — so deep, in fact, it is usually unconscious and habitual, rather than a conscious choice made each time. When this individual arrives for equine assisted services, to allow them to practice ignoring and being ignored would only reinforce the patterns that brought them to our help in the first place. In order for us to support a client in working toward secure attachment, we must support them in practicing secure relating.

Pause a moment and notice your response to the ideas of "ignore" "resist" and "cooperate" - see if you can list some behaviours that might fall into each category. Which category feels hardest for you to engage with confidently? When someone makes a request for connection from you, how do you respond? (Likely, you will respond differently depending on the relationship and your state of being when the request is made...so how might you respond to a trusted loved one? How would that differ from how you might respond to a boss, or a new friend, or an unfamiliar horse? How do you respond when experiencing stress or when a lack of trust exists?)

PRACTICING SECURE RELATING

When we think of the basic attachment cycle — a request made and met — in what way would a request be met that would build secure attachment? Hopefully, you would say that for secure attachment others would respond to us, generally, in healthy connection. When we are young, we have little control over this. We do what we can to survive. As adults, however, we are on more equal footing. We can make deliberate choices about how to get to a place of connection with someone, particularly in environments of support, like in a therapy or coaching session.

If someone makes a request for attention from someone else — *and let's be clear, this is someone they want to be in relationship with, even if only briefly* — and the person making the request is ignored... what should happen next? What is the only choice available in order to move toward connection with that individual? The only option that moves someone toward connection when ignored is to *increase the energy (or pressure) of the request*, incrementally and in an appropriate manner. Consider if, when ignored, the person making the request gives up (like one with dismissive attachment tendencies might do) ...nothing will come of the interaction. Connection will not occur. What if the energy of the request remains the same when ignored? The best-case scenario is nothing happens, the worst-case scenario is we nag and nag at the same level of request until the other individual blows up or removes themselves from the situation, in frustration and annoyance.

What if, in response to the request, the response is resistance — the other individual notices the request but is engaging with it in a way that is not healthy for the relationship (think negotiating, gaslighting, tantrumming, stalling, etc.). The requestor could give up the request, allowing the resistance to be successful (those leaning toward the more dismissive attachment style may do this). Or the requestor could demand connection, and force someone into either more resistance, or likely, appeasement/compliance (we may see this from those who lean toward entangled attachment). Or, finally, the requestor could allow the request to remain, (hold space or hold the expectation) while the resistance played out.

Imagine what could happen if during negotiation, gaslighting, tantrumming, or any other form of resistance, one were to calmly hold space for the other while also holding onto the request for connection. The other individual is not forced into anything, there is no threat for them AND the requestor is able to still make their needs known. Being able to calmly hold onto an expectation/request during resistance opens a path for connection that is not available if one gives up or presses the matter with force. This is an aspect of the both/and approach of secure relating.

So, then, what is appropriate when connection is the response to the request? Consider if the request increases or remains even after connection is achieved, then the other individual likely regrets their connection ("Well that didn't change anything!"). This can be confusing and lead to a sense of powerlessness. The only appropriate response to connection is to release the energy of the request — to allow the request/need to have been met, and rest in that connection.

Let's take an example of asking a horse to come away from his hay in order to connect with us (and perhaps come to session). If we ask the horse to engage with us and we are ignored, we must increase the energy of our request if we are ever to connect (remember this is about acknowledging our worthiness for *connection*, NOT insisting on a certain task). If the horse resists (walks away, perhaps), we must stay with the horse and maintain our expectation so the horse can eventually, without threat and of his own choosing, come into connection with us. And, if we ask our horse to engage, and he does, we can smile, soften, and rest in that connection...releasing our successful request for connection.

While this may seem simple on paper, as you consider this scenario of asking a horse to come away from his hay — explore in your mind (and in your sensations) what that might be like for you to hold your request, to increase your request, and then finally to rest in connection — it is not so simple when our own histories and patterns get involved.

These are the principles of connection, and the appropriate responses are the ways in which we can engage with others in a secure style. If we flip the script and find the request is being made of us — the appropriate response is of course, connection — however, how that request feels to us in that moment, and how connection feels as a response, will vary significantly based on our histories. But, ultimately, moving toward secure attachment means finding connection when appropriate requests are made of us and in making requests for connection from others.

Also consider that the cycle of request and response can occur in our internal systems (like requests made within our own bodies...drowsiness is a request for sleep, as an example), our community systems (like at work), and in our spiritual relationships as well. We dive more into these ideas in our training and mentoring. When you consider all of the relationships that exist in an individual's life, there are innumerable ways to either reinforce old patterns of relating, or opportunities for bringing a more secure way of being into everyday life.

Pause a moment and reflect on the ideas presented here. Track sensations in your body as you consider how it would feel to increase the energy of a request when someone ignores you? How would it feel to maintain an expectation or request when someone resists? How would it feel to rest and relax when someone cooperates with your desire for connection? (Extra challenge: How might it feel to rest and relax into connection if you had to work through ignoring or resistance prior to achieving that connection?)

SERENA MAKES A REQUEST...AND STICKS WITH IT

In order for Serena to shift her old patterns of relating, one of the things she needs to practice is making a clear request and sticking with it. This, of course, is not easy. When Serena decides she is ready to make a request and stick with it, there are still challenges ahead. When she is ignored and old beliefs arise, her body wants to give up. Her instinct is to withdraw, curl in on herself, and let the request go. In these moments, she often acts as if she doesn't want or need the connection (dismissive). Her therapy team supports her in regulating her body through movement, rhythm, and the strength of their connection, so that she can return to a sensation of calm and enough strength to try again. This takes repetition and practice over long periods of time.

Eventually, Serena is able to make a clear request, increase her energy when ignored (but without moving to force through her old ways of crowding, doting, and touching without consent) and one day, Flower feels sufficient energy from Serena that she wakes up and looks over at her. Serena was able to find regulated energy in her body through the use of drums, other instruments, and rhythmic movement. Success! This is a moment of connection. This is a moment to release all of the request, all of the energy that was pointed in Flower's direction, so they can enjoy the softness of connection.

But Serena's body finds another old pattern, she finds she cannot release the request and rest. When Flower turns toward her, Serena moves forward into Flower's space. Her anxious, entangled tendency causes her body to want to control what happens next. It feels too vulnerable to relax and let Flower come to her. Flower stops, confused by the shift in Serena. To invite Flower over without controlling gives Flower choice, but then to step into her head space as she is walking closer feels like a "block" that controls Flower's movement. This is another stage of the relationship that requires time, regulation, and practice. Serena now has to practice releasing the request and relaxing when connection is offered.

With time and support from the therapy team, Serena begins to be able to make a clear request, increase pressure when needed, wait and breathe when needed, and then release and relax when connection comes (secure attachment). The more she can do this, the more her body finds this to be its new pattern. Serena can ask for Flower's attention, stick with her request, and enjoy connection when it is offered. Eventually, Serena and Flower are able to walk side by side in the pen. The two have found a secure way of connecting and relating, where flexibility and autonomy are allowed.

IN CLOSING

Each one of us is a unique blend of our ancestry, personal experiences, environment, culture, and communities. There is no one size fits all approach to healing, no technique, activity, or intervention that works for everyone. A therapist or facilitator carries a significant responsibility to learn, reflect, introspect, and practice presence and attunement with their clients and therapy team. It is within this space of connection to self, connection to others, and standing upon the footing of our emerging understanding of human beings, that we can offer ethical and practical approaches to healing.

The principles of connection are meant to be a guiding framework for secure relating — how each aspect of the principles is enacted will be unique to the relationship in that moment. Therefore, each session and each relationship will have its own flow; its own dance with the principles. We at The Natural Lifemanship Institute hope to have provided, with this chapter, a framework for how to begin this process of healing, while acknowledging that true transformation of attachment is a journey that can last a lifetime.

Final Reflection: As you finish this chapter, pause and breathe deeply into your abdomen. What might be some areas of personal development that would benefit from attention from you? Write, sketch, or name out loud one goal you would like to work toward in your relationships. Then, draw in another deep breath. Notice your feet. Feel your body supported by the furniture that holds you. Look around the space in which you occupy and remember that life is a journey that takes a lifetime. It is the relationships we make along the way that make all the difference. What is one way you can offer yourself connection, right now?

Thank you for joining us in this exploration of healthy relationships and how Equine Assisted Services with The Natural Lifemanship Institute can support growth and healing both for you and for your clients. We would love to hear from you while on your journey and hope to cross paths with you in the future.

Chapter 5:

NEUROBIOPSYCHOSOCIAL IMPACT OF EQUINE INTERACTION & TECHNIQUES TO SUPPORT CONNECTION

BLAIR MCKISSOCK

ABOUT BLAIR MCKISSOCK

Ph.D. CTRS, Animal Assisted/Outdoor Research and Recreation Therapies, Yoga Alliance 500hr E-RYT, HorseWork Master Facilitator and Faculty

Blair McKissock has been working in nature-based education and therapy for over 25 years. As an undergrad, she became a certified recreation therapist (RT) with specialties in outdoor and animal assisted interventions completing field experience in dolphin assisted therapy and adventure therapy. Just after college, she became a PATH Int'l therapeutic riding instructor combining her lifelong relationship with horses and her work as an RT. She continued working as an experiential education facilitator and trainer.

She earned her Master's in Education studying the motivational impacts of animal interaction on academic achievement and student wellness. For the next 10 years, she worked to develop evidence based equine assisted curriculum, professional resources and online education opportunities having had the extraordinary opportunity to travel the country for six months and train in several methods of equine assisted work including EAGALA, Equine Guided Education, and Eponaquest.

Shortly after, she joined forces with Debbie Anderson of Strides to Success to create HorseWork to provide equine assisted learning education and resources. Together they partnered with PATH Int'l to develop guidelines and professional competencies for Equine Assisted Learning (EAL). It was during this time that all of her work began to converge as wonderful connections between experiential education, nature-based therapy and equine assisted learning and therapy.

These connections also showed up in her direct service working with veterans with Post Traumatic Stress (PTS) and other survivors of trauma in EAL and yoga when people experienced moments of feeling "connected". She wanted to understand this more in depth and pursued her Ph.D. in Applied Ecopsychology studying the nature of connection itself and how connecting with a horse impacts people with PTS.

Blair is a regular conference presenter internationally, speaker and facilitates professional development workshops supporting the growth of equine-assisted businesses. She stays active in academics as an adjunct faculty in Public Health and remains an active researcher on several projects. Currently she serves as the Director of Education and Research at Strides to Success in Indiana and is the co-founder of HorseWork. She continues to research and document the efficacy of equine-assisted learning and therapy and train the next generation of facilitators.

INTRODUCTION

Animals enrich our lives. It seems simple and obvious but, this is a loaded statement. In human-animal interactions, we are learning to understand what this means and the implications of our depth of understanding. On the surface, we know that just being in the presence of an animal or being in nature makes us feel good (Beck et al., 2003). If we did not, none of us would be drawn to a helping profession that involves a four-legged co-facilitator and natural environments.

The more we explore, the more we begin to understand that the concept of connection goes beyond just feeling good in the company of an animal. There is actual science happening here that we are learning to understand, yet our ancestors knew as common knowledge. Historical instances of the use of animals for therapeutic purposes go back as far as the third century where the Greeks used horses to rehabilitate soldiers (Rault et al., 2020). Similar principles have been used in medical practice where animals helped to create a psychological impression on a patient to improve the rate of healing. The achievement of these therapeutic benefits correlate to changes in physiological characteristics of humans such as breathing, response to stimuli, heart rate, and the functions of organs such as the lungs and digestive system. Recently conducted studies support the view that human-animal interactions impact physiological processes (Lindström et al., 2015).

Most physiological processes that are impacted by human-animal interactions occur unconsciously and involve the nervous system, hormones, the brain, and initiated actions. One example of an alteration of physiological processes is the vagus nerve that regulates muscle contractions, the operation of the digestive system, respiration rate, and motor functions (Scopa et al., 2019).

This chapter explores the impact of equine (horse) interactions on neurobiopsychosocial processes on the body, conditions for connection, and how facilitators can support conditions for connection in Equine Assisted Services (EAS).

The concept of human-animal interaction goes beyond the simple understanding of pet ownership to make the humans feel better. The next level of understanding involves a reciprocal relationship where we acknowledge the sentience of the animal while simultaneously acknowledging something within ourselves. We begin to understand that we cannot control or dominate nature into submission for our gain. That is an illusion. Instead, there is an understanding that was once "known" but forgotten when we moved into the modern age and away from nature. Indigenous people have "known" we are not visitors in nature; we are OF nature.

That understanding of interconnectedness comes in those moments when we feel connected to life. Our brain relaxes, our body relaxes, and we experience genuine connection. Many of us who practice equine assisted work have experienced those moments when a client connects with the horse, and everything goes still and silent. That connection happens because a shift occurred down-regulating the nervous system allowing for vulnerability and openness that can't happen in states of stress. In that down-regulated state, we are more resilient, more at peace among the chaos, and we can reconnect with that expanse of nature. From that normal state of functioning, we can experience the ultimate state of flow.

Modern humans live their lives in a state of chronic stress partly from the stimulation overload of modern life and the lack of rest in the brain. The life we live is very disconnected from the natural world, leading to what I like to call "nature dysfunction". This dysfunction leaves us hungry for connection of any kind. Have you ever experienced that void or emptiness somewhere down deep that you can't explain? No matter what you do, you can't fill it or make it go away? In our modern world, humans have tried to fill that void in some positive and some not so positive ways.

As EAS professionals, we have the unique opportunity to help our clients experience connection to the equine partners in our practice. We can help them experience a healthy state of functioning by helping to trigger a shift from a sympathetic nervous system (SNS) dominant state to a parasympathetic system (PNS) dominant state. The horses will visibly respond to this shift giving us another opportunity to teach positive relationship skills. Stress inhibits connection, normal functioning, and decision-making. Chronic stress leads to dysfunction in everyday life. When working with the horses, we can teach ways to self-regulate the nervous system, intentionally triggering different functioning states — ultimately fostering the discovery of the pathway back to interconnectedness and back to self.

There is no single theoretical foundation for why horses can have such a profound impact on humans, and we have a long way to go before arriving on an agreed framework. This chapter is not meant to be an academic presentation of a theoretical foundation. Instead, it serves to present ideas on what could be happening in the human body when horses and humans interact and suggest ways to help people get into that space. It is my hope that the content serves to put forth work that has been done by some of the amazing pioneers of our field and serves as the subject for future conversations and exploration of new frontiers in human-animal behaviour.

The general pathway that humans follow in their interactions with a horse begins with curiosity. This curiosity is the key to engaging someone in the process of change, which is generally why people seek Equine-Assisted Services. A human must be willing to engage and be curious to connect in a relationship (Kashdan et al., 2004). Good thing humans have a built-in attraction and natural curiosity about nature. The Biophilia Hypothesis (Wilson, 1984) posits that humans have a natural inclination to affiliate with life, a natural attraction if you will.

Even when a client is afraid to interact with the horses, they still have some curiosity that can be encouraged to eventually reduce the fear enough for connection. Some scientists argue that it may be more the novelty of the horse or its size that attracts people and engages them. In the end, the client shows up and demonstrates some curiosity that keeps them coming back, which is half the battle. It is this moment when there is a willingness on behalf of the person to initiate the physiological cascade within their body, that there is a shift from a threat state to a non-threat state.

The effectiveness of animal interaction, specifically equine interaction, is partly due to the psycho-physiological impact on the human body, reducing the fear and anxiety of social situations that people with Autism Spectrum Disorder (ASD) often experience. Biophilia initially creates the innate attraction for connection and interaction (Wilson, 1984). Following the initial connection during interaction, a cascade of physiological reactions occurs. Although it is not clear in what order it takes place, this cascade effect contributes to our understanding of why animals can help humans acquire social skills and the attainment of treatment goals (Malinowski et al., 2018).

When a client interacts with the horse, they experience a drop in blood pressure, an increase in heart rate variability (HRV) (Gerkhe et al, 2011), and a reduction in cortisol (Malinowski et al., 2018). The increase in HRV indicates a toning of the vagus nerve, which triggers the autonomic nervous system (ANS) to downregulate, stimulating a shift to the parasympathetic nervous system (PNS). During this interaction, there is a release of the hormone oxytocin, creating a positive, empathetic feeling (Beetz et al., 2012), increasing motivation to engage in future social interactions. The fear and anxiety associated with the upregulation of the sympathetic nervous system (SNS), or SNS dominance, in individuals with ASD is related to dysfunction of social, emotional, and cognitive deficits (Song et al., 2016).

Interaction with horses helps the client experience positive feelings associated with social interaction and self-regulation. What follows is a description of the neurobiopsychosocial cascade that happens when we shift from an SNS dominant state to a PNS dominant state and proceed to a nature-connected moment.

THREAT STATE

We live the majority of our lives in a state of stress. Our predictive brain spends much of its time deciding if the current situation or environment is safe. It is the same for our equine partners. We learn what is safe by our experience. Our brain remembers. The stronger the experience, the more intense the memories, the more likely we will not repeat a negative one such a burning your hand on a stove (van der Kolk, 1994). For people with trauma, this is more pronounced.

The chronic state of stress comes with a heightened state of awareness, over contracted muscles in the body, as well as high levels of adrenaline and flight or fight hormones. When we are in this state, our thinking brain is offline, affecting our decision-making and ability to maintain relationships.

When we are in a threat state, our sympathetic nervous system (SNS) is triggered. The SNS is activated by an increase in respiration. When we encounter a stressful situation, we either hold our breath or begin to take shallow breaths. Short quick breaths trigger the vagus nerve to send a signal to all of the major body systems to go offline in order to provide energy to the muscles to fight or flee a situation; much like our equine partners.

The difference is that when the stress is over for the horse, they take steps to shift back to a baseline state. Humans can get stuck in the threat state, (e.g. a feedback loop) where the cycle is continually repeated. The increase in respiration triggers the vagus nerve, which increases heart rate to increase oxygenated blood to the muscles in preparation for flight or fight. There is also a change happening in the brain. When the vagus nerve is triggered, the HPA axis is triggered. This junction of the hypothalamus, adrenal gland, and prefrontal cortex becomes activated. The prefrontal cortex and amygdala are trying to determine if the immediate situation is a threat to safety. They scan memories to see if this is something that has been encountered before. If it is not something was encountered before, the imagination fills in the gaps with other memories to make the best "guess" as to the action required.

For people with PTSD, everything is a threat. Suppose the conversation between the pre-frontal cortex and the amygdala determines there is an active threat based on previous experience. In that case, they signal the hypothalamus to release corticotropin-releasing factor (CRF), which activates the pituitary gland to release adrenocorticotropic hormone (ACTH), which activates the adrenal gland to send out cortisol and epinephrine to the body. The freeze state is a psychological state when the threat response is so strong that the body can't handle it and the thinking brain goes completely offline, leaving us in a freeze response while the flight/fight hormones are circulating throughout the body.

Reduced regulation of the HPA axis from chronic stress and trauma is associated with increased levels of cortisol and other glucocorticoids that can have destructive impacts on the hippocampal neurons resulting in difficulties in learning, memory skills, and attention while increasing the risk of depression (Turner et al., 2010). All of the stress hormones that flood the body heighten our sight, hearing, and other senses making them more acute to the environment to respond. It floods our muscles with oxygen and gives them a boost to increase our chances of survival. The body hums with energy.

Typically, when the body reaches a certain level of cortisol, it creates negative feedback and tells the body to switch back to the normal baseline state or activation of the parasympathetic nervous system (PNS). However, in our current lifestyle, the body never recovers from stress. We continually bombard it with stressful situations and stimulations to where the body becomes desensitised to the effects of the cortisol, and the body does not shift back. Chronic states of stress decrease our heart rate variability (HRV), an indicator of health. It also has many other adverse effects on the body and immune system that compound as we age. The emotions of anxiety and fear that humans associate with these stress states make it nearly impossible to connect. The physiological factors that help us to connect with other life are inhibited. If we loved the threat, we would not be willing to fight it.

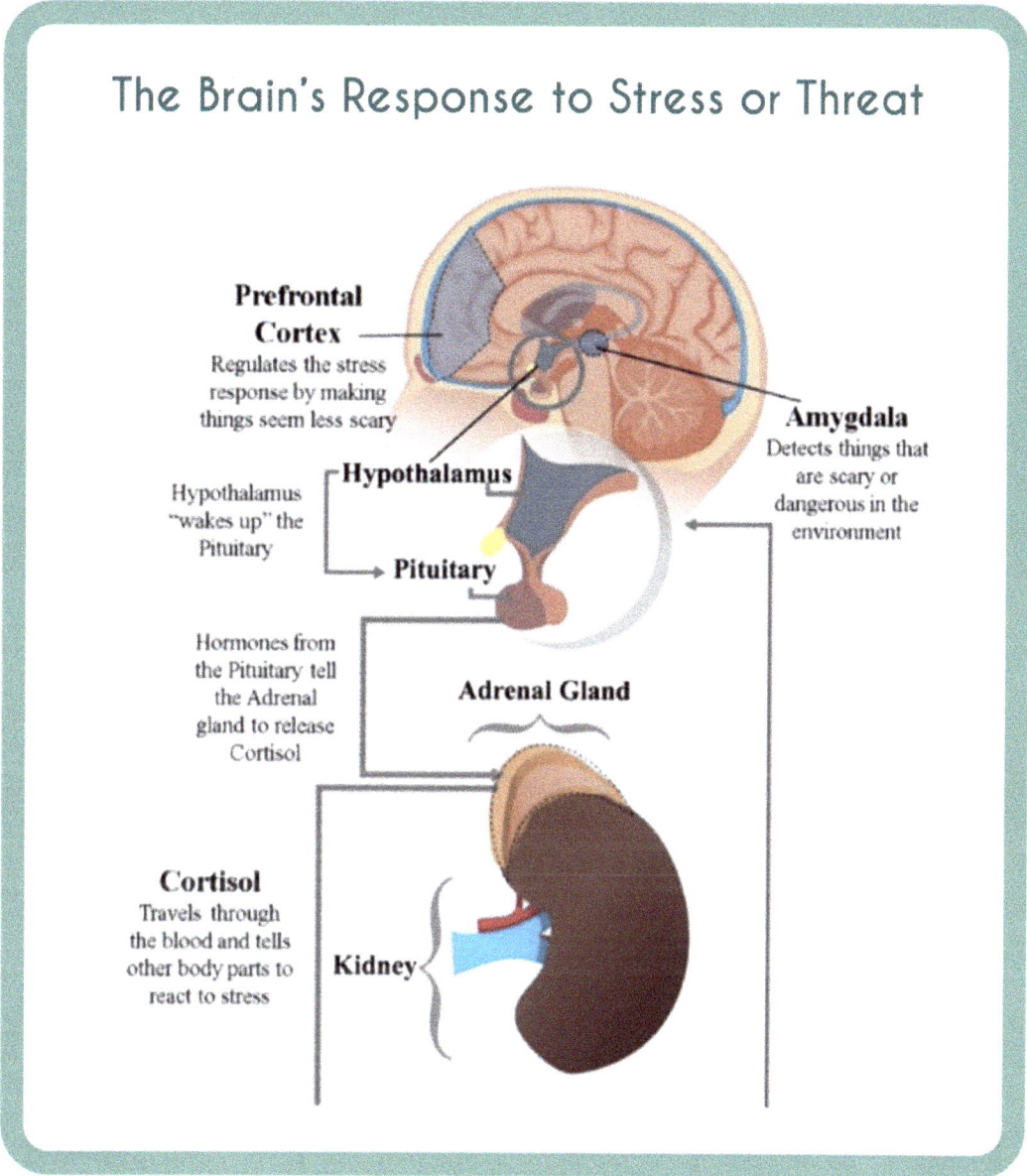

The Brain's Response to Stress or Threat

Prefrontal Cortex
Regulates the stress response by making things seem less scary

Amygdala
Detects things that are scary or dangerous in the environment

Hypothalamus "wakes up" the Pituitary

Hypothalamus

Pituitary

Hormones from the Pituitary tell the Adrenal gland to release Cortisol

Adrenal Gland

Cortisol
Travels through the blood and tells other body parts to react to stress

Kidney

CASCADE TRIGGER

So, what about the state of relaxation that allows us to connect? Approaching a horse, may be intimidating and novel for most of our clients. This "new" situation causes something to shift in us, allowing for just enough of an opening for the shift to happen. The newness of the situation throws off the thinking brain and allows for curiosity and vulnerability. Usually, the climate of the barn and the demeanour of the facilitators promotes just enough trust for the client to feel secure. Clients do not have to feel entirely safe, just secure enough to try. Their willingness to engage in the experience is the key. No one can be forced into relaxation and connection. It is self-elicited.

The notion of intentionally triggering the relation response is nothing new. Yogic practices dating back 2000 years elicit relaxation responses and demonstrated a profound understanding of the nervous system. In the modern era, Autogenic Training was used as a technique for triggering the relaxation response in the early 1930's. There is, however, still so much to be learned about the impact of human-animal interaction, specifically equine-assisted interaction, on the human nervous system and physiology. We know from our ancestors that the human has to cue the body when it is out of danger. However, triggering the relaxation response is different for everyone. Working with horses and being in relationship with them can help facilitate the relaxation response along with strategies and exercises. For example, an act such as grooming causes a relaxation response where the brain activates the parasympathetic nervous system.

If we as facilitators, hold the space for this moment between the client and the horse, their nervous system will begin to shift. We can trigger this by encouraging clients to take a deep breath. The act of deep inhalation triggers the vagus nerve to slow the heart rate and to activate the rest and digest mode in all of the major systems it innervates. Deep inhalation helps to balance the gases in the body including oxygen and carbon dioxide and reinflates the alveoli at the bottom of the lungs allowing for a greater exchange. There is a balance of oxygen and carbon dioxide in the body necessary for normal functioning.

The more we can develop a habit of deep breathing or diaphragmatic breathing, we can help to increase the tone of the vagus nerve. High vagal tone is another indicator of psychological wellbeing (van der Kolk, 1994). When we start with respiration, we also begin the cascade of reactions within the body that shift us from the SNS dominant state to the PNS dominant state. Once the cortisol levels begin to come down, the blood flow increases to the brain and ventricles, stimulating the brain and supporting neurogenesis or developing new neural pathways. This is why being in a relaxed state is good for change! During this process, norepinephrine is released, enabling vasoconstriction. Due to vasodilation caused by norepinephrine, the resulting relaxation response results in a reduction in blood pressure, reduction of respiratory rate, increased blood flow in the muscles, the release of tense muscles, and better oxygen consumption (Toray, 2004).

When we are relaxed and engage in an activity with the horse, the brain will modulate the neurotransmitters that make us feel good and more even. The positive feelings and relationship with the horse serve as further motivation to continue working toward their goals.

Once the PNS shift occurs, a connection can happen. Keep in mind, it may take several sessions with our equine partners before clients can reach that state. It does not automatically happen. The more we can help clients trigger the shift through the practices we teach about engagement and being in a relationship with the horses and other equine partners, the more they will develop a habit that will carry over to their daily lives. This leads to more confidence in a person's ability to self-regulate and greater resilience.

ATTACHMENT AND CONNECTION

Preliminary research suggests that when someone connects with another living being, they can experience intense feelings of contentment, love, and a sense of being connected with something greater than themselves. They feel complete or whole. Cohen calls these moments "Riding the Green Wave" (Cohen, 2007). After the initial shift to a PNS dominant state occurs, then social connections can happen. Several physiological changes occur during the process (Hausberger et al., 2008). For example, the stabilisation of heart rate and breathing processes results in reduced stress, lower anxiety level, better motor coordination, and a general improvement of motor skills. According to Fine, Beck & Ng (2019), teaching someone to develop positive behaviours and mindsets such as breathing and meditating or other forms of effective behaviours, impacts the establishment of retroactive feedbacks. These feedbacks have stimulating and strengthening effects on the vagus nerve. The vagus nerve operates by controlling neuroceptive processes in two ways: activating defensive mechanisms or relational mechanisms (Turner, et al., 2010).

The work of Bowlby, Harlow, and others sought to understand the mechanisms of attachment among all species. Their work showed us that connection is essential for all life, not just for humans. Ultimately, their work gave us the keys to trigger the same biological responses as those experienced between a mother and child (Zilcha-Mano et al., 2011). Bowlby (1969) defined attachment as a biologically-based, evolving psychological system that sets the foundation for motivational, emotional, and memory processes. Myron Hofer, MD (1995) constructed a causal model of Attachment Theory by integrating the constructs of attachment, biopsychosocial framework, and physiological cascade to generate a causal pathway of connection between two living beings (Vincent et al., in progress). When a person is under stress, abnormal attachment and bonding occur. It can create a relationship that is based on co-dependency and fear. However, attachment and connection created in a relaxed state is grounded in trust, security, and safety.

When working with clients in EAS, if we can shift out of the SNS dominant state and into the PNS dominant state, our body systems begin to relax. The vagus nerve sends the signal to the body systems to return to baseline in the body and return to normal functioning (Dusek, 2009). When we return to normal functioning, our thinking brain or the prefrontal cortex comes back online. When we then begin to connect with an animal, two critical things happen which promote connection and attachment: the activation of mirror neurons in the brain and the release of oxytocin. Mirror neurons helped infants mimic the actions of a mother as part of the learning process (Keysers, et al. 2017). Mirror neurons are located throughout the brain. When we connect, the neurons in the frontal lobe begin to fire. Mirror neurons are triggered by individual activity that requires focused attention or when observing another engaged in an activity (Lamm & Majdandžić, 2015). They also play a role in relationships and connection. When the mirror neurons fire, they promote the release of oxytocin, the primary hormone in bonding and attachment. It is not a direct causal relationship, but the two functions occur together and are not mutually exclusive. Of course, this is a bit of an oversimplification of mirror neurons and oxytocin, however, given the right set of circumstances, we can support the triggering of these responses when pairing humans and horses together.

This also supports how being with horses can help humans experience vulnerability, connection, and the positive emotions associated with connection and relationship. When we are stressed, we don't experience deep connections. However, if we as facilitators can foster a relaxed and safe environment, support relaxation in our clients, and then help them experience connection, we can change their lives. So many of the clients we work with individuals or in groups in mental health or learning context have trouble connecting with others. When we create intense positive sensory experiences with the horses, those good memories are just as strong as the intense negative ones. Recall of strong positive memories can create the same feelings of peace and calm when they are recalled equal to the strong sensory experience of a recalled negative or trauma memory. "Emotional memories are forever" (van der Kolk, 1994). So, let us help people create positive ones.

The remainder of this chapter will discuss ways that we can help to trigger the PNS shift and support "Riding the Green Wave" connection with an explanation of the BreathBodyBrain™ method and using an example of a client's first session.

INTENTIONAL TRIGGER OF THE SNS DOMINANT STATE

The BreathBodyBrain™ method is a simplified outline of exercises to trigger the PNS shift and teach them to clients. It was developed over 25 years of growing HorseWork Education at Strides to Success combined with many years of teaching yoga.

Many of the clients who choose Equine Assisted Services, are searching for a means to meet their goals when other ways have failed in the past. For some, traditional office-based therapy has not been successful, or they have become burned out from therapy. For others, they are looking for a novel approach to meet their personal goals.

BreathBodyBrain™ (BBB) uses a top-down, bottom-up approach to trigger the relaxation response in the body by stimulating the vagus nerve and increasing vagal tone. This method integrates beautifully with EAS because of the horse's responsiveness to human body language, personal energy, and intention.

As the client brings their energy down, the horse will tend to respond through connection and engagement. This continuous reinforcement of the intentional use of PNS triggers helps to create habits that will transfer to everyday life. When we teach a single technique but don't create a new habit, the client will go back to old habits and patterns when presented with stressful situations. Integrating the BreathBodyBrain™ (BBB) practices with Equine Assisted Services (EAS) also helps the client learn how to down-regulate the nervous system to bring the thinking brain back online to improve decision-making and relationship skills.

First, it is taught by utilising the easiest and simplest way to tone the vagus nerve, breathing, then moving into the bodywork and brain-based work. Each part builds upon the previous step to help the client spend most of their time living in a homeostatic state and learning how to trigger the flow state.

BREATH

Breathing is living. It is our most basic functions and one of the most powerful tools in building resilience to the stress of everyday life. There are three primary breathing practices taught in the BBB method.

The first is to sigh. Throughout the day, we sigh unconsciously as a way to then reinflate the tiny alveoli sacs at the bottom of the lungs. Sighing is for the most part involuntary. We sigh as many as twelve times an hour! An increase in the sigh can indicate higher stress levels and our body's way of trying to self-regulate. When we are in a state of stress, we tend to breathe from the top third of our lungs or hold our breath, reducing the amount of oxygen exchanged through respiration. When we inhale deeply, we contract the diaphragm and stimulate the dorsal branch of the vagus nerve. This signals to the body and brain that there is no danger or that the threat has passed. You will see horses do this after a spook and when they are relaxed. The deep inhale also helps to off-gas the metabolised stress hormone circulating in the body. It is simple and very effective.

The second breathing technique is to pause at the top and bottom of a deep breath. A pause after a full inhalation, as well as the pause after the lungs are empty serves to help move the stress hormone out of the body and allow the body to release tension.

The third technique is to extend the exhale by a couple of seconds, then inhale and teach them to count the whole breath. Teach the client to count the inhale for 4 or 5 seconds, and the exhale for 6 or 7 seconds, depending on what they can tolerate. The extension of the exhale is another signal to the body and brain that you are in a state of safety and security. Try each of these before interacting with the horses, as part of an exercise or activity with the horses and as part of the giving gratitude.

BODY

Bodywork tends to be a bottom-up technique stimulating "various somato-, viscero-, and chemo-sensory receptors that influence central neural processing and mental activities via ascending pathways from the periphery to the brainstem and cerebral cortex" (Taylor et al., 2010).

The point of bodywork is to invite the client to shift from thinking to feeling; to get them out of their head and into their body to develop an interoceptive awareness. Our program starts with finding your feet. This literal grounding method is a way of feeling the connection to the ground through the feet and feeling the connection. Grounding gives the client a sense of stability and security, allowing for relaxation.

The second part of our program is to move the body. We teach people to move their body to improve blood circulation and move the stress hormones within the body out through the lungs where they are metabolised and leave the body. When we are in a threat state and stay still, the freeze mechanisms in the body are activated, creating a feedback loop of stress. Moving is a way of breaking that loop.

The last strategy is a simple body scan. Invite the client to move their awareness from the bottom of their body upward. Bottom-up muscle relaxation and body awareness help to bring the conscious mind into the body and slow the thoughts in the head. It activates peripheral sensory afferents or sensory neurons that help develop interoception (Craig, 2002) or an awareness of the body's interior landscape.

Keep all body practices trauma-sensitive by giving the client both a choice to participate and control over stopping and starting the exercise. Invite them to notice any sensation and not judge or try to change what they feel in their body. These exercises are great during grooming, leading or mounted exercises with the horse. The horse's body will respond in kind to the client's body as they release tension in their muscles and relax.

BRAIN

Brain activities are my favourite to work with. It can be enlightening to learn that what we think creates an emotional response actually creates a physical response in the body. This knowledge, empowers the client to control what they think, and change the way they feel. It is also one of the most difficult to change. Neural pathways are created in the brain as we develop encoded with memories and experiences that form beliefs about who we are and what we value. It can be very difficult to replace negative beliefs and habits; however, we can create new habits to slowly replace old ones through practicing simple strategies while working with the horses. As a horse owner, these strategies can be just as effective for us as our clients! These brain activities are considered a top-down pathway activated by focused attention and the intention to relax. Think of it as literally working from your brain down to your body.

The first strategy for the brain is to practice finding space between the urge to act and the action. This means to slow things down and to pause before we act or practice non-direct line thinking. For example, when we approach the horse that is in their stall, move slowly and take a moment to ground the body and sigh.

Next, release expectations to accomplish a task such as haltering a horse and simply take your time with each step paying attention to each cue from the horse. Pause before opening the stall door and remind the client, the purpose is not to halter the horse but to initiate a relationship and build trust with the horse. Haltering is just one step. Practice enjoying the doing of a task instead of accomplishing it.

The next strategy is to use a tactile cue to elicit a relaxation response. Teach clients that door-knobs are just as crucial as doorways. When we touch a doorknob, it is a reminder to come back to the present through the touch felt-sense of the doorknob. Walking through the doorway is an act of leaving what happened on one side of the doorway behind in order to be open and present to what is on the other side.

The last strategy is to practice positive situational thinking. This is a common cognitive-behavioural technique used in both counselling and coaching. In the context of Equine Assisted Learning, the facilitator practices the reset technique when the client experiences frustration with the horse either due to disengagement or the horse's response to mixed messages from the client. Reset technique interrupts the negative thinking pattern related to the situation and gives the client a chance to regroup. Then the facilitator teaches the client to reframe the current situation positively and processes how the client might apply the new positive frame in their everyday life. The Reset technique reduces both impulsiveness, and escalating frustration, in a stressful situation.

COMBINED STRATEGIES

There are also many strategies that combine breathing, moving the body and brain work at the same time. If you have ever worked with methods such as Brain Gym™ or Emotional Freedom Technique, they utilise body movements that activate certain regions in the brain to help with behaviour change. The same is true for EMDR therapy. The rapid bi-lateral eye movement activates the prefrontal cortex and the hypothalamus. This allows the client, with guidance from the therapist, to recall intense traumatic memories and resolve the traumatic experience reducing the negative emotions associated with it (Pagani et al., 2012). These triggers of trauma memories can be combined with mounted EAS seamlessly to stimulate interception and proprioception when combined with the 3-dimensional movement of the horse.

Yogic practices are an excellent example of utilising breath (Pranayama), movement (Asana) and meditative practices. The use of mudras, or symbolic hand gestures, are also effective. My personal favourite mudra is **Vajrapradama Mudra**. Try holding your palms toward your chest, interlace your fingers with the fingertip on the outside of the hand and the thumbs straight up. Hold your hands against your heart. This is the mudra of trust and unshakable confidence.

Touching fingertips together in different combinations and bringing hands together promotes cross-lateralisation and sensorimotor integration in the brain as well as increased focused attention. Pair that with a positive thought or mantra and a positive emotional response is created. Simple mudras can be used as gestures when working with the horse to convey a client's intention symbolically.

There are 100's of triggers, exercises, and strategies that a facilitator can integrate into their practice with the horses to support their clients. Once you understand the principles, it is easy to get creative and integrate this work to enhance equine-assisted mental health and learning practices for the client's benefit.

EXAMPLE SESSION

To translate sometimes nebulous concepts into something concrete we can look at a sample session, describing how a facilitator would promote triggering a relaxation response in a client to support connection with a horse. It is assumed that anyone working in EAS has the proper training and experience to do so. If anyone is still learning or training to become an EAS professional, try the sample session yourself and see how the horse responds. The session is meant to be trauma-sensitive and follows the COASTR model of facilitation (McKissock et al., 2022). Everyone experiences things differently; the only truth that matters is your own. We teach from our own experiences, and that's what makes us better facilitators.

TRAUMA-SENSITIVE SESSION SAMPLE

CREATE A SAFE SPACE (CHECK IN)

There are specific strategies that can be implemented to create a safe space where people will be more likely to open up to sensory awareness and connection. Being trauma sensitive means giving the participant choice and control over the direction of a session and providing information to create predictability and transparency. Basic structure of the session follows the COASTR model of facilitation (McKissock, et al., 2022)

Physical Space should be open and inviting, as natural as possible and be clear from debris. Smaller workspaces should be available away from other participants for those who wish to feel more privacy.

CHECK-IN (C OF COASTR)

The facilitator should show the participant around the facility and give a complete tour of the facility to provide a sense of safety and transparency. Closed doors left unexplored can cause stress for people with PTSD.

Go over the norms and expectations while at the facility.

Introduce the basic concepts for connection: grounding, permission, gratitude, and reflection.

Create a low energy atmosphere for connection

As part of the process, participants and horses should both be involved in the selection of the partnership, which horse to pair with the participant. This process is very intentional and thoughtful but ultimately up to the facilitator.

The first connection is special and should be treated with a sense of reverence.

The facilitator should keep their voice low and speak with a calm even cadence.

Set the tone by playing soft music in the background or creating a space outdoors which might include the soundscapes of nature, the smells of the barn, a sense of space, sense of emotional place, of community, and a sense of belonging, support, trust, and thankfulness.

Give the participant time a moment to "arrive" before bringing the horse in.

OPENING (O IN COASTR)

Explain the activity and the process.

Ask the participant to take a moment and set an intention for the session.

After a few moments, the horse should be brought in by an equine specialist and given the same opportunity to settle into the space.

After a few more moments and when the equine specialist feels like the horse is settled as evidenced by their demeanour, head carriage, and body language, bring the client close to the horse.

PNS SHIFT TRIGGER

Lead the client through exercises to ground their body, deepen the breath, open the senses, and calm their mind. This can be any mindfulness exercise.

Take a moment to ask the horse's permission to connect. Any act of permission such as horseman's handshake or mindfully asking for permission is appropriate. This helps to create the mindset that horses have the choice to connect and it helps build trust so they can be open and vulnerable.

Have client check in with their sense of pressure and notice what they are able to sense.

Check in with their emotional senses and their sense of pressure. (For people with PTSD, they need to gauge their own anxiety and energy levels to gain mastery over their ability to self-regulate. This includes seeing if there is too much pressure or energy on them or the horse taking them out of their comfort zone and pushing them into anxiety. The pressure comes from any part of the dynamic and may have an effect on all parts of the dynamic.)

ACTIVITY (A IN COASTR) FACILITATED CONNECTION

Invite the participant to begin approaching the horse, paying close attention to how the horse changes as they approach.

Take a moment to look at the horse's body language.

Participants should be taught to greet horses from the side or the "friendly zone."

This is commonly the shoulder area. Approaching from the front can be confrontational to both horses and people, especially those with PTSD.

The participant should offer their hand to the horse and see if they move their head over to greet them.

If the horse is willing to engage, the participant can move to the next stage of connection where they lay both hands on the horse's shoulder and stay present with the experience.

This physical connection can lead into whatever activity or interaction the facilitator has planned for the participant, but a shortened version should be used every time you greet a horse as it moves the person out of direct line task-oriented thinking and into the present moment creating a sensory awareness.

SHIFT (S IN COASTR)

If the horse is not engaging or the client is experiencing anxiety of any kind, take a moment to rest. This technique is a way for the client to reground and centre their body through the breath and grounding technique taught earlier. The "Reset" is overall, a helpful facilitation technique if things aren't going as planned.

REFLECTION (R IN COASTR)

The facilitator and participant should walk the horse out of the workspace with the equine specialist.

Then move to another area for reflection.

Reflection usually consists of open-ended questions posed by the facilitator to ascertain what the participant experienced. If the facilitator is a mental health provider, they would process the session using their skills and expertise. If the facilitator is not a mental health provider, they would process the experience using experiential education questioning.

Keeping with the experiential model, there is no right answer and no judgment of any kind. This is simply time to reflect on the process, experience, and next steps.

Ask the participant about what they experienced during the exercise and what senses that they noticed. The facilitator can print out the list of 5 senses to go over with the participant.

The facilitator should encourage the participant to begin keeping a journal of each of their sessions to record their somatic, sensorial, emotional experiences and reflections on their experiences.

SUBSEQUENT SESSIONS

The sessions following this first one should be created to align with the participant's goals and allow freedom to follow what happens in the moment with the horse.

The example listed above only demonstrates an unmounted interaction. It is noted that unmounted and mounted interactions can and should be part of the process for clients. However, every situation, barn, participant, horse, and facilitator are different. If the facilitator includes mounted work in their protocol, they should be qualified to instruct riders safely in a mounted session just as they should be qualified to facilitate any type of interaction with horses.

CONCLUSION

We know from research that goes back to the early 90's (Hama, et al., 1996) that spending time with the horse can decrease heart rate, slow respiration and increase heart rate variability (Gerkhe, 2000; Hama, et al., 1996). Most of these concepts are not new. But what is becoming clearer is what happens in the brain and body when we connect. If we can as facilitators create the right circumstances and learn how to trigger the physiological responses, then we can increase the likelihood that our clients can connect with the horses. When clients develop a level of confidence connecting and being in relationship with the horses, then we can help them translate the skill to other people to help them develop healthy human relationships and improve their quality of life.

REFERENCES

Beck, A. M., & Katcher, A. H. (2003). Future directions in human-animal bond research. *American behavioural scientist*, 47(1), 79-93.

Beetz, A., Uvnäs-Moberg, K., Julius, H., & Kotrschal, K. (2012). Psychosocial and Psychophysiological Effects of Human-Animal Interactions: The Possible Role of Oxytocin. *Frontiers in Psychology*, 3. https://doi.org/10.3389/fpsyg.2012.00234

Bowlby, J. (1969). *Attachment and Loss: Attachment*. Basic Books, New York.

Craig, A. D. (2002). How do you feel? Interoception: the sense of the physiological condition of the body. *Nature Reviews Neuroscience*, 3(8), 655–666. https://doi.org/10.1038/nrn894

Cohen, M. J. (2007). *Reconnecting with nature: Finding wellness through restoring your bond with the earth* (3rd ed.). Ecopress., Lakeville.

Dusek, J. A., & Benson, H. (2009). Mind-body medicine: a model of the comparative clinical impact of the acute stress and relaxation responses. *Minnesota Medicine*, 92(5), 47–50.

Gehrke, E. K., Baldwin, A., & Schiltz, P. M. (2011). Heart Rate Variability in Horses Engaged in Equine-Assisted Activities. *Journal of Equine Veterinary Science*, 31(2), 78–84. https://doi.org/10.1016/j.jevs.2010.12.007

Hama, H., Yogo, M., & Matsuyama, Y. (1996). Effects of Stroking Horses on Both Humans' and Horses' Heart Rate Responses. *Japanese Psychological Research*, 38, 66-73.

Hausberger, M., Roche, H., Henry, S., & Visser, E. K. (2008). *A review of the human–horse relationship*. Applied animal behaviour science, 109(1), 1-24.

Hill, L., Winefield, H., & Bennett, P. (2020). Are stronger bonds better? Examining the relationship between the human–animal bond and human social support, and its impact on resilience. *Australian Psychologist*, 55(6), 729-738.

Hines, L. M. (2003). Historical perspectives on the human-animal bond. *American Behavioral Scientist*, 47(1), 7-15.

Hofer, M. A. (1995). *Attachment and psychopathology*. In (Ed.) Attachment theory: Social, developmental, and clinical perspectives, 367-406. The Atlantic Press, Inc., Hillsdale.

Hosey, G., & Melfi, V. (2014). Human-animal interactions, relationships and bonds: A review and analysis of the literature. *International Journal of Comparative Psychology*. International Journal of Comparative Psychology, 27(1).

Kashdan, T. B., & Roberts, J. E. (2004). Trait and State Curiosity in the Genesis of Intimacy: Differentiation from Related Constructs. *Journal of Social and Clinical Psychology*, 23(6), 792–816. https://doi.org/10.1521/jscp.23.6.792.54800

Keysers, C., & Gazzola, V. (2017). A Plea for Cross-species Social Neuroscience. *Current topics in behavioural neurosciences*, 30, 179–191. https://doi.org/10.1007/7854_2016_439

Lamm, C., & Majdandžić, J. (2015). The role of shared neural activations, mirror neurons, and morality in empathy – A critical comment. *Neuroscience Research*, 90, 15–24.

https://doi.org/10.1016/j.neures.2014.10.008

Lindström, N. B., Allwood, J., Håkanson, M., & Lundberg, A. (2015). Multimodal human-horse interaction in therapy and leisure riding. In Proceedings of the 2nd European and the 5th Nordic Symposium on Multimodal Communication, August 6-8, 2014, Tartu, Estonia (No. 110, pp. 61-71). Linköping University Electronic Press.

Malinowski, K., Yee, C., Tevlin, J. M., Birks, E. K., Durando, M. M., Pournajafi-Nazarloo, H., Cavaiola, A. A., & McKeever, K. H. (2018). The Effects of Equine Assisted Therapy on Plasma Cortisol and Oxytocin Concentrations and Heart Rate Variability in Horses and Measures of Symptoms of Post-Traumatic Stress Disorder in Veterans. *Journal of Equine Veterinary Science*, 64, 17–26. https://doi.org/10.1016/j.jevs.2018.01.011

Pagani, M., Di Lorenzo, G., Verardo, A. R., Nicolais, G., Monaco, L., Lauretti, G., Russo, R., Niolu, C., Ammaniti, M., Fernandez, I., & Siracusano, A. (2012). Neurobiological Correlates of EMDR Monitoring – An EEG Study. *PLoS ONE*, 7(9). https://doi.org/10.1371/journal.pone.0045753

Rault, J. L., Waiblinger, S., Boivin, X., & Hemsworth, P. (2020). The power of a positive human–animal relationship for animal welfare. *Frontiers in Veterinary Science*, 7, 857.

Scopa, C., Contalbrigo, L., Greco, A., Lanatà, A., Scilingo, E. P., & Baragli, P. (2019). Emotional transfer in human–horse interaction: new perspectives on equine assisted interventions. *Animals*, 9(12), 1030.

Song, R., Liu, J., & Kong, X. (2016). Autonomic dysfunction and autism: Subtypes and clinical perspectives. *North American Journal of Medicine & Science*, 9.

Toray, T. (2004). The Human-Animal Bond and Loss: Providing Support for Grieving Clients. *Journal of Mental Health Counselling*, 26(3).

Turner, D. C., Wilson, C. C., Fine, A. H., & Mio, J. S. (2010). The future of research, education and clinical practice in the animal/human bond and animal-assisted therapy. In *Handbook on Animal-Assisted Therapy* (pp. 547-578). Academic Press.

Vincent, A., O'Reilly, A., McKissock, H. B., (Manuscript in Progress). Animal Assisted Interventions and Community Programs.

Wilson, E.O. 1984. *Biophilia: The Human Bond with Other Species.* Harvard University Press, Cambridge.

Van der Kolk, B. A. (1994). The Body Keeps the Score: Memory and the Evolving Psychobiology of Posttraumatic Stress. *Harvard Review of Psychiatry*, 1(5), 253–265. https://doi.org/10.3109/10673229409017088

Zilcha-Mano, S., Mikulincer, M., & Shaver, P. R. (2011). An attachment perspective on human–pet relationships: Conceptualization and assessment of pet attachment orientations. *Journal of Research in Personality*, 45(4), 345–357. https://doi.org/10.1016/j.jrp.2011.04.001

PART 2:
Animals
ANIMAL ASSISTED THERAPY

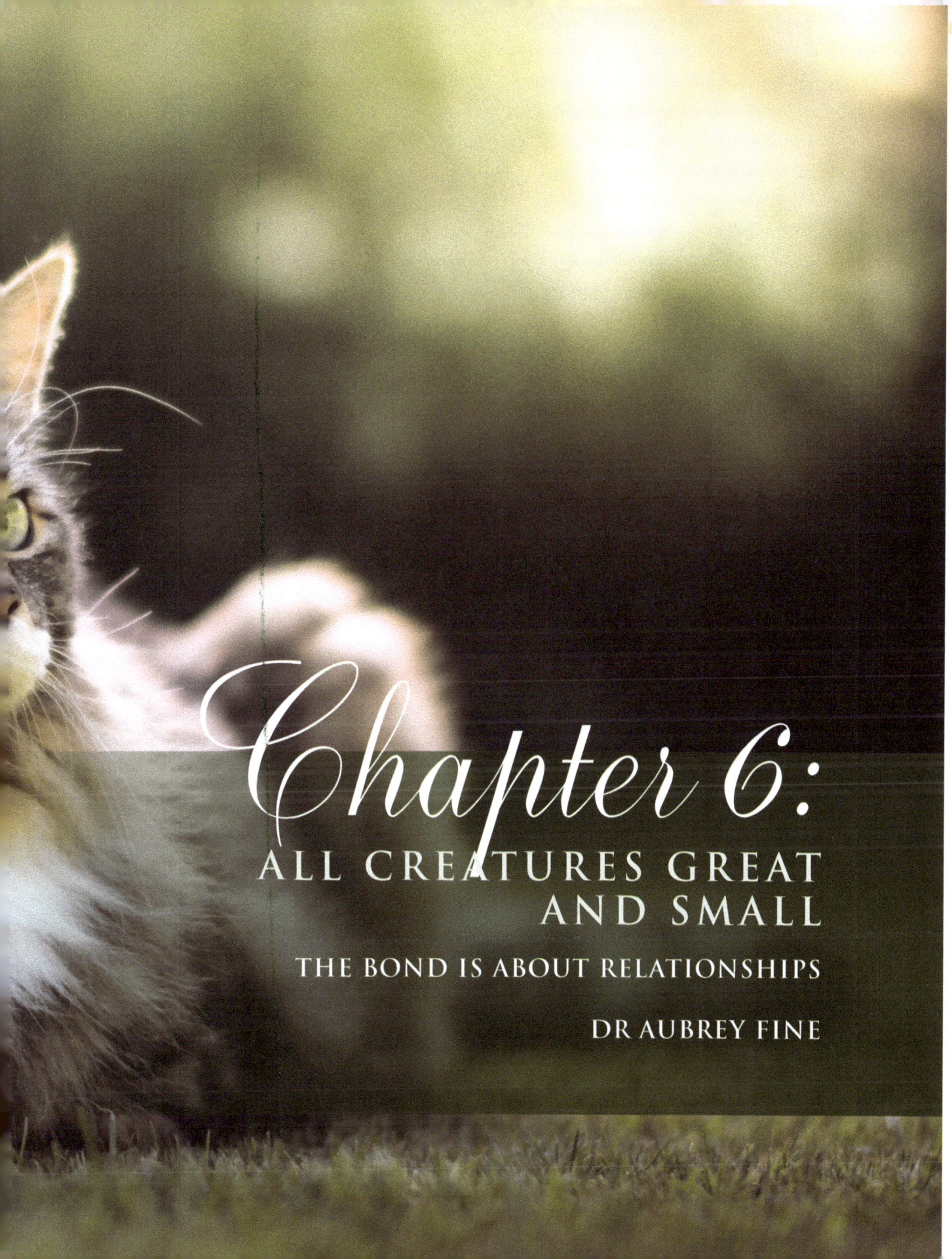

Chapter 6:
ALL CREATURES GREAT AND SMALL

THE BOND IS ABOUT RELATIONSHIPS

DR AUBREY FINE

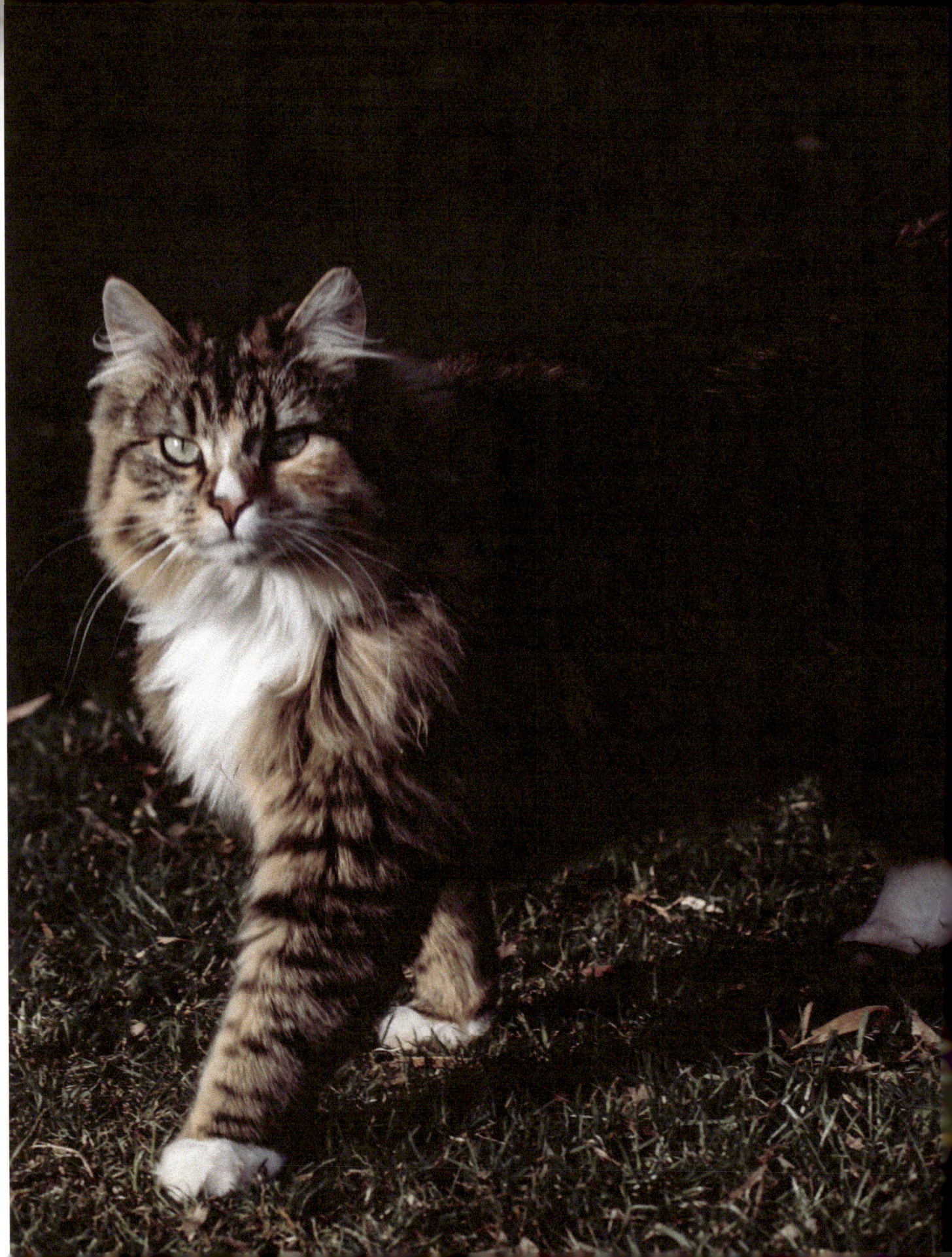

ABOUT DR AUBREY FINE

Ed.D., Professor Emeritus/Licensed Psychologist, CA Poly State University, Pomona, CA, USA

Dr Aubrey Fine is a native of Montreal, Canada. He received his graduate degree from University of Cincinnati in 1982. Dr Fine has been on the faculty at California State Polytechnic University since 1981 and is presently a Professor Emeritus and a licensed psychologist. In 2001, Dr Fine was presented the Wang Award given to distinguished professor within the California State University system (23 universities).

Aubrey has been recognised by numerous organisations for his service and dedication to children, animals and the community. In July of 2016, he received the William McCulloch Award for Excellence in HAI Education and Practice from the International Association of Human Animal Interaction Organizations, in Paris, France. Additionally, he was awarded the Educator of the Year in 1990, from the Learning Disability Association of CA as well as receiving the 2006 CA Poly Faculty Award for Community Engagement.

Aubrey's primary research interests relate to the psycho-social impact of human animal interactions and animal assisted interventions, social skills training and children with ADHD, and resilience in children. Dr Fine is the author of several books including the Our Faithful Companions, Parent Child Dance, Therapist's Guide to Learning and Attention Disorders, Fathers and Sons, The Total Sports Experience for Children, Give a Dog Your Heart, The Handbook on Animal Assisted Therapy (5th edition released in July 2019) Afternoons with Puppy, and The Welfare of Animals in Animal Assisted Therapy (Springer 2021).

He also has had a featured monthly column in Dog Fancy Magazine on the human animal bond entitled the Loving Bond. He has been a guest on numerous national TV and radio shows including on programs on ABC, Discovery Network, KTLA, NPR, PBS, Fox and CNN. Dr Fine's work has also been featured in the Wall Street Journal, Time Magazine, People magazine, Allure Magazine, Associated Press, Los Angeles and New York Times. He was noted as one of the pioneers in Animal Assisted Therapy in the New York Times.

Dr Fine is the chair of the Human Animal Bond Advisory Committee of Pet Partners as well as the past chair of the steering committee on Human Animal Interactions for the American Veterinary Medical Association.

INTRODUCTION

W hen I was invited to give a short opening keynote address at the *Nourished Conference* in January 2021, I didn't imagine that a chapter would be constructed from that presentation. Like all of you, we have our own stories. This article is about my personal journey in reflecting on the significance of animals in my life. My journey began unexpectedly, because I was a child who never had pets.

Many of you may recognise that the title of this article is borrowed from the book and famous BBC series called *All Creatures Great and Small*, based on a country veterinarian, who wrote stories about his human and animal clients and their significance in both of their lives. Many years ago, I had a chance to meet James Herriot's grandson in Scotland at a conference. He brilliantly captured some of the wonderful tales that he recalled about his famous grandfather. His talk was brilliant and heart-warming, perhaps just like his grandfather. A quotation I found years later was where Herriot stated "*If having a soul means being able to feel love and loyalty and gratitude, then animals are a lot better off than a lot of humans.*" Many of you, I believe feel the significance of what Herriot was trying to share.

I applied the title of *All Creatures Great and Small* to this chapter because over the years I have shared my life with so many animals, but there were two that had a more significant impact which greatly changed my life. Most of this paper will be highlighting these special beings. My **small** (using Herriot's metaphor) was my first pet Sasha who was a gerbil that I acquired in 1973. She was a gentle soul who serendipitously changed my life. The other animal that blessed my life is a large beautiful Arabian horse that I met seven years ago. Who would have thought that this city slicker would become a best buddy to a horse? Her name is Amber. You will get to meet her in this article as well.

When I grew up in Canada, I was actually afraid of animals. My mother didn't like them, and her reactions towards them had an impact on both my sister and I. If we saw dogs while walking down a street, we would immediately walk away. My mother discouraged any interest or interactions with our furry neighbourhood creatures but as I aged, I decided that I was ready to have animals in my life.

It was 1973. This truly was a serendipitous beginning (as I noted earlier). I named my first pet Sasha. Sasha was a little gerbil, and once we became acquainted, we got along splendidly! At that time, I was a College student in Quebec. I was working for an organisation part time and was directing a social skills program for children with learning disabilities. One day I thought I would bring Sasha to the program to meet the children. I thought it would be a unique experience for the children to meet a little creature, but I didn't really plan for what I was about to witness.

The program included about 30-40 children, as well as several staff. I still remember that cold morning when I brought Sasha into the program. Sasha was greeted enthusiastically by lots of children. They asked many questions, including, "Why are you bringing this little animal to the program?" "What kind of animal is she?" Some even asked if they could hold her. One boy, Steven (pseudonym), was so convincing in his request that I allowed him to hold her, but I gave him a few specific guidelines that he had to follow. "I'm going to get you to sit down, and you have to promise me you will stay still and not move when I place her in your palms."

Typically, Steven was a very impulsive child but he agreed with my terms, and he sat down with his legs crossed on the ground right next to me. I told him to take his two hands and put them together right next to his tummy with palms up. Then I took Sasha out of the cage, got her comfortable with me first and then placed her onto his open palms. Surprisingly to me, as Steven became noticeably calmer, Sasha appeared more comfortable. Sasha started to meander up his chest to the joy of that little guy. I still remember watching him, with his eyes wide open. His gentle hands were her foundation.

Forty-eight years later what I remember the most, was not the entire interaction, but the highlight of watching a little boy beam with pride as he told me, "You see I promised you I wouldn't move, and I haven't." It was at that moment that I really began to recognise what we conceptualise today as the power of the human and animal bond. It was this incident that intrigued me enough to spend the next 48 years of my life studying not only human animal interactions, but more specifically what is known today as Animal Assisted Interventions.

Let us segue for a few moments from my personal journal to explain the human-animal bond and provide a brief glimpse into the physical and psychological benefits that are derived from our relationships with animals.

WHAT IS THE HUMAN-ANIMAL BOND?

So, what is the human-animal bond? Many of you have likely heard numerous definitions, but perhaps are unfamiliar with the roots of the definition. One should appreciate that the metaphor used for the *human animal bond* (HAB) was initially coined as a term to capture the spirit of the infant-parent bond. The term HAB was borrowed by our early leaders from that unique relationship. The first "official" use of the term "human-animal bond" was highlighted at the *Proceedings of the Meeting of Group for the Study of Human-Companion Animal Bond* in Dundee, Scotland, March 23-25, 1979 (Fine and Beck, 2015).

Perhaps a strong element that exists within the bond is the keen sense of kinship that seems to connect the animal with his/her human counterparts. Many believe that for a bond to be formed the association between humans and their pet animals must be mutual and significant to both parties.

Perhaps the most utilised definition was established by the *American Veterinary Medical Association (AVMA)*. According to the *AVMA*, "The human-animal bond is defined as a mutually beneficial and dynamic relationship between people and other animals that is influenced by behaviours which are essential to the health and well-being of both. This includes, but is not limited to, emotional, psychological and physical interactions with people, other animals, and the environment" (JAVMA 1998 p.1975).

Although the AVMA definition gives us tremendous insight into our desire to interact with animals, some contend that additional traits such as love, admiration and connection must be incorporated in the definition. When writing the book *Our Faithful Companions*, I came across a Greek term that is used to describe familial love which I believe exemplifies that devotion felt within this human-animal relationship. The Greek term is *Storge* (Fine 2014). Recent research by anthropologists have suggested that kinship doesn't have to be a biological relative like a cousin, a grandparent, sister, brother, a parent. But that "kin" could represent individuals in our lives that have meaning to us — for example a person we call our "aunt" might be our mum or dad's best friend. Similarly, animals whose lives have meaning for us can assume closer familial kinship.

Such familial closeness occurs to me when I come home, and the dogs and birds greet me. Years ago, when we had a larger menagerie of animals in our home, it was such a joyous welcome I received. The dogs were excited about my presence and would bark, and the cockatoo would begin shouting, "He's home!" It is not as if my wife was running to the door and saying, "He's home!" *Storge* encompasses this love that we're focusing on. Over the years I've witnessed this form of familial love, not just in my own personal relationships with animals, but in watching people all over the world and how they related with their animals. Pets were once relegated to being kept in spaces outside the home (garage, backyard) but such arrangements have dramatically changed. Many of our pets are now sharing our living spaces and bedrooms.

THE HUMAN-ANIMAL BOND AND ITS HEALTH BENEFITS

I strongly believe that science is catching up to what many of us have believed for centuries: having animals in our lives is good for our wellbeing. Ever since the pioneer research by Erika Friedmann and her colleagues (1980, 1983), multidisciplinary researchers have investigated numerous benefits of pet companionship, including data that petting a dog lowers blood pressure and/or heart rate (e.g., Shiloh, Sorek, & Terkel 2003; McGreevy, Righetti, & Thomson 2005).

Since the early years of this discovery, several other studies have discovered that positive contact with animals can also produce numerous healthy physiological and psychological outcomes, including decreased cortisol (stress hormone) levels, an increase of numerous neurotransmitters as well as altering oxytocin, an endorphin that promotes a sense of happiness (Odendaal & Meintjes 2003). Table 1 synthesises some of the literature and highlights some of the physiological and psychological benefits of pet companionship.

TABLE 1: HEALTH AND PSYCHOSOCIAL BENEFITS OF PETS

Reprinted with Permission (Fine, 2014)

STUDY DESCRIPTION	AUTHORS/YEARS PUBLISHED
Petting an animal causes decreases in blood pressure and/or heart rate.	Eddy, 1996; Friedmann, Beck, & Lynch, 1983; Shiloh, Sorek, & Terkel, 2003
Stroking a pet can lower heart rate.	McGreevy, Righetti, & Thomson, 2005; Vormbrock & Grossberg, 1988
The presence of a pet dog or cat can lower levels of heart rate and blood pressure in stressful situations such as completing mental arithmetic.	Allen, Blascovich, & Mendes, 2002
The risk factor for coronary heart disease was significantly lower for pet owners than nonowners, particularly for males.	Anderson, Reid, & Jennings, 1992
Lower levels of serum triglycerides (high levels of which are associated with increased risk for heart attacks in elderly pet owners compared to nonowners.	Dembicki and Anderson 1996
Pet owners had significantly lower systolic blood pressure. Pet owners had significantly lower plasma triglycerides.	Jennings 1995
Walking with a dog increases and enhances the opportunities to initiate and sustain chance conversations with strangers than walking alone.	McNicholas & Collis, 2000 and McNicholas 2000
Pets can reduce feelings of loneliness and isolation.	e.g., Headey, 1998
Women living entirely alone were more lonely than those living with either pets or other people.	Zasloff & Kidd 1994
Elderly people with pets have also been shown to have fewer symptoms of depression than those without pets.	Roberts, McBride, Rosenvinge, Stevenage, & Bradshaw, 1996
Interactions with animals can also produce hormonal changes.	Odendaal and Meintjes (2003)

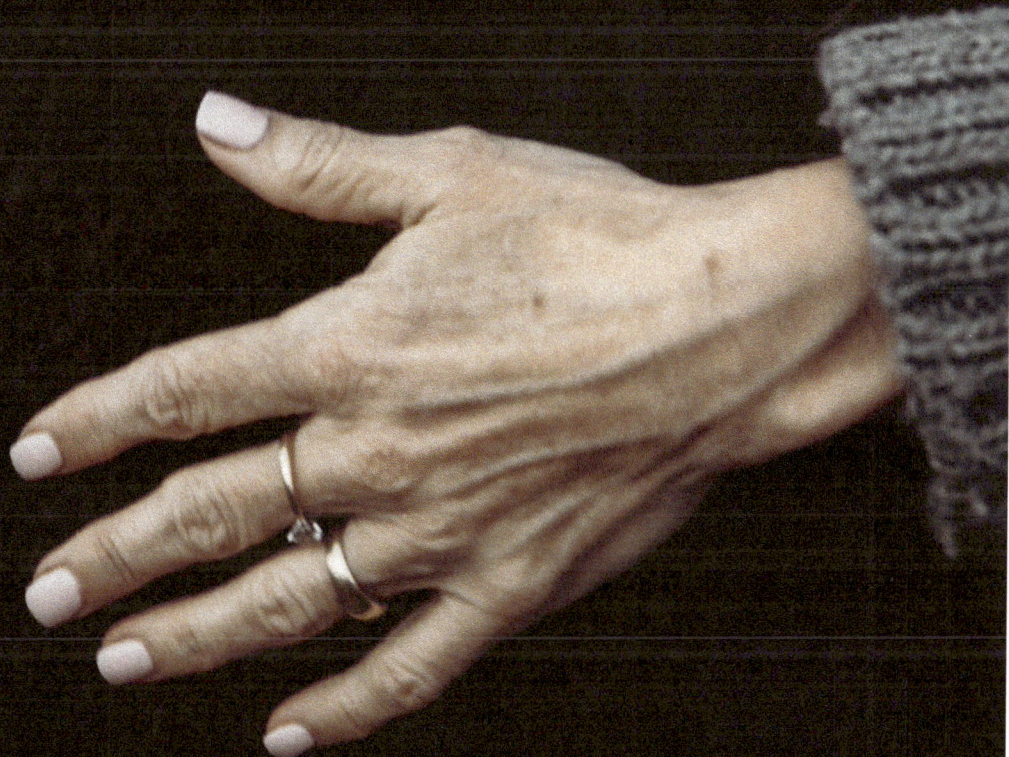

MEETING MY GREAT

Let me switch gears now and return to talking about my **great** and how we met as well as how she changed my life! In May of 2014, I attended a photoshoot to get some pictures of me and a horse. The conference at which I was presenting asked me to have a few pictures taken so they could use them as publicity for my presentation. My University was built on the land of Mr Kellogg. Mr Kellogg, whom many of you know as a cereal magnate, had some property in Southern California where he established his Arabian horse farm. In the middle of the 1930's he donated that land to the State of California and eventually that land became one of the 23 universities of the California State University system. On the campus today, we have about 65 horses.

I remember the day vividly. As I arrived to meet the photographer at the Equine Centre, I could see the horse they selected had a beautiful red coat and was wearing some of her Arabian garb. Although I had previously visited the horse centre on occasion, I really did not have a strong connection with any of the horses. My expectation for the morning visit was to meet one of the horses, capture the moment and just leave.

However, fortunately, that didn't happen. I realised when I met Amber that I did not even have any treats with me to encourage her to relax and become more comfortable to pose with me. Being some-what perplexed before taking the pictures, I turned to a college student nearby and asked, "Do you have anything I can give Amber, so she may be more interested in meeting me?" The student reached into her backpack and said, "Well I have a pear here would that do?" I smiled and said, "Yes." Not being greedy, after I shared a piece of the pear with Amber, I immediately returned the rest to the student. "Here's your pear back," I said as the student chuckled and said I could keep the rest for Amber.

Who would've thought that my whole relationship with a horse would begin with sharing a pear and taking a picture? I didn't want to be the person that would visit these magnificent creatures just to take a picture and walk away, so I promised the student I would come back and help with grooming Amber.

I was so impressed after our brief interaction that I wanted to get to know Amber a little bit. I don't believe the student really thought that I would follow up but I did and that's how our journey began. Over the years the students have acted as my mentors and babysitters to ensure my initial interactions with Amber were safe and positive. Over time we have become so much more comfortable with each other. I always tell people, you haven't lived until a horse runs full gallop in the pasture, just to come to you to say hi and snuggle.

To capture our early encounters and to synthesise the relationship we have formed, I often think of the quotation from the film Casablanca, where Rick tells Louie, "I think this is the beginning of a beautiful friendship." In so many ways, that quotation exactly captures our enduring relationship!

Amber and I have become very good friends. Our connections have led to a wonderful friendship and that friendship has led to our bond. My priority in our enduring relationship is the friendship we share when we greet each other and just spend time together. Indirectly, all the health benefits we talked about earlier are experienced almost every time Amber and I are together. My wife often tells me when I feel a bit down or grouchy to, "Go and visit Amber, she'll make you feel better." I know our visits really do make me feel wonderful. Biologically, my oxytocin is flying and flooding me, because of the significance I feel in regard to our connection. Some people who know me, will tease me and call Amber my girlfriend.

A funny story happened several years ago when I found out that Amber was pregnant. I was so excited and eager to get home to tell my wife. I didn't have my cell phone with me, so after spending some time with Amber, I drove home. When I arrived, I ran into the house exuberantly shouting to my wife, "Honey, guess what? My girlfriend is pregnant!", not realising there were several people in our home, including a contractor who was working in the kitchen. His facial expression was a contortion of shock, genuine surprise, and almost comical "Oscar awards" quality. His face revealed his sense of confusion but he quickly realised that Amber was not a human girlfriend, but an 1100 pound Arabian horse that had captured my heart.

So, our connections really have led to unique friendships that have evolved over the years, even during the restrictions of COVID. My friend Alan Beck once stated, "The indelible bond we share with animals incorporates opportunities filled with empathy, inspired by these connections." It is with that empathy, that these connections really unite all creatures; Great or small, human and non-human.

Since I shared Amber's pregnancy, I may as well finish the story. I was very involved with her care during that period and was so excited about having a first grand horse. In fact, Amber's first foal was my first grandchild. Ironically, Amber gave birth two weeks before, my daughter-in-law gave birth to a beautiful child, whom I adore greatly. During Amber's pregnancy, I had a graduate class on the topic of human-animal relationships and asked the class if any of them would be interested in coming to a horse's baby shower. We had plans to go to the equine centre for a practicum on horse behaviour and equine assisted services. I suggested they could come early for the celebrations and meet some of the horses, including my dear friend Amber. I must confess that I was surprised at the enthusiasm the students shared.

A few of the students set up baby shower games, including selecting a name for the new foal and guessing how many carrots were in a bottle. They even made Amber a baby shower cake, filled with oats, barley, molasses, carrots and apples. Amber seemed delighted with the extra attention and snacks and shared them with all her friends. It's ironic that after the course was completed, the most significant comment, echoed in many of the student evaluations was that the party helped them conceptualise the importance of the human-animal bond. Some students noted they never realised the significance until they celebrated a baby shower with a horse. "Being part of it made the bond come alive."

Daniella, my first grand horse is now five years old and I was there at her birth at 2am on the 15th April. Daniella is a gentle giant with whom I also have a unique bond. Daniella has now had her own foal. I was unable to be there, but ironically Daniella's foal, Fey (barn name) was born on my birthday and unbeknownst to any of the staff, the foal was given the name of my mother (Fae). How eerie, but so special.

Over the years I have truly appreciated how blessed my life has become because of my Great and Small, and all the other animals that I have been surrounded by (I must confess that each of them is also equally as important). As I conclude, I end with Anatole France's quotation: "Until one has loved an animal, a part of one's soul remains unawakened." I often think of my early years growing up in Canada and believe that perhaps my life and soul were not yet totally awakened, because of my limited interactions with animals. I didn't appreciate the significance of their lives, and how they would have such a strong impact on my life.

Everyone needs a champion and I believe that our champions can be animals. Over the years, both my two special friends (my small and great) have truly been champions for me. We need to celebrate the gifts that we share with them and cherish the times together. These moments will leave you speechless — tranquil portals to other living entities.

REFERENCES

Allen K., Blascovich J. & Mendes W.B. (2002). *Cardiovascular reactivity and the presence of pets, friends and spouses: the truth about cats and dogs.*

Psychosomatic Medicine: *Journal of Biobehavioral Medicine*, 64 (5), 727-739.

American Veterinary Medical Association. *The Human-Animal Bond* www.avma.org/KB/Resources/human-animal-bond/Pages/Human-Animal-Bond-AVMA.aspx

Anderson W.P., Reid C.M. & Jennings G.L. (1992). Pet ownership and risk factors for cardiovascular disease. *The medical journal of Australia*, 157 (5), 298-301.

Dembicki D. & Anderson J. (1996). – Pet ownership may be a factor in improved health of the elderly. *J. Nutrition for the Elderly*, 15 (3), 15-31.

Eddy T.J. (1996). – RM and Beaux: reduction in cardiac response in response to a pet snake. *Journal of Nervous and Mental Disease*, 184 (9), 573-575.

Fine, A. H. (2014). *Our faithful companions: Exploring the essence of our kinship with animals*. Crawford, CO: Alpine Publications Inc.

Fine, A. H., & Beck, A. (2015). Understanding out kinship with animals: input for healthcare professionals interested in the human/animal bond. In A. H. Fine (Ed.) *Handbook on animal-assisted therapy: Theoretical foundations for guidelines and practice* (3rd edition) (pp. 3-15). San Diego, CA: Elsevier Inc.

Friedmann, E., Beck, A.M., Lynch, J. (1983). Looking, talking and blood pressure: The physiologic consequences of interaction with the living environment. In: New Perspectives on Our Lives with Companion Animals (A.H. Katcher, A.M. Beck, eds). San Francisco, CA: *Pets Are Wonderful Support.*

Friedmann, E., Katcher, A.H., Lynch, J.J., & Thomas, S. A. (1980). Animal companions and one-year survival of patients after discharge from a coronary care unit. *Public Health Reports* 95(4), 307-312.

Headey B. (1998). – Health benefits and health cost savings due to pets: preliminary estimates from an Australian national survey. *Social Indicators Research*, 47, 233-243.

Jennings G.L. (1995). – Animals and Cardiovascular Health. 7th International Conference on Human-Animal Interactions, Animals, Health and Quality of Life, Geneva, Switzerland.

McGreevy, P.D, Righetti, J., Thomson, P. (2005). The reinforcing value of physical contact on the effect on canine heart rate of grooming in different anatomical areas. *Anthrozoos*, 2, 33-37.

McNicholas, J., & Collis, G.M. (2000). Dogs as catalysts for social interactions: robustness of the effect. *British Journal of Psychology*, 91, 61-70.

McNicholas, J., Collis, G.M., Kent, C. and Rogers, M. (2001) The Role of Pets in the Support Networks of People Recovering from Breast Cancer Presented at the 9th International Conference on Human-Animal Interactions, People and Animals, A Global Perspective for the 21st Century, Brazil, September 2001.

Odendall, J.S. and Meintjes, R.A. (2003) "Neurophysiological Correlates of Affiliative Behavior Between Humans and Dogs." The Veterinary Journal 165(3): 296-301.

Roberts C.A., McBride E.A., Rosenvinge H.P., Stevenage S.V. & Bradshaw J.W.S. (1996). The pleasure of a pet: the effect of pet ownership and social support on loneliness and depression in a population of elderly people living in their own homes. In Proceedings of Further Issues in Research in Companion Animal Studies (Nicholoson, J. & Podberscek A., eds). University of Cambridge: Callender.

Shiloh, S., Sorek, G. and Terkel, J (2003) Reduction of state-anxiety by petting animals in a controlled laboratory. Anxiety, Stress & Coping Vol. 16, Iss. 4,387-395.

Vormbrock J. & Grossberg J. (1988). – Cardiovascular effects of human pet dog interactions. Journal Behav. Med., 11 (5), 509-517.

Zasloff R. & Kidd A.H. (1994). Loneliness and pet ownership among single women. Psychological Reports, 75, 747-752.

Chapter 7:

ANIMAL ASSISTED PSYCHOTHERAPY FROM A HUMANISTIC PSYCHOTHERAPY LENS

THE RELATIONSHIP THAT HEALS

MEG KIRBY

ABOUT MEG

Degree Psychology / Sociology, Masters Social Work, Diploma Gestalt Therapy, Mental Health Social Worker and Psychotherapist of 23 years, Founder, Director, Head of Learning of The Equine Psychotherapy Institute, Victoria, Australia

Meg Kirby is an author and international leader in Equine Assisted Psychotherapy and the growing field of Animal Assisted Psychotherapy. She is passionate about the ethical considerations of working with animals in a therapeutic environment. Meg heads The Equine Psychotherapy Institute, Australia's leading educational and training organisation for equine assisted psychotherapy and animal assisted psychotherapy, delivering live, online and postgraduate equivalent training to Australian and international students. Meg is also the founder of AWARE Therapy™. She is a lifelong advocate for animal welfare and the environment. In 2021, Meg founded her Kind Kangaroo Sanctuary, and is pioneering and teaching an ethical approach for including kangaroos in animal assisted psychotherapy.

INTRODUCTION

This chapter will introduce the reader to animal assisted psychotherapy, and describe the humanistic psychotherapy approach that is unique to the author's approach - a contemporary gestalt psychotherapy, relationally-oriented, somatic-based and trauma-informed model of animal assisted psychotherapy. It will offer a case vignette to support a beginning understanding of the theoretical and philosophical components of the approach; and finally, introduce the reader to kangaroos and the pioneering approach of the authors' inclusion of kangaroos in animal assisted psychotherapy, including the ethical and legal complexities of including wildlife in animal assisted therapy interventions.

AUTHOR CONTEXT, HISTORY, AND INTRODUCTION TO PSYCHOTHERAPY

A little about me to help you understand the development of the psychotherapy approach, and more specifically animal assisted psychotherapy approach, that I have developed over the last decade, and teach both, in Australia and internationally.

I have been a psychotherapist in Australia for 25 years, practicing with children, adolescents, adults, parents, families, and organisations. My psychotherapy practice began within the allied health discipline of clinical social work or mental health social work (MHSW), in the broader context of inpatient and outpatient child, adolescent and family psychiatry (as it was referred to in Australia at the time). Child, adolescent, and family psychiatry is now referred to as child and family mental health, in the government and public sector.

Fascinated by the deep inner workings of the mind and psychological, social and systemic origins of ill-health and psychiatric conditions, I was drawn to child and adolescent psychiatry specifically. At the time, it was known to be the last bastion for understanding the client or patient from a *psychotherapeutic, developmental, and trauma-informed lens*. Adult psychiatry at the time had already moved away from a developmental, trauma-oriented, and relationally focused psychotherapeutic approach to a recovery, management, and medicalised approach, focusing on assessment and diagnosis, medical intervention, crisis intervention, case management and general support and management of disorders.

After graduation in both psychology and social work degrees, I practiced as a mental health social worker first at Monash Medical Centre Adolescent Inpatient centre, and then, the Austin Hospital out-patient child, adolescent, and family psychiatry team. During this time, I received further training through Monash University in Developmental Psychiatry, which was a one-year training program for clinicians practicing at Monash Medical Centre, mental health services. Included in the training, and part of the approaches I was exposed to by fellow clinicians I worked alongside in the psychiatric teams and units, included analytical child psychotherapy, psychodynamic adolescent psychotherapy, family therapy (including a variety of schools of family therapy being practiced by clinicians), psychodynamic parent therapy, systemic adolescent therapy, cognitive-behavioural therapy, behavioural therapy, and play therapy, to name a few.

Luckily for me (and my passion for personal development and psychotherapy) my beginning mental health social work career was steeped in psychotherapy and therapeutic approaches to mental health and psychiatric disorders. From my psychology and social work degree education, I knew that I was drawn to *the third force in psychology* of humanistic psychotherapy and psychology approaches. These approaches were aligned with my personal values and interest areas, and the ethical, systemic, and social justice imperatives embedded in a social work sensibility.

Third force psychology or humanistic psychotherapy approaches focus on clients' inner feelings, subjective experience, needs, fulfillment, search for meaning, happiness, identity, and potentialisation or self-actualisation. Third force psychology consciously attempted to address issues that were seen to be neglected in the dominant approaches of the time, including Freudian psychoanalysis (focused on unconscious sexual motives) and behavioural therapy (focusing on behaviour only). In humanistic psychotherapy approaches, the clients' subjective experience is centre-stage, and the therapeutic relationship is fundamental (and is oftentimes included in the therapeutic dialogue between therapist and client). The inherent power imbalances in the therapy-client relationship are included in the therapeutic dialogue, and in this way power differentials are minimalised, addressed, ameliorated, or utilised to shape the therapeutic process, as useful and appropriate.

I chose to practice mental health social work and simultaneously study a further three-year diploma in Gestalt psychotherapy at the Gestalt Institute of Melbourne (after my initial psychology, social work and developmental psychiatry qualifications). Thus I could receive the *specialised psychotherapy training* I needed to practice *humanistic psychotherapy* within my public mental health social work practice context and future private practice.

PSYCHOTHERAPY

Twenty years ago, in Australia, there was a particular clinical anecdotal wisdom or narrative handed down in certain therapy circles, in relation to counselling and psychotherapy. Specifically, this narrative held that *psychotherapy*, was viewed as a depth-oriented therapeutic approach that attempted to identify and work with very fundamental unconscious processes, attachment patterns, unaware patterns and deep feelings, dynamics or *unfinished business* that a person had been carrying with them

through their life (these were developmental adaptions, protective mechanisms or defences utilised to survive in the context of significant early life relationships and trauma events). *Counselling* was viewed as a more surface-oriented and cognitive therapeutic approach to reflecting on life's difficulties, presenting symptoms, and finding solutions.

I was very much drawn to the deeper work of psychotherapy, including the search for meaning, psychological wellness, empowerment, and diving into the fundamental workings of the "'whole person" in their search for growth, healing, and actualisation.

> " *I was very much Drawn to the Deeper Work of Psychotherapy, including the Search for Meaning...and Psychological Wellness.*

After completing training in Gestalt psychotherapy and a further 11 years of working in child, adolescent and family psychiatry, and private practice as a psychotherapist and mental health social worker, I immersed myself in learning four USA based models in equine assisted psychotherapy and equine assisted learning over a period of three years. I was very surprised, in general, how lightly the word "psychotherapy" was being used. Some equine assisted psychotherapy approaches included very little or no psychotherapy theory or practice methodology in the approach.

Over time and practice, I integrated my depth of psychotherapy knowledge and expertise into some of the equine assisted psychotherapy concepts I had been taught and developed a consistent and unique psychotherapy approach to including horses into clinical and therapy practice.

Later, in 2011, I developed and taught this model of equine assisted psychotherapy in Australia. From 2011 to the current day, I offer education and training at The Equine Psychotherapy Institute for both Australian and International students in online and in-person formats. Our latest endeavour has been to deliver the *Postgraduate equivalent of Equine Assisted Psychotherapy*, which is approved by the psychotherapy peak body in Australia, the Psychotherapy and Counselling Federation of Australia (PACFA).

The Institute has now also developed training and education in animal assisted psychotherapy, supporting registered professionals to include a variety of species into the psychotherapy process, across varied indoor and outdoor environments and settings.

HUMANISTIC ANIMAL ASSISTED PSYCHOTHERAPY

My personal context and the Australian context give you, the reader, some understanding of what the word, and the practice of psychotherapy means to me. Fast forward to the present day, and the terms counselling and psychotherapy are now used interchangeably by many, however the history and term *psychotherapy still means something very particular to me* (and many psychotherapists in Australia). You will not be surprised to know that I use the word psychotherapy, in the context of animal assisted psychotherapy (and equine assisted psychotherapy) to mean something very specific.

If you train with me and our multi-disciplinary clinical staff team at the Institute, you will train in a *depth-oriented humanistic psychotherapy approach that is inherently relational, somatic, trauma-informed, developmentally oriented, and ethical.* This is the essential uniqueness of our animal assisted psychotherapy approach that I will introduce you to today.

ANIMAL ASSISTED PSYCHOTHERAPY

Animal assisted interventions are still emerging in Australia, and include a range of therapy, activities, education, learning, support, and assistance for people, incorporating animals. Animal assisted therapy, at its broadest definition includes animal assisted occupational therapy, physiotherapy, speech therapy, mental health nursing, psychology, social work, counselling and psychotherapy. *Animal assisted psychotherapy is a sub-speciality of animal assisted therapy*, where animals are included and are a central feature of the psychotherapy process.

I was so delighted when I met Nancy Parish Plass via her ground-breaking book, *Animal Assisted Psychotherapy: Theory, Issues and Practice*, in 2013 (and then in real life when I hosted her here in Australia). This was the first book (that I had read) that brought a clear psychotherapy lens and spotlight, specifically *psychodynamic psychotherapy* with children lens, into the broader animal assisted therapy and animal assisted interventions field or context.

As Nancy Parish-Plass so clearly discusses in her chapter on *making order out of the chaos*, the umbrella term of animal assisted interventions must be understood first and foremost, in order to understand what animal assisted psychotherapy is and what it is not. To further complexify matters, many people research and practice with *assistance animals* and refer to them as *therapy animals*, and clinicians, academics and public alike can unintentionally mistake this (the inclusion of assistance animals or activities with animals) as therapy or psychotherapy.

Many people unfortunately also believe that the animal needs the training, rather than the human professional or clinician, which leads to further confusion of what the work of psychotherapy including animals, is actually about. I value Nancy's work so much because her voice (writing and academic work) brings psychotherapy centre-stage in the animal assisted therapy discourse.

What I am bringing to the table in this chapter, so to speak, is animal assisted psychotherapy from a *humanistic psychotherapy* lens. So, I will share my model of animal assisted psychotherapy with you the reader, with a deep respect for other animal assisted psychotherapy approaches. I hope to give you an introduction to my approach of animal assisted psychotherapy and a case study to reflect on. I believe, with more examples of animal assisted psychotherapy approaches, it becomes clear how animal assisted psychotherapy is *fundamentally different* to other animal assisted interventions including other Animal Assisted Therapies (AAT), Animal Assisted Learning (AAL), Animal Assisted Education (AAE), Animal Assisted Coaching (AAC), Animal Assisted Activities (AAA), and, other animal related services such as Assistance Animals (e.g. Assistance Dogs).

So, as defined previously, *animal assisted psychotherapy is a sub-speciality of animal assisted therapy*, where animals are included and are a central feature of the *psychotherapy* process. Let's get a broad picture of what this can look like, as the application of animal assisted psychotherapy can be very diverse. This unique psychotherapy process with animals can occur indoors in a therapy room, or outdoors, in the natural environment. It can include only one species of animal (say for example, including only dogs, or only cats, or only horses or only kangaroos). It can include a variety of species in the same therapeutic space, such as two cats and a dog in a room-based session, or, hamsters, rats, birds, and a dog in a play-based, room session.

Psychotherapy with animals can be facilitated outdoors, for example, in a paddock or yard, with horses, dogs, and cats, or, chickens, sheep, and goats incorporated into the session, or on a bush or forest walk, with wild kangaroos, magpies, frogs and kookaburras in a session. These inter-species sessions mean that the practitioner needs extensive knowledge of a range of species. In a zoo-based or wildlife park-based session, the zoo animals are captive in their separate enclosures and the wildlife may approach or be separated in their species-specific enclosures. Sessions can include a range of animals and species, including domestic animals, farm animals, and wildlife.

Animal assisted psychotherapy can occur at the psychotherapist's private property, in the case of a private psychotherapist offering sessions, or it can occur in government or non-government mental health and clinical services. It may occur in the field, forest, or bushland in public spaces, or in other organisational and business settings (as described above in the example of sessions taking place in zoos or wildlife parks).

The diversity, range, quality and effectiveness of the session is dictated by the psychotherapists' professional code of conduct and ethics, training, approach and experience, the facilities, setting, and therapeutic space or spaces, the psychotherapist's knowledge of animal behaviour and their species-specific knowledge, the animals behaviour, expression, subjective experience and relational tendencies, and the psychotherapists' specific training and supervision in animal assisted psychotherapy.

HUMANISTIC ANIMAL ASSISTED PSYCHOTHERAPY AND THE AWARE THERAPY™ FRAMEWORK

It sounds funny to be using the term *humanistic*, whilst talking about the human-animal bond and human-animal relating, however, from a *psychotherapy* point of view, humanistic psychotherapy, refers to a specific approach to psychotherapy that is different from other psychotherapy approaches including psychoanalytic, psychodynamic, and other behavioural therapy approaches (as previously mentioned).

To understand our humanistic animal assisted psychotherapy approach, is it useful to understand our underpinning psychotherapeutic framework. AWARE Therapy™ is a unique and inclusive psychotherapy approach I developed as a specialist equine, animal, and nature assisted psychotherapy framework. The AWARE Therapy™ approach underpins all teaching, training, and clinical practice at The Equine Psychotherapy Institute (2011-2022). It is a psychotherapeutic synthesis of relational Gestalt psychotherapy, mindfulness psychotherapy, Buddhist psychotherapy, cognitive-behavioural therapy, neuroscience, trauma-informed approaches (including somatic experiencing principles and practices) combined with wisdom teachings of horses, animals and the natural world.

The 10 *theoretical and practice focuses* that articulate the AWARE Therapy™ approach include - **A**wareness; **W**isdom **A**pproach (horse wisdom, animal wisdom, nature wisdom); **R**elationship; Regulation; Resourcing; **E**xperiential; Experimental; Embodiment; Ethical and Enrichment. This psychotherapy approach is discussed and showcased more comprehensively in my book "Equine Therapy Exposed: Real Life Case Studies of Equine Assisted Psychotherapy and Equine Assisted Learning with Everyday People and Horses" (Kirby, M, 2021) alongside rich and varied clinical and non-clinical case studies of the work.

In brief, awareness, mindfulness, embodiment and the phenomenological method of observation, inquiry, and interspecies dialogue, sit as a cornerstone in this approach. Clients are supported to become aware of their Self — sensations, feelings, thoughts, beliefs, values, wants, meanings and desires and patterned way of thinking, relating, and behaving. Clients are supported to become aware of the Other (the animal/s) — who they are, how they feel, move, behave, what they may want, and what their boundaries, consent and desires are. Clients are invited and supported to become aware of the environment, how it may resource, regulate, or impact them in any moment, and how this mutual impacting is happening in the here and now. Clients are invited to become aware of the relationships that they create with the animals and other people, the relationships the animals offer, the unmet relational needs they may have in their history or current experience, and the relational templates that they may have been carrying with them in their lives.

The rich and experiential environment of animal assisted psychotherapy means that there are multiple relationships happening at any one time, so awareness and relationship are the backbone of the session, and the relationship is the "live experiment". In a very real way, the trained psychotherapist can see how the client does life and does relationship! How they approach, perceive, interpret, make

meaning, behave, and step into relationship in patterned ways. The client's sense of self, dysregulation, regulation and capacities to resource, and become aware, mindful, and connected (with self, other and the environment) is experienced, witnessed and engaged with, by the therapist or practitioner. The practitioner offers a safe *therapeutic relationship* and range of *therapeutic interventions, experiences and experiments* to contain and direct the process of psychotherapy and the therapeutic goals.

The animals are the engaging and safe relational system, the live relationship, a microcosm of the live "field of relationships" that are included centre-stage and alongside the practitioner and the broader environment. The animals feel, respond, relate and behave, as they do in their species-specific behaviour and inter-species behaviour, and this subjective experience, responses and behaviour of the animals may impact the client in a variety of real-life and relationally authentic ways. This may include but is not limited to the animals impacting the client in ways that may evoke, trigger, co-regulate, model healthy behaviours, touch, hold, move, play, provide emotional safety, non-judgemental feedback, offer safe attachment, provide a projective mechanism (like all relationships perhaps unwittingly do), and bring different qualities of presence, energy, reaction, and responses, to the therapeutic space.

The practitioner is charged with the responsibility to provide services that are client-centred, relationally oriented, physically and emotionally safe for all parties, and mutually beneficial for the client and the animals, that ultimately provide a therapeutic space and safe container to process issues, address clients' therapeutic goals, and fulfil the professional contract (within the professionals' scope of practice and ethical codes of conduct).

Given all of the above, we never know exactly what will happen, how it will happen, what the client will experience, what the animals may feel or do, and what may get evoked or unfold in the client, and the client-animal-therapist-environment field or system of relationships and relational moments. This work is incredibly creative and rich, and it demands a lot of skill and competency in the psychotherapist, and a very clear theory of change and practice methodology. Therapists, counsellors, and mental health clinicians practicing animal assisted psychotherapy, must first and foremost understand and be trained in psychotherapy, before or alongside the specialist training and practice in animal assisted psychotherapy.

Our humanistic animal assisted psychotherapy sessions can be unstructured, as traditional psychotherapy is, where the therapeutic process unfolds as the emergent themes, issues, and relationships present dictate. Or the sessions can be more focused on or inclusive of psycho-educational elements (for example, learnings related to physiological regulation, feelings and emotions or affect regulation, body, personal space, touch, and value boundaries, etc.). This psycho-educational lens is introduced to the client through an animal wisdom lens — where the therapist is tracking, sharing and inviting curiosity and reflection into the animals modelling or demonstration of what may be thought of as healthy behaviours. For example, self-regulation capacities such as observing animals expressing feelings versus avoiding feelings, or observing animals regulating their nervous system through the out-breath or other movements like turning away, stretching the jaw or other specific movements or actions, versus intellectualising.

The therapeutic choice-point of considering unstructured or structured psychotherapy interventions is assessed through multiple lens such as the client's presenting issues, the client's wants and needs in the moment, the therapeutic goals and contract, etc. This ongoing assessment defines whether the therapist follows a more unstructured process or includes some structured or psycho-educational elements in the sessions, in the service of the client's needs.

Psycho-educational elements can be incredibly valuable for therapists to utilise and include in session, as there are diverse and varied ways that animals can model healthy capacities in any moment. This can include observing animals' self-regulation and healthy expression behaviours and observing the animals' capacities and tendencies to release or use healthy defence responses, when the setting, context and environment supports the opportunity for the animal to do so. For example, after a naturally occurring stressor (such as a loud flock of birds flying over a mob of kangaroos), the psychotherapists and clients can observe and discuss how the animals' physiological processes work or demonstrate in the moment how they release excess energy, stress or conflict, naturally. Additionally, this may serve to demonstrate how animals, within both their authentic, species-specific system of relationships (e.g. with herds of horses or a mob of kangaroos), and within the natural environment or ecosystem they are inhabiting, can successfully self-organise, self-regulate and group-regulate (i.e. regulating together as a shared experience or as a group or community response).

Another example is where a client discusses how they have become aware of a tendency or pattern of holding in their anger (in their intimate relationships in their life in ways that have become personally harmful), and then in the very next moment, the therapist and client observe two horses, one expressing anger and boundary-setting communications! One horse communicates "move away from this pile of hay now" with flattened ears, tightened nostrils and snaking their neck out toward the other horse, whilst the other horse acknowledges and responds to the anger/boundary communication or expression, by stepping back, releasing with a big out-breath snort, and turns back to another pile of hay that is a couple of metres away. This opportunistic moment of psychoeducation can be harnessed (through observation, curiosity, inquiry and dialogue) in many, varied, unstructured and structured ways to address the clients' therapeutic goals and concerns, and therefore heighten potential clinical outcomes and effectiveness.

All animals and the natural world, I believe, provide an *innate wisdom* and *non-verbal, educational opportunistic dialogue* for clients to tap into not just their own meaning, subjective experience, and inter-subjective experience, but also their own, perhaps untapped, human-social-mammal wisdom. Clients can then potentially digest, integrate and utilise this animal wisdom and experiential learning in other life-spaces and relational contexts with humans and non-human mammals and animals. The animals and the natural environment bring an aliveness, emergence, and rich relational and experiential dynamic to the sessions. The animals' presence magnifies, stimulates, and directly provide *heightened awareness, authentic relationship*, and *natural education opportunities*, in this unique psychotherapy process.

ANIMAL WISDOM

Animals can model and remind or teach us about:

Being in the moment, living in the here and now	Animals live in the present moment, not the past or the future. Imagine what your life could look like if you stayed more connected to the present, and not worrying about the past (which is no longer here!) and/or planning for the future (which isn't here yet!).
Regulate the nervous system and calming signals	Animals use calming signals to reduce stress, tension, or energy in their body. For example, a horse may use their out breath to release excess tension (down regulate), a chicken will shake their body after an experience, and a kangaroo may scratch or lick their forearms.
Feelings as information and Self-regulation	Animals feel feelings (as waves of energy – energy in motion) and act on the need beneath the feeling. For example, chickens experience fear and may call out to their flock members or flee for cover, horses feel anger and harness the energy to set new boundaries with their herd members through energy and body language, sheep feel joy, and they express their experience of aliveness and excitement in the moment. Then, they let go, next moment!
	So, feelings are not judged, where one feeling is judged as better than another. They are experienced as information, expressed, and actioned, in relation to the current environment. Feelings are data of the relational field to guide and orient around expression, survival and thriving. Feelings point to an underlying need or message, guide "action" (or response) and completion of needs.
	Thus, animals remind us of the function of feelings and the neutrality of feelings, once honoured, felt, and actioned, healthy self-regulation can continue. Humans are reminded of the layers of judgements and fixed beliefs that can function to interrupt the natural "cycle of experience".
	Once feelings are noticed, named, and fully felt, they can be safely released, releasing the animal or human to respond to the next moment of life experience, and continue the healthy cycle of experience.
No judgement	Animals do not judge, they are not interested in what you are wearing, what degree you earned, or what you ate for breakfast! Animals offer contact or connection, without judgement. All people yearn to be seen, and met, with acceptance.
Unique talents and gifts of individuals	Animals are all uniquely different, as are human beings, they know and express their uniqueness. Noticing and valuing an animal's unique colour, appearance, behaviour or temperament can provide a doorway for people to notice their own tendencies and uniqueness, and perhaps even value their own uniqueness!

Belonging and herd/ mob/ pack/ flock life	Many animals live in connection with their group and each member has a 'place' in the herd/ mob/ pack/ flock. Animals can remind us of our inherent need for belonging and "place in our community" and, our later life developmental life-stage need to "give back" or fulfil our service for the greater good of all humans and beings.
Instincts and sensing	Animals live from their bodies, their senses, feelings, and instincts, and have abilities to "feel from a distance". As animals, they are unaffected by the challenge of integrating cognitive capacities and conditioning of societal living, as humans are. Animals can help us re-discover our true nature, help re-connect us to our sensations and senses, feelings and instincts, and capacities to "feel from a distance", re-connecting with our subtle sensing capacities.
	Spending time learning the language of animals can support us to re-learn what was once ours, and thus we have an opportunity to become more whole and integrated. Integrating these sensing, feeling, and instinctual capacities with our capacities for thinking, can foster a creative intelligence far beyond what we have already experienced.
Experimenting —there are no mistakes	Animal Wisdom can remind us to experience life in every moment and remember that life can be about - living, learning, choices, taking responsibility, fulfilment, and connection to something greater than ourselves. When we experiment, try something new and see what happens, we learn, we choose, we move out of our conditioned psychological and societal patterns, we have a chance to fulfil our potential and contribute to the greater good, to humanity and the natural world we live in.
Play	Play is one of the most effective tools for keeping relationships fresh and exciting. Playing together brings joy, vitality, and resilience to relationships. Through regular play, we learn to trust one another and feel safe. Animals play with us and with each other, and can be a wonderful model for adults who have forgotten to play, and a wonderful support for children in initiating unstructured play, spontaneous play, curiosity and playfulness.

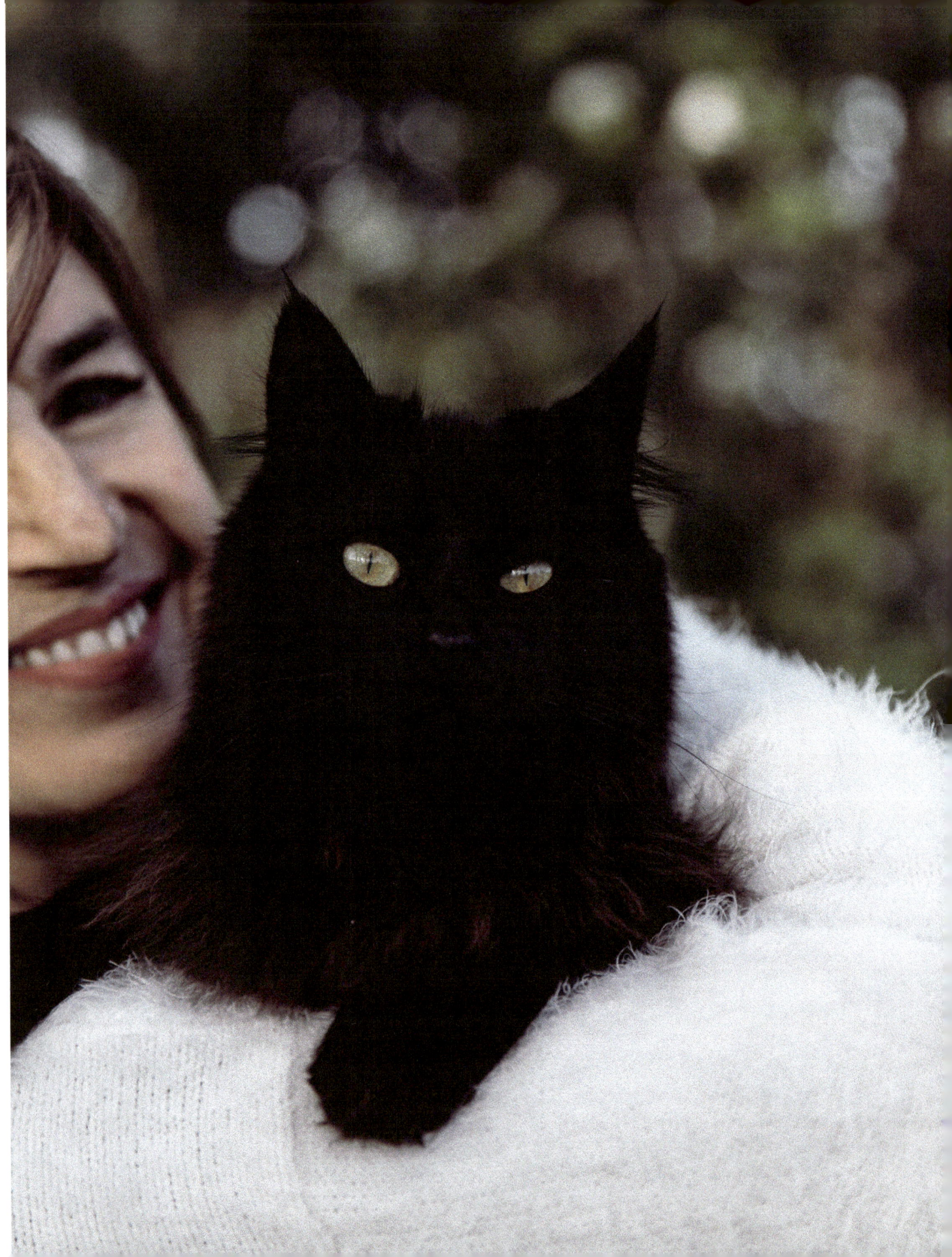

THE ANIMALS' CONTRIBUTION TO CLIENT CHANGE

The role of the animal emerges in the session and the trained practitioner tracks and facilitates the unique way the animal is contributing to client change in many ways.

The animal can offer or become a change agent in the following ways :

The Client (Self)	Client projection onto the animal, so the animal in this moment becomes the client, or an extension of the client.
The Client (Internalised Other)	Client projection onto the animal, where the projection is a significant other from the client's history (referred to as transference).
Co-regulator	Regulating this client's nervous system — the animal's physiology acts as a co-regulator, supporting the client's own nervous system to regulate.
Unique Feedback	Bio-feedback mechanism and behavioural response to clients offers data about how client impacts others.
Role Model	Modelling to client — healthy ways of behaving i.e., living in the present rather than the past (in one's mind or story).
Emotional Safety and Trust	The safe, non-judgemental other (animal) supports safety and stress reduction in the physiology and psychology of the client.
Engagement, Motivation, Interest and Catalyst	Supporting clients' attendance and further engagement, interest and motivation in personal exploration and change.
Educational Support	The wisdom of animals and the behaviour of animals can teach clients about many things.
Evocative cue or trigger	The animal's presence triggers present of part feelings and/ or supports an activation in clients — here the animal may also represent the unsafe other or be a catalyst, evoking unprocessed emotional and psychological material.
Safe Attachment	The animal provides the human with an experience of attachment needs such as, safe movement, touch and holding (and the client may have a corrective experience).

Nature	The animal provides a literal and metaphoric doorway for clients in meeting biophilic needs (to feel and be connected with the natural world and themselves in nature).
Authentic Relationship	An honest and direct relational other
Non-judgemental and accepting other, providing confirmation	Here the client experiences feeling seen, heard, valued and loved by another being (this may include an oxytocin download).
Challenging Other	The animal's behaviour, presence or movements provide a new or novel experience to negotiate, think through or contemplate, which stimulates problem solving, creativity, responding to the current field and other skills that overall build health and resilience.

ANIMAL ASSISTED PSYCHOTHERAPY CASE STUDY

A Unique Therapy for Every Client: a case reflection of long-term animal assisted psychotherapy with an adult with complex trauma and fixed character tendencies, including depression, and life-long anxiety.

Elizabeth is 55 years of age, identifies as female, and has been attending animal assisted psychotherapy regularly over the last 5 years. She came to therapy referred by her general practitioner (doctor) with a mixed diagnosis of depression and anxiety after attending sessions over many decades with other professionals including counsellors, psychologists, and a psychiatrist.

Elizabeth has a complex history including pervasive emotional and physical neglect and potential abuse. Some memories Elizabeth has shared include feeling disconnected from her father. Elizabeth cannot recall having any conversations with her father growing up.

Elizabeth's mother was an intellectual and found solace and meaning in reading. Elizabeth shared feeling close with her mother but felt that she was unable to notice or care for her basic needs, including food, clothing, and other basic daily living needs. Elizabeth recalls often feeling cold and alone. Both parents have now passed away, and Elizabeth has many of her mother's books and collectables.

Elizabeth continues to be connected to her sister, whom she sees yearly. Elizabeth's sister is on the autism spectrum, and Elizabeth has often wondered if she, herself, may be autistic. Elizabeth's sister disclosed she experienced sexual molestation and recalls other inappropriate sexualised behaviour from her father. Elizabeth feels she too experienced sexual molestation or inappropriate sexualised behaviour relating with her father but cannot remember any specific incidents or details.

Elizabeth lives alone however has recently developed a new relationship with a man whom she reports feeling a great degree of deep care, love, and stability, that surprises Elizabeth every day. This is a tremendous change for Elizabeth, who prior to therapy, had never had a long-term relationship.

Over the last 5 years, together we have had therapy sessions with the horses, in the bush, in the room with animal feline (cat) supports Fleur and Sabrina, and canine support with my dog, Bear. The session I am going to expand further on was our first session in the kangaroo sanctuary, which unfolded after Elizabeth's request to have a session in the sanctuary.

What I discovered very early on in working with Elizabeth in therapy was that she needed to have 100% control over the focus, setting, interactions with the animal and myself and conversation topics. What I *could not do with* Elizabeth, was offer any structure, activities, or specific interventions, as this was experienced by her as manipulative. Elizabeth stated that it felt too staged, forced or manipulative. I cannot utilise invitations or experiments such as, "let's take an outbreath together" (to regulate our nervous systems), or "would you like to meet the herd in a way that feels safe and right for you and tune into the animals' personal space boundaries today?" or "spend some time with Crystal and notice what is she feeling right now, and notice what it feels like being together" etc. These kinds of interventions are received well by many clients, however, for Elizabeth they are triggering, and she experiences a heightened sense of resistance, defence, and anger.

In the early sessions, when I offered anything specific and invitational like that, she would look away, avoid, re-focus the conversation, or look at me in a way that non-verbally indicated a NO. I would *hear* her, respond by changing approach, and engage in a way that felt to be within her comfort zone or window of tolerance (most likely re-focusing on *discussing* something that came to Elizabeth's *mind*). I was careful of not moving her outside her window of tolerance, or challenging her too quickly or inappropriately, which would risk a rupture in our therapeutic alliance. I would continue tracking Elizabeth's non-verbal and verbal boundaries with me and my interventions, and initially refrained from moving outside of cognitive functioning and interventions into more disturbing inquiry or experiments (i.e. exploring Elizabeth's emergent awareness and experience, including feelings, sensing, somatic experience or nervous system functioning, activation, or dysregulation).

In the early sessions, after tracking Elizabeth's non-verbal boundaries and communications in relation to my interventions, I started to say out loud, "that is NOT something that interests me Meg", whenever she gave me a sign it was *not* something she wanted to do. In this way, I hoped to give her the signal that I was attempting to notice, track and respect her wishes, feelings or needs, and give *a voice* to her indirect communication or non-verbal boundaries (and perhaps her need to avoid or protect from certain experience and relational intimacy). Then, I hoped, she could agree, disagree and laugh, as she needed to initially.

After years of working together, Elizabeth and I are now able to freely and non-defensively discuss exactly what she wants, does not want, what she feels, what is a "yes or no" for her in the moment and celebrate. Elizabeth has built a tolerance for more freely and directly expressing her feelings, wants, needs, boundaries in safe dialogue with me and the animals. It has been a long journey, and

a very important relational discovery and experiential learning process. Elizabeth now experiences *I can be safely seen and heard* in relationship with myself and the animals, on occasions. This is a significant therapeutic shift.

As a practitioner I have had to stay focused equally and spontaneously on regulation and resourcing interventions, awareness interventions, insight and meaning-making interventions, and relational and relationship-based interventions. Elizabeth has helped me, as an animal assisted psychotherapist, to throw out any *constructed interventions* and apply our humanistic theory of change and practice methodology spontaneously and creatively so that the psychotherapy process now feels like art. I really tune into what is emerging in the here and now, what is happening for Elizabeth, the animals, the environment, and myself in the here and now, and follow and track that with my inquiry, curiosity, and observations.

So many of the more specific and structured experiments (relational experiences with animals) that I teach and utilise with other clients, were unacceptable and inappropriate for Elizabeth. For example, I could not offer - any interactions with the animals designed to regulate, any activities with equipment or props, or any planned activities or invitations to express particular feelings or patterns with the animals. I certainly could not use our Horse Wisdom or Animal Wisdom programs (these are more structured session plans, with a social-emotional learning topic and skill development area, that we teach at the Institute to utilise for certain clients).

During session, everything needed to be absolutely spontaneous with the animals, it needed to be and feel emergent (i.e., unfolding in the moment), and it needed to be conversational, casual and dialogic in style. I had to utilise our institute theory of change and practice methodology in a precisely unique, process-oriented and unstructured therapeutic approach.

I began to understand that Elizabeth would be the one to introduce themes and issues (that matter to her on the day), and I was to track, follow and explore these themes or issues as they emerged in her conversation. In the beginning, we spent time observing the horses; watching the kittens play; meeting or playing with particular individuals in the herd; approaching, touching and stroking certain individuals who Elizabeth was watching, discussing, or wanted to get closer with; getting curious about and discussing the individual's animals' behaviour, feelings, tendencies and dynamics together, and discussing their relevance to her experience, patterns, needs and context (that were meaningful for Elizabeth); being intimate, touching and caressing for minutes and minutes and feeling and anchoring into the emergent resourcing opportunities as they arrived; going for walks with Stormy, Raj, Crystal and other horses in the forest trails; and, taking Bear, my Japanese spitz, for a walk whilst noticing her needs and tendencies.

All of these relational experiences with the animals, the relationship building, the interaction, what, when and how, was all dependent on and developed by Elizabeth's wishes, wants, energy, and the animals' natural engagement, behaviour and the relational moments that unfolded as Elizabeth would meet, connect and engage with the animals.

Over the years, we co-developed a spontaneous and unstructured way of working together that looks something like the following. Texting ahead and checking in with Elizabeth around what kind of session she was wanting, indoor, outdoor, and with whom (horses, cats, dog, or kangaroos). When Elizabeth arrives, we have a cup of tea together and in the check in phase of the session, we connect in with what she has experienced in her life since last session, and what she feels is meaningful to discuss or explore further in the session. We together track the animal/s we are present to or relating with, and Elizabeth shares her questions, impressions, the meaning, and experience in relationship with the animal/s and what is shaping up in the relating in the here and now. I work hard to give equal attention to what Elizabeth wants to *discuss* (cognitive-focused interaction and exploration which can lead to insight) regarding current challenges, feelings and significant themes, needs and meanings that are important to her; the *emerging process* (experience-based, experiential interaction and exploration which can lead to awareness, mindfulness, and a regulated nervous system); and, exploring emerging feelings, senses, and changes in the here and now in both Elizabeth's experience, the animals' experience, and, the relational exchange or between.

When I met Elizabeth, she presented with an entrenched pattern of over-thinking, focusing on definitions, facts, insights from a variety of books, politics and all things related to cognition, to the exclusion of her senses, feelings or the current environment or present moment of experience. Elizabeth was raised in a family system where this was the cultural norm. As a child and as an adult, Elizabeth felt she was shy, introverted and books were her safe haven, both as a child and now as an adult. Elizabeth utilised books and knowledge as the royal road to truth and fulfillment.

Elizabeth has had an ongoing history of finding it difficult to find work, even though she is an academically accomplished woman. Elizabeth shares that she often felt depressed, distressed or anxious, unable to move into action and complete basic living tasks such as eating, household chores, gardening or meeting work deadlines. In session, Elizabeth is currently addressing her hoarding tendencies, as she has all of her mother's collectables and things she has collected over the years, which makes it difficult to find space to entertain, to find space in her home for house-hold basics, or function in a healthy way in her relationship with her partner.

In the very beginning, Elizabeth would talk endlessly about her ideas, memories, tangential thoughts, definitions, tid-bits of history, and knowledge she acquired over the years. I would offer my curiosity, presence and deep listening predominantly, and my I-thou relating (including practicing inclusion, confirmation and commitment to dialogue which largely equates to unconditional positive regard, attuned responsiveness and really understanding her inner world and perspective whilst I stay connected to my authentic experience of being in relationship with her). Over time, after setting boundaries with me (albeit non-verbally mostly) and orienting me to her agenda, Elizabeth began to get used to the role of the animals in the therapy space, and look for the animals to be supporting her in some way *cognitively* (in exploring some new or relevant themes, metaphor, idea and meaning) and *experientially* (in breathing with them, touching and connecting, regulating with them, tuning into the feelings with them, and allowing them to lead the way into the present moment in relationship).

The animals would engage in ways that I was not welcome to. The animals would naturally interrupt her, engage with her spontaneously and authentically in their approach, behaviour and quality of relationship, and over time, non-verbally assisted her to be experientially more present, tolerate different needs (*others needs* in relationship), and draw her attention to calmness and different feelings, when they emerged, supporting her to come to the present moment with a freshness and new meaning. The animals modelled and assisted Elizabeth (over time) to start to *feel grounded and connected, experientially, with herself, the environment and life.*

The animals immersed Elizabeth in authentic *relationship and heightened contact (intimacy)*, slowly, and for greater and greater lengths of time. This was also tolerable and naturally engaging, motivating, and interesting for her. The animals' supported change in a myriad of ever-changing ways, by being a catalyst and support for engagement and motivation; co-regulating her nervous system; evoking nervous system activation and feelings; providing safe, consensual touch, movement and holding; modelling healthy ways of being and relating; giving unique relational feedback; providing emotional safety and trust; becoming a projective medium to explore personal themes and patterns; and much more (as referred to in The Animals Contribution to Client Change chart).

> *New neural firings and neural pattern development oriented around life is safe, life is good, I matter, and, I can be intimate with others.*

We have recently entered a new chapter in the therapeutic process where Elizabeth has now started to naturally feel and report when she feels (spontaneously) coherent, grounded, resourced, and regulated in her nervous system, whilst with myself and the animals. I track and observe, as her out breath now (spontaneously) supports her nervous system to regulate. I join in, when it appears or feels naturally relevant. I now watch how quickly she can utilise myself, the environment, the animals, and the emergent experience of being-together, as a way to explore and experience life safely, supporting not just a new *experiential truth* and emergent meaning and insight, but also new neural firings and neural pattern development oriented around *life is safe, life is good, I matter, and, I can be intimate with others.*

This is a big shift that took many years. There are no quick fixes when you are working with complex neglect and entrenched personality or character patterns (based around what we call *deflection* — the unaware tendency and protective strategy to avoid and regulate awareness, contact and inti-

macy through over-intellectualisation and a conceptualised sense of self and life). Intellectualisation, narrative and over-thinking was Elizabeth's family norm, it was her sanctuary, it was her world. It was her protection from the harshness of the sensing world, where she did not get her basic developmental needs met, where she did not feel seen, held, mirrored, responded to or emotionally attuned to, as a child or emerging adult.

One of Elizabeth's dominant coping patterns of course has been her tendency to get caught up with reading books, to the exclusion of all else. Sometimes she does not eat, shower or complete work. Insight alone, has not been enough to shift this pattern. Understanding the cultural tendencies, understanding her history, her need for psychological safety, the disassociation, and the comfort and certainty that is achieved by reading and intellectualising, only goes so far. Disclosure, cognitive understanding, and insight are not enough for Elizabeth or clients like Elizabeth to sustain deep therapeutic change. I believe, the psychotherapy must be experiential, relational, awareness oriented and experimental. Humanistic animal assisted psychotherapy can provide this.

Elizabeth has tried many therapies and modalities including cognitive behavioural therapy, supportive psychotherapy, and medication over the years. What we have discovered in our animal assisted psychotherapy is that it is ultimately, the *time, the safe authentic and engaging relationship with the animals, lots of open exploration, curiosity and dialogue, creative process and (spontaneously emerging) "corrective experiences" (where Elizabeth experiences safe attachment needs being met) is what supports therapeutic change.*

The corrective experiences that I and the animal partners have given Elizabeth include (a repetition of) experiencing *early unmet needs, being met. These include* core developmental needs for feeling seen, feeling heard, feeling valued, expression of feelings, practicing agency, welcoming frustration and anger and harnessing the energy for action, feeling emotional and psychological safety in relationship, practicing being aware and present, and getting "lost" in the spontaneous moment of experience (as opposed to getting "lost" in her thoughts, ideas). This therapeutic change is slow, and happens over years of new *relational experiencing*, years of re-wiring the brain, the body, the behaviour, and the whole being (including developing a new sense of self, and hope). Years of coming to know a *different way of knowing safety*, comfort and discomfort, regulation, resourcing, relating, inspiration, and truth- through experiencing it. Over time, Elizabeth is experiencing life differently — using her mind differently, and engaging with her senses, feelings, spontaneity, and the present moment. Elizabeth is becoming more aware, present, and connected to herself, others, and life.

ELIZABETH AND THE KANGAROO SANCTUARY

More recently, Elizabeth asked to meet the kangaroos in her next session, and I agreed. She knew about the Kind Kangaroo Sanctuary and had been keenly watching the development of the enclosure, the building, the re-vegetation and finally, and the arrival of my new mob of kangaroos, as she attended each session.

As we first entered the enclosure, a quiet, alert, and aware state of being came over Elizabeth. The kangaroos greeted her by the cabin door. Elizabeth began to immediately move to her mind and ask me questions about the kangaroos, and then, she paused herself, and took an out-breath, and allowed herself to settle back into the moment of relating with the individual kangaroos as they approached.

Harry and Luca the youngest male kangaroos approached Elizabeth. The other kangaroos were lying quietly, listening, but not engaging. Luca approached and began to grab Elizabeth's hands with his tiny paws and throw back his neck in a playful or interactive gesture. Elizabeth was delighted and was transfixed on the little kangaroo and his behaviour. Elizabeth and Luca played for some time and then Luca went back to his pouch bed and lay down. Elizabeth talked quietly, slowly and her thoughts started naturally slowing. Elizabeth appeared to have an increased ability to move fluidly across her thinking and experiencing in the here and now.

Luca approached Elizabeth another time, after settling for about 15 minutes, again engaging her with his hands, body, chest and throwing his neck back. Elizabeth scratched him and rubbed him all over. Elizabeth was overcome with a quiet, meditative style of relating that was unusual, and extensive. Time could pass as we both sat in silence, in presence together, in presence with the kangaroos. The dialogue she shared with me was around feeling transfixed by the *gentleness* of the animals. Elizabeth shared her observations that the kangaroos were naturally curious, with an "ability to initiate, to step towards the unknown" (the unknown, in this case being Elizabeth). Elizabeth described them as "sensitive" and had such a "quiet, gentle way about them".

As I observed Elizabeth, the sensitivity, quietness and gentleness appeared to be impacting her, as her dialogue slowed and quietened. She appeared to rest in moments of silence, and there was an unusual space and spaciousness in our therapeutic dialogue and the therapeutic space. It felt like the kangaroos, in their unique way of behaving as a prey species, with both a heightened, alert awareness and playful curiosity, appeared to foster a heightening of awareness and a different capacity for presence in Elizabeth.

In the integration stages of the session, Elizabeth offered, "how different, unexpected, individual they are". "The horses are prey and herd animals too, but the kangaroos feel so very different...maybe because they are more equal (in size) to us." Elizabeth shared that she was really struck by the mob of kangaroos being a very united group or family, that had a more "cohesive feel" than she had experienced or felt with our herd of horses (which is a larger herd, with many sub-herds and pair bonds within the herd of twelve horses).

Elizabeth attempted to put some more words to what she experienced and what was meaningful for her in this animal assisted psychotherapy session with the kangaroos. She reflected, "It required a different level of mutual trust to engage with them" Elizabeth also commented that given the kangaroos are an "indigenous" (Australian) animal, "I feel they connect in a way that introduced or other domesticated animals don't do for me."

Elizabeth went on to discuss how kangaroos as a native species, feel very soothing and "right" to be with, to be in relationship with, particularly in the sanctuary space where we were seated. Eliz-

abeth also went on to discuss her concern for indigenous animals, climate change, and her concern for the environment and people's relationship with nature. This did not appear to dysregulate her nervous system, instead connecting her to her core values around sustainability and principles of global responsibility.

By the closure of the session, even though Elizabeth had moved back into some cognitive based reflection and discussion of activating topics of concern, I could still feel the impact of the kangaroos — her talking was slower, less pressured, there were lots of pauses and silences, lots of out-breaths and natural moments of re-regulation of her nervous system (using her outbreath and expression), and, she left the sanctuary space with an embodied presence, a regulation and awareness, that was palpably different somehow to other sessions. We had new themes to meaningfully explore next session (if relevant) around, quietness, gentleness, sensitivity, difference, trust, and feeling "right".

> *The power of animal wisdom, the presence of animals, and the real, authentic relationships that the animals offer, is potentially profound and effective in supporting therapeutic change.*

In psychotherapy, each session builds on the next. Each month or year of experiential psychotherapy naturally accumulates and reinforces the changes experienced. So now, as an experienced psychotherapist and animal assisted psychotherapist, I no longer seek quick fixes, but rather I look for tangible evidence of *experiential change during each session*, as well as *shifts and developments across the sessions, over time*. I believe, it is very important that psychotherapists do not get sucked into the six sessions fix all claims, and the short-term solution-oriented approach of our (so called) modern times. Also, I believe it is equally important to stay alert to the sometimes very immediate, experientially evident, shifts and changes that can happen within one animal assisted psychotherapy session.

The *trained* animal assisted psychotherapist is the glue, the weaver of the therapeutic process, and ultimately responsible for the safety, growth and wellbeing of their client, the animals, and the natural space that they inhabit and work from. The rich tapestry of sound therapeutic rigour, creative process and relationally oriented therapeutic space provided by the humanistic animal assisted psychotherapist, the animals, and the natural environment, together weaves a professional, unique, and effective therapeutic service that can meet the needs of a range of clients in ways that is sometimes hard to achieve with other more traditional approaches and settings.

ETHICAL CONSIDERATIONS WITH ANIMALS AND WILDLIFE

In closing this chapter, I want to briefly touch on some of ethical considerations of including animals in psychotherapy, and specifically, including wildlife in the context of animal assisted psychotherapy.

My personal journey has led me (and the Institute) to not just be a regular financial donor for animal-based charities, including Animals Australia and World Animal Protection, but more recently to volunteer at a wildlife shelter, to learn about kangaroos, and, to begin to advocate for kangaroo welfare. This has been a very heart-felt journey for me, both personally and professionally. My mentor at the Wildlife Sanctuary has inspired and supported me to learn about, and ultimately fall in love with kangaroos. This journey has led me to learn about macropods as a species, apply for a wildlife licence to keep eastern grey kangaroos (the kangaroos that are indigenous to our local forest), continue to develop my wildlife sanctuary under guidance and mentorship of an expert in the field, and, ultimately learn how to include them in animal assisted psychotherapy sessions with *select clients*, with a *fundamental focus on the feelings, needs, consent and agency of the kangaroos*, at all times.

Our animal assisted psychotherapy training includes and requires of student practitioners:

- An in-depth education and application of our AWARE Therapy theory of change and practice methodology, including our signature Animal Wisdom Program.

- An in-depth education and study of the relevant species-specific knowledge and skill (of the animal and species that they are wanting to include in their practice), including safety protocols.

- A demonstrated application of our code of ethics and code of conduct (which includes fundamentally ensuring the animals are not just physically safe, but most importantly the welfare, wellbeing, and enrichment of the animals' quality of life is the central feature).

- Specialised education on our unique approach to "I-Thou Inter-Species Relating" that requires practitioners are continually tracking and including their animals' subjective experience, consent (including the animals' ability and freedom to turn away, move away, express and seek distance, space and support), feelings, needs, behaviours, and tendencies in session, and outside of session.

- Alongside, fulfilling other professional, legal and ethical responsibilities.

Ultimately, the *way the humanistic animal assisted psychotherapy professional thinks, feels and works*, across theory and practice, is what supports and provides for the safety, welfare, wellbeing and enrichment of the animals included, in session.

Kangaroos are enclosed in a sanctuary environment where all their species-specific needs are met. In session, they are invited into a therapeutic proximity and space (with the practitioner and client) that includes freedom and agency to choose to approach, meet, interact and dis-engage, withdraw, seek distance, space, as they choose. The kangaroos are included in session, as an opportunity for clients and animals to meet, relate and potentially build a relationship, and for clients to build awareness and mindfulness as relevant to their therapeutic goals.

All contact with kangaroos is based on *consent* and *being-oriented relating* only. We do not teach or utilise *training with kangaroos* (e.g. positive reinforcement based training or negative reinforcement-based training) in session *to support client learning, growth, or change*. All interactions between clients and kangaroos in this way is relational only, not activity or task-focused, and always initiated by the kangaroos.

Thus, in our approach, the animals' consent and mutual benefit is implicit and imperative in the session. Kangaroos are included in our approach, as the "relational other", where clients are offered an opportunity to learn, grow, make meaning, and develop mindfulness skills with the kangaroos. We offer clients an opportunity to step into a "live relationship", an authentic relational opportunity, or authentic relationship (where relevant and where contact over time may blossom into relationship and intimacy) with animals that they may have never met before, and who are indigenous to the land, country and Australia — the land the clients live, work and call home.

We do not utilise tasks, activities, or educational opportunities (through training the animal, for example). We do not utilise animals and set up *tasks for client to achieve, activities for the client to learn from,* or opportunities for the client to *teach the animal commands, tricks or behaviours* or use *animal training* to support growth or learning. We do not recommend to practitioners that kangaroos or wildlife are included in animal assisted psychotherapy. We do, however, model an ethical way of including wildlife in sessions.

The power of our humanistic animal assisted psychotherapy approach rests on *being to being* relating as the catalyst for new awareness, growth, and change. The work that we teach and practice is founded on the ethical premise "it is the safe, consensual, mutually beneficial, being-oriented, and enrichment-based, inter-species relating in the here and now (in the *wider I-Thou inter-species system of relating* — including the human practitioner, client, animals, and environment system) that contributes to client change and healing". I believe, given our *unique and specialist theory and practice methodology*, we are well placed to ethically include kangaroos, wildlife and a variety of animals in our sessions.

In fact, it has been refreshing, exciting and deeply aligned with my values, to include animals in the psychotherapy context, that people can't control, ride, halter, lead and where people do not bring along the commonly held misunderstandings and myths that *the value of animals is largely based on their service or ability to learn tricks* or *perform* for humans. This frees the humanistic psychotherapist up to explore the real work of psychotherapy incorporating animals — awareness, authentic relationship and deep inter-connection that has the potential to enrich, potentially heal and nourish all people, animals, and the planet.

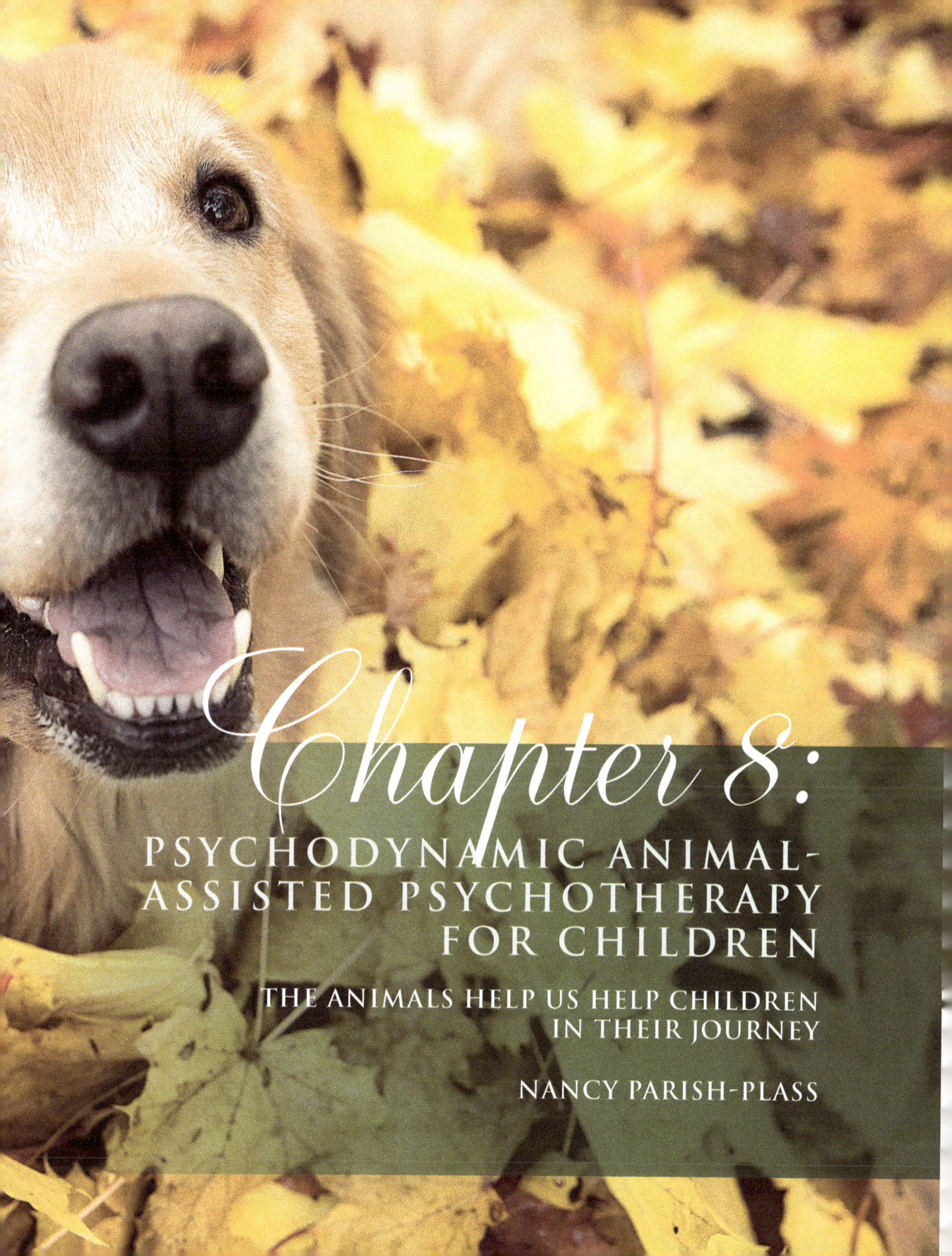

Chapter 8:

PSYCHODYNAMIC ANIMAL-ASSISTED PSYCHOTHERAPY FOR CHILDREN

THE ANIMALS HELP US HELP CHILDREN IN THEIR JOURNEY

NANCY PARISH-PLASS

ABOUT NANCY PARISH-PLASS

MA Social Work Child & Youth – Chairperson of the IAAAP – The Israeli Association of Animal-Assisted Psychotherapy – Haifa, Israel

Nancy Parish-Plass studied psychology at Smith College and the University of Illinois at Urbana-Champaign, before working in early childhood education in Kibbutz children's houses in Israel. She later received extensive training in Animal-Assisted Psychotherapy (AAP) at the pioneering Oranim College and in advanced studies in psychotherapy at the Machon Magid Hebrew University School of Psychotherapy for experienced therapists in the field of mental health.

Parish-Plass is the founding and current chairperson of the Israeli Association of Animal-Assisted Psychotherapy, and she is spearheading the struggle for legal recognition of the field in the Israeli Knesset. Her specialty is in the area of animal-assisted psychotherapy with at-risk children, and she was most influenced in her professional development by memories of her relationship with her horse Baby Doll and her dog Tammy, as well as by all the children with whom she has worked.

INTRODUCTION

While working in the field of Animal-Assisted Psychotherapy (AAP) for the past 20 years with children in various therapy settings — for normative, at-risk, and maltreated children, the other psychotherapists and social workers on staff were often astounded by the special connection I had with my clients, and by the content that came up in therapy. Colleagues often noted that some of these children had been resistant to therapy, or were serial dropouts from therapy in the past, yet waited impatiently to come to their weekly sessions with me. They also noted how some of these children had been in therapy before, but only with me did serious content come up, allowing the clients to work through that content. Was it something about me? Was it the animals? Was it me with the animals? These questions have been welling up inside of me since my student days during my field placement, when the director was almost immediately taken aback by the effect that my sessions were having on the children and what they confided in me, despite the fact that I was only a student.

Those questions led me on a journey, searching for answers through further study, conversations with AAP colleagues, clinical supervision, reading research studies, conducting research, attending conferences, lecturing, and writing. This process helped me to integrate all of the knowledge I gathered during my journey and to reach further insight into how I and others can help "the kids" even more. "The kids" have thrown light on these questions and helped me reach some discoveries and conclusions. The children are no less a part of my journey than the animals and I have been a part of theirs.

The best psychotherapists are not mechanics who carry out therapy "according to a rule book" but rather understand that growth occurs within a process that may take many unexpected twists and turns. Working mechanically, without understanding, will lead to superficial results. Not only do we need to understand WHAT to do, but we must understand HOW IT WORKS, and WHY what we are doing is helping. Only then will we be able to negotiate unexpected directions, and do it better. Furthermore, if we work mechanically, following rules of WHAT to do, instead of feeling the client, then the client may feel like a machine that we are trying to fix. A mechanic and a machine do not have a relationship. Psychotherapy can only occur in the context of a relationship.

Most of my writing is in an academic format, full of references to research studies and to theoreticians, in hopes of stimulating further academic research and gaining more serious recognition of our wonderful field. This chapter will be more "reader-friendly" and written for current AAP therapists and any others who are interested in Animal-Assisted Psychotherapy practices. It is my hope to introduce readers to the myriad of mechanisms that might be occurring under the surface of the AAP process that haven't been previously recognised. These insights may encourage AAP therapists to recognise the variety of opportunities afforded to clients by AAP and how to take advantage of these opportunities.

This chapter is based on my previous publications. Readers who are interested in delving into the research and theoretical background of the information and ideas presented here are invited to read the material listed at the end of the chapter.

FIRST OF ALL.....JUST TO GET THINGS STRAIGHT

AAI – LET'S MAKE ORDER OUT OF CHAOS

Animal-Assisted Interventions (AAI) is an umbrella term for the many wonderful interventions that may be carried out in order to use the human-animal bond to further the welfare of humans, while being aware of the ethical concerns surrounding animal welfare[1].

According to IAHAIO (the International Association of Animal Interactions Organizations), AAI includes AAT (Animal-Assisted Therapy), AAA (Animal-Assisted Activities), AAE (Animal-Assisted Education), and AAC (Animal-Assisted Counselling and Coaching). Each has their own definitions, goals, mechanisms, processes, professional training and approach towards preparation of the animal for the intervention.

Animal-Assisted Therapy (AAT) is the intersection between two different areas: Animal-Assisted Interventions (AAI) and therapy. Obviously, not all therapy modalities are AAI's, and not all AAI's are therapy.[2] This is an important point, for until recently (and often presently), in popular media and even in professional literature, any AAI was referred to as AAT. Whether the writers were referring to visits with animals by non-professional volunteers or to reading programs assisted by dogs in libraries, the activity was referred to as AAT. Further confusion between these interventions is caused by the reference

---

[1] The subject of ethics is critical to our profession and is unique among other therapy professions, for it must also address the issue of the ethical treatment of the animals who accompany us in our sessions. In the Code of Ethics for our professional organisation here in Israel, we refer to ethics towards clients, ethics towards animals, and ethics towards all that occurs in interactions between clients and animals in AAP sessions. For this Code of Ethics, see the citation in the bibliography at the end of this chapter.

[2] Even in the area of mental health professions, there is confusion surrounding the boundaries between sub-professions. Certainly, not every mental health worker is a therapist. Similarly, there are many mental health practitioners who integrate animals into their work very successfully, yet they are not AAP therapists. For instance, a social worker who makes home visits (not for the purpose of therapy) might bring her dog to visit an otherwise intransigent homebound senior citizen who lets her in only because of the dog. Also, in the field of counselling, there are AAC counsellors, accompanied by their dogs, whose emphasis is on psychoeducation or on problem-solving, and not on psychotherapy. Therefore, their work would be referred to as AAC and not AAP.

to "therapy animals", and the person and the animal together are often referred to as a "therapy team". By this logic (or "mislogic"), if someone is bringing a "therapy dog" to an activity, and together they are a "therapy team", then the activity "must" be therapy, and therefore, the person carrying out the activity "is" a therapist, at least in the mind of many of those carrying out the activity and those participating in it. However, therapy is a process that can only be facilitated by a qualified therapist with the relevant professional credentials and academic training. It is therefore, unethical to refer to such interventions as therapy.

Animal-Assisted Therapy (AAT) is not a profession but rather an umbrella term; AAT can include animal-assisted occupational therapy, animal-assisted speech therapy, animal-assisted psychotherapy, and more. Each of these modalities have distinct definitions, goals, mechanisms, techniques, processes, professional training, and preparation of the animals for their participation in the therapy process. It is essential to realise that the animal is NOT the therapist, or even the co-therapist. A therapist is aware of the issues which brought the client to therapy, the goals of the therapy and the path to those goals. The therapist has intention at any given point in the therapy process. The animal has no awareness of these issues and has no intent of fulfilling the goals of the therapy.[3] The animal brings her or his self into the session, and in certain types of therapy, her or his training, which helps to facilitate the therapy process.

AAP is the intersection between AAT and psychotherapy.

FIGURE 1: ANIMAL-ASSISTED INTERVENTIONS

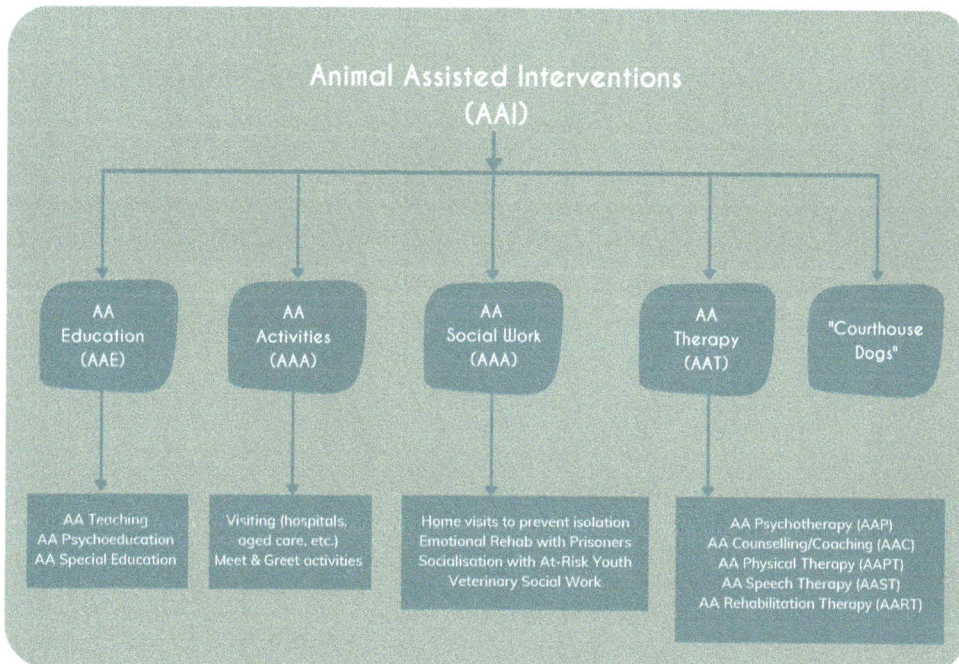

---

[3] I am not saying that animals feel no empathy. However, there is a certain unfounded, in my opinion, romanticism that says that animals know what to do to help people and more so are intent on helping people. I feel that this is "humanising" the animal, anthropomorphising, for our own needs for someone to see us, for someone who wants to and can help us.

FIGURE 2: INTERSECTION BETWEEN AAT AND PSYCHOTHERAPY

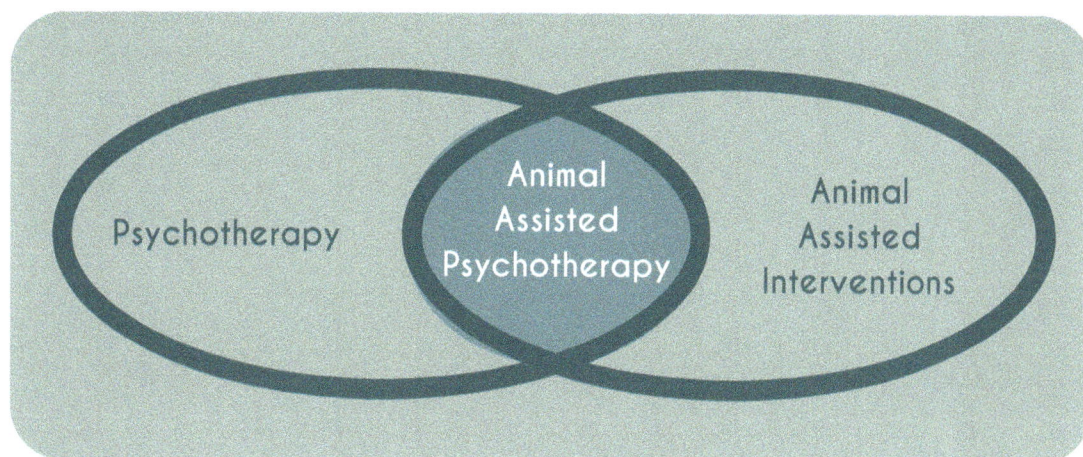

WHAT IS PSYCHOTHERAPY?

The goal of psychotherapy is to modify behaviours, cognitions, emotions and personal characteristics in directions that increase the client's functioning, quality of life, and meets client goals. According to the American Psychological Association, the techniques employed to reach these goals involve informed and intentional application of clinical methods and interpersonal stances based in psychological principles.

This chapter focuses on one type of psychotherapy — psychodynamic psychotherapy with children. Psychodynamic psychotherapy facilitates EMOTIONAL EXPRESSION of the deeper issues that underlie the presenting symptoms (behaviours, cognitions). That is, symptoms (behaviours, cognitions) are an expression of deeper issues, and therefore the goal of psychotherapy is long-term change by working on the behaviours, cognition, as well as the symptoms. The stance of psychodynamic psychotherapy is that psychological problems come from past problematic relationships. Re-enactment of these problematic relationships occurs within the therapist-client relationship, bringing issues to the surface and allowing for exploration. Painful content can thus be worked through and processed, leading to insight and change. Psychotherapy takes place through a medium. For adults, that medium is conversation, explaining the common description of psychotherapy as "talk therapy".

PSYCHODYNAMIC PSYCHOTHERAPY WITH CHILDREN

The medium for psychotherapy with children is play. A subconscious process, play can be an expression of the child's past or present experiences and emotions. "It's not real. I'm only playing." This sense of "only playing" expands what Winnicott calls potential space, the intermediate area between one outer reality and our inner emotional world, the place where we can imagine, experiment with different ideas, explore and express our emotions and experiences to our self and others without fear of consequence and reality crashing down on us. Essential to the establishment of the potential space and a child's ability to take advantage of it, within the therapy process, is a sense of safety — both physical and emotional. Should the child feel threatened in any way, the potential space collapses and imaginative play ceases.

Winnicott would have been fascinated to learn that there Is a neurobiological system facilitating the sense of safety needed for the existence of the potential space. The default mode network (DMN) is a neural network, connecting various regions of the brain, which continues to function even when we are in a resting state; not involved in goal-directed activity, or inward concentration. Should a novel situation or possible threat arise, the DMN alerts us to the need to move our attention outwards. This feeling of safety, provided by the sense of having a "guard at the door", allows us to consciously focus on our internal selves and experience an imaginal space in the flow of time, including context of our relationships with others.

Although considered to be therapeutic in and of itself, play is often not enough for the therapy process to occur. Play must be mediated by a therapist, between the child client and his or her inner world as content comes up within the play. This may be done through the therapist's reflections of what is said and done by the child within the play and sometimes through conversations about that play, depending on the child's cognitive and emotional abilities to participate in such conversations.

Furthermore, it is critical for the therapist to ensure a safe atmosphere for the establishment and conservation of the potential space to prevent its collapse. The therapist must prevent the intrusion of threatening reality into the play which might result in the collapse of potential space and therefore the end of meaningful play. For instance, in a play sword fight, no one should ever actually get hurt. If the child brings up especially emotionally-threatening content in play, it is essential for the therapists to help the child preserve the state of "as if", or pretending. This allows the child to keep much-needed defences that facilitate emotional expression through play until the time arrives that he or she feels comfortable enough, motivated enough, to connect the play to his or her experience, worries, or fears and relate them to the therapist.

The play therapy setting includes various medium in order to further expand the potential space, stimulating play and emotional expression in general. These mediums include creative art materials, dolls and doll house, toys, games, and materials encouraging dramatic role-play. Often, if not usually, the play will become deeper and bring up more content when there is a partner in the play, allowing the child to become a sort of director, giving directions to the therapist of what role to play as well as how to act and react within that role.

Play therapy has many opportunities for achieving the goals of psychotherapy for children:

- Play provides a window to that which cannot be expressed – content that may not otherwise be accessible

- Play may provide the environment that allows communication to occur as well as serving as a channel for communication, expression of emotion, ideas, experience, wishes to self and others

- Discussion of the content, while remaining in the context of play, allows defences to stay intact, which bypasses emotional barriers to discussion of painful reality

- Play with an empathetic and sensitive therapist leads the child to feel understood, resulting in a sense of security and safety, leading to more emotional and behavioural regulation and a willingness to enter deeper into the process

- Play facilitates process of working through painful and confusing issues and content

- Play allows for experimentation of different behaviours and outcomes, leading to insight and positive change

- Play allows for practice of new and more appropriate cognitive and behavioural patterns, which may then be exported from the therapy setting into real life, leading to an overall healthier wellbeing and better functioning and quality of life

THE THERAPEUTIC ALLIANCE IN PSYCHOTHERAPY

A crucial factor in psychotherapy, without which meaningful processes and change are less likely to occur, is the therapeutic alliance. For adults, the therapeutic alliance is comprised of three elements: the client's relationship with the therapist characterised by trust, agreement between client and therapist concerning the goals of the therapy, and agreement between client and therapist concerning the tools and techniques used to reach these goals. For children, who may not have the cognitive abilities to understand or interest in the goals of therapy, the trusting relationship with the therapist is the main component of the therapeutic alliance.

Research has shown that the therapeutic alliance predicts or is strongly related to the therapy outcome. This has been found to be true across therapy modalities and populations. Furthermore, a strong therapeutic alliance established at an early point in the therapy process is especially related to positive therapy outcome. Conversely, a weaker therapeutic alliance is correlated with high dropout rate from therapy. After the initial positive perception of the therapist is established, other factors that positively affect the therapeutic alliance include the therapist's skills in containing anxiety, relating to problem-solving from the perspective of a child client, and creating a sense of privacy and confidentiality. Working on past and present relationship problems through the client-therapist relationship, in a situation characterised by intimacy together with autonomy, facilitates the exploration of the client's emotional issues within the therapy process.

Some children however, may be resistant to forming a therapeutic alliance with their therapist. Parents bring their children to therapy due to emotional, social and behavioural problems. Depending

on the way the concept and goal of the therapy is presented to the child, the child may feel that the parents, and the therapist, are trying to "fix" them; they may close down, become defensive and reject the idea of a relationship with the therapist. Due to their life experience, some children have a general lack of trust in adults and may be characterised by insecure attachment. These children may see all adults as emotionally unavailable, rejecting, or even dangerous.

Somehow, the therapist must create a sense of safety for the client within the therapist-client relationship. One possible solution for resistance to the establishment of the therapeutic alliance is a focus on what is referred to as the third thing. That is, the therapist may suggest that they both focus on something outside of the therapist-client relationship that can be studied and observed by both therapist and client. This third thing serves as a neutral area where communication is indirect. It allows for less threatening, authentic and warm sharing of one's inner world, forming a bridge to the therapeutic alliance and emotional expression. Examples of a third thing may be a hobby, sports, a book, love for nature, or an animal.

ANIMAL ASSISTED PSYCHOTHERAPY

Animal-Assisted Psychotherapy (AAP) has the same goals as psychotherapy with many of the same mechanisms and processes. Some of the mechanisms, however, have unique qualities, while others are in and of themselves unique to AAP. This uniqueness allows the therapist to reach the client and advance processes that otherwise may not occur.

MECHANISMS: THE INTEGRATION OF ANIMALS INTO THE THERAPY SETTING CREATES A SAFE ENVIRONMENT FOR THERAPY PROCESSES TO OCCUR

AUTHENTICITY OF THE AAP ENVIRONMENT

Arriving to a first therapy session is likely to be daunting for a client. The situation is artificial, the client knows there will be expectations of him or her but is unaware of what they might be, and a sense of hierarchy is inherent. The presence of the animals facilitates a more natural, less artificial atmosphere in the therapy setting, making it less threatening to the client. Animals are inherently authentic in their behaviour and emotional expression. They may show curiosity in the client, initiate interaction, avoid the client, or simply ignore the client. Animals naturally behave, interact, and express emotions without any agenda to manipulate or make an impression on a client.

Furthermore, the authentic behaviour of the therapist in interaction with the animals such as: spontaneously patting the dog, laughing at the rats' antics, worrying about a sick hamster, leads to an impression of a more natural and authentic therapy environment where authentic and spontaneous emotional expression is accepted and even the norm. The therapist might describe the animals in a way that is accepting of who they are, allowing the client to perceive the atmosphere as one of overall acceptance. A dog's initiation of interaction with the client, encouragement from the therapist towards both client and dog, together with the reflections by the therapist of the dog's behaviour and emotional expression, serves as an invitation for the client to join the social situation and take part. The roles of "therapist" and "client", which might be daunting to the client, are likely to be blurred or even erased, making the atmosphere feel even less artificial and more personal.

ANIMALS PROVIDING A SENSE OF SAFETY

Attachment theory, which has been strongly backed up in research, discusses what is needed for the formation of a healthy attachment between a mother and baby, in order for the baby to form future healthy relationships, leading to optimal psychological health. The four characteristics of secure attachment are proximity maintenance (the desire to be near the people to whom we are attached), secure base (from which the child may be curious and explore the environment with a secure feeling), safe haven (to which the child may return for comfort when feeling threatened in any way during that exploration) and separation distress (anxiety that occurs in the absence of the attachment figure). The basis for attachment theory has been found not only in psychological research but also in research in the area of interpersonal neurobiology.

Research has shown that an animal may serve as both a secure base and safe haven for a client in the therapy setting. The implication of this finding is that the presence of the animal is likely to create a sense of safety from which the client may explore his or her inner world and dare to express it. If especially threatening memories or associations are touched and the client becomes overwhelmed, he or she may go back to the animal for cuddling and safe interactions in order to feel safe and calm again.

This sense of safety provided by the animals is intricately related to and positively influences many mechanisms in psychotherapy, explaining the uniqueness of the contribution of animals to the field of psychotherapy. The influence of this sense of safety provided by the animals' presence on mechanisms of psychotherapy will be detailed in the following sections.

ANIMALS AND ALL THEY BRING WITH THEM – A UNIQUE MEDIUM IN THERAPY

As opposed to other mediums (conversation, art, music, books, etc.), the medium of Animal-Assisted Psychotherapy (AAP) is ALIVENESS. That is, animals move (e.g. run or fly), they eat, defecate, urinate, are born and give birth, get sick, recover, require medical assistance, shed hair or moult feathers, feel as well as show emotion and pain, play, fight, and eventually die.

They stimulate our senses and have senses themselves that can be observed through their reactions to what they sense — they make noise and react to noise, can be smelly and smell (food, grass, us and each other), they move and cause us to move, may be soft/scaly/bristly when we touch them, have colour. They seem like..., they remind us of.... The animals' behaviours, emotions and characteristics are similar to those of humans, yet not the same, therefore they represent reality at a safe psychological distance, allowing for threatening content to arise. "It's not me.... it's the animal." The animals and all they bring with them serve as a very rich and multidimensional medium, stimulating for the client associations, memories, sensations, emotions, and content, all of which have their roots in the client's inner world. When brought up in play or discussion, they serve as a window into that inner world, which is critical to the therapy process.

There is evidence to suggest a neurobiological explanation for the stimulation of the client's inner world through animals. The amygdala is the emotional centre of the brain which holds our implicit memories, that is our unconscious memories for which we have no words but are expressed in our physical sensations, emotions, perceptions, and behaviours for which we have no explanation and therefore may confuse us.

Successful psychotherapy depends on the ability to gain access to these implicit memories and to give them words, part of the process of translating them to explicit memories that can be worked through in order to form a meaningful narrative. This is especially critical in the case of interpersonal trauma, which causes damage to neural pathways that are responsible for the translation of implicit memories of the amygdala to explicit memories in the hippocampus. According to research, seeing animals activates the right amygdala highly significantly more than seeing people or landscapes, therefore stimulating these implicit memories.

The presence of the animals in our sessions is likely to facilitate the expression of these implicit memories and associated reactions, which can be used to work through the issues that brought the client to therapy. Our goal as therapists is to gain access to the client's inner emotional world. Animals supply that access through their effect on the amygdala.

Animals will always be accompanied by certain accessories that may bring associations and content for the client. A dog's leash may bring up the subject of control. A hamster's cage may represent home, jail, a safe place from the outside world, or a trap. Their food brings up associations related to eating, whether it be caring for another or eating disorders. Medicine that the animal might need to take may bring up associations of caring or illness (I give medicine to my animals with the help of my clients, whenever I can).

I once shared my therapy room with a therapist from a different therapy modality. An empty cage had been left there and the client remained focused on why the cage was empty for the entire session. Did the animal die? Was the animal kidnapped? The therapist was shocked at the content that an empty cage brought into the session, content that was critical to the child's issues and emotional problems that had not come up before.

ANIMALS AS A SOCIAL MEDIUM IN THERAPY

All other individual therapy modes have only one live relationship in the room, however, AAP includes the client-therapist relationship, the client-animal relationship, and the animal-therapist relationship. I practice AAP, with a number of animals in the room, which offers multiple relationships and social dynamics including: individual relationships of the client with each animal, individual relationships of the therapist with each animal, and individual relationships of each animal with every other animal. There are certain presenting issues, such as interpersonal trauma, for which a relational therapy is highly recommended. Animal-Assisted Psychotherapy (AAP) is a relational therapy par excellence!

Different animals have different personalities, creating a myriad of types of relationships with the client, the therapist and each other, in which everyone in the room acts, reacts, interacts with each other. The result is a laboratory of relationships allowing for transference and re-enactment in the here-and-now of many different relationships and parts of relationships from the client's life.

Thus, the AAP triangle (or quadrangle or more) brings to life the client's inner social experiences and inner object world. Therefore, the AAP setting has the potential to be a microcosm of the client's social world. Once the content comes up in this process, it can be worked through and insights reached. Once words have been attached to the experiences and emotions, through mediation by the therapist between the client and his or her inner world, symptoms often disappear, meaningful discussions can take place, which lead to cognitive and behavioural change. These changes can be practiced within the safe therapy environment through the client's interactions with the animals and mediated by the therapist's reflections.

Animal Assisted Psychotherapy (AAP) is reminiscent of group therapy, which is also based on working on one's issues through interactions and relationships in the therapy setting. As in group therapy, the AAP client may at any point choose to be a participant or an observer. That is, the client may participate in any given interaction in the room — with the therapist and/or animal(s), or may choose to observe and contemplate the interactions between the therapist and animal(s) or between the animals. Both these choices are opportunities for advancing the therapy process. Unlike group therapy, the focus of individual AAP is one client.

PHYSIOLOGICAL AND NEUROBIOLOGICAL EFFECTS ON HUMANS OF THE PRESENCE OF ANIMALS

Participating in the therapy process, including being in touch with difficult content from one's inner world, may be anxiety-producing for many clients. This may be explained by a process in which a threatening situation increases the release of cortisol, a hormone produced in the brain which in turn leads to a rise in blood pressure and heartrate, causing a feeling of anxiety and giving one the physical strength to fight or flee in a dangerous situation. This response may create difficulty for the client to be in touch with, share and discuss emotionally charged issues, to show authentic emotions, and to create the therapeutic alliance that is so critical to the therapy process.

Research has shown that the presence of animals is likely to lower cortisol levels, blood pressure and heartrate. This research explains the evidence that the presence of animals has an anxiety-reducing effect on humans, allowing clients to be less anxious in the therapy setting, in a relationship with the therapist, and when in contact with troubling content from their inner world.

Furthermore, there is evidence pointing to a rise in the human's level of the hormone oxytocin in the presence of animals. Oxytocin has been shown to result in higher levels of affiliation, trust in others and emotional sharing, all critical to the therapy process. A rise in oxytocin may result in disclosure of content important to the therapy process. This is particularly important in the case of maltreated children, who are often referred to therapy for emotional, social and behavioural problems with no clue that their experiences of maltreatment are the source of these problems. The increased trust and emotional sharing as a consequence of the animals' presence may result in disclosure of maltreatment.

Oxytocin has also been implicated in facilitating connectivity in neural systems. The effects of the changes in cortisol and oxytocin levels induced by the presence of animals will be elaborated on in later sections.

THE THERAPEUTIC ALLIANCE IN AAP

As mentioned above, the establishment of the therapeutic alliance is critical to the psychotherapy process and will be much less likely to occur, if at all, if the therapist is not perceived by the client as safe, as well as a source of safety. My experiences in therapy have shown me that AAP has been instrumental in the establishment and also continuation of the therapeutic alliance.

One child from a "normative" background, who had refused to interact with a previous therapist over the period of a year and a half, quickly became very talkative with me, telling me about all the dangerous secrets of his family's dynamics. When I was working at a group residential treatment setting, many children who had dropped out of other therapy, or had refused to go in the first place, would bang on my door, saying, "I want to come to therapy with Mushu!" (Mushu was my wonderful dog with me in therapy for 16 years.) After my first two years there, I was routinely given the most resistant children. In seven years, only one child dropped out of therapy after a year.

This phenomenon has intrigued me from my first year of therapy. Furthermore, and I am sure that this is related to the therapy alliance unique to AAP, my experience and that of my colleagues seems to show that more children make first-time disclosures of maltreatment to an AAP therapist than to therapists from other therapy modalities. When I decided to return to my studies and received an M.A. in Child and Youth Clinical Social Work, my thesis was on the subject of the therapeutic alliance in AAP. Not surprisingly, I found that for children in group residential treatment settings, the therapeutic alliance was established earlier and stronger in AAP than in other therapy modali-

ties. My upcoming research will ask the question as to whether more children indeed do make more first-time disclosures of maltreatment to an AAP therapist than to other therapists. This is especially important due to the fact that many studies show that maltreated children keep their secret. They remain alone in their experiences and the maltreatment goes unreported. According to studies of Adverse Child Experiences (ACE's), the consequences of lack of reporting are: continuation of the maltreatment, severe emotional and behavioural problems, addictions, higher suicide rates, physical health problems, and in some cases, significantly shorter life span due to health problems indirectly related to the maltreatment.

How can we explain the explanation for the findings of my thesis? My first inclination, and I feel this until today, is that it lies partially in the client's perception of safety that exists in the AAP setting. As mentioned earlier, the animals provide both a safe haven and secure base in the therapy setting. In addition, the presence of the animals lowers the anxiety that clients may otherwise experience in the artificial therapy situation, which may be due to the naturalness the animals contribute to interactions or to the lowering of anxiety-producing cortisol in the client. This may allow the client to remain in the therapy setting and hopefully participate in the therapy process, however, feeling safe in the setting does not necessarily point to feeling safe with the therapist.

The concept of a third thing, that interest which is in common to both therapist and client, can also include interest in animals. This gives a sense that they share a feeling and can participate together in their common interest, in real time, encouraging the development of a relationship. The activity of caring for the animals, worrying together about their emotional and physical welfare, and together trying to understand them, is likely to help the client perceive the therapist not only as safe, but also as a source of safety. I must emphasise that this is not only possible for clients who like animals, for not everyone does. However, even in this case, the client sees that if the animals are sick or hurt, the therapist cares for them. Therefore, the therapist will still be perceived as an empathetic and compassionate person. In a study showing subjects videos of therapists either with or without a dog and then asking them which therapist they would prefer to meet with, there was a significantly higher preference for the therapist accompanied by a dog. It is interesting that this was true even among subjects who professed no love for animals.

This study brings up an interesting question. Does this desire of the subjects for a therapist with a dog have any implication for the therapeutic alliance? Apparently, it does. As I mentioned earlier, many children with avoidant attachment who had not been in therapy with me expressed a strong desire to come to me (and my animals!) for therapy, and those that did eventually enter into therapy with me formed a very strong therapeutic alliance. There is research evidence that an expectation of a therapeutic alliance indeed predicts the successful establishment of the alliance.

I will add to the equation a situation in which an animal who is frightened may run to the therapist for safety and comfort. Animals may show excitement when the therapist approaches them. Through identification with an animal as small or dependent on others, clients are likely to see the animal's behaviour as a cue of safety. If the animal perceives the therapist as a safe haven, then this might serve as proof that the therapist really is safe.

There are many clients, especially those who were maltreated by the very adults who claimed that they were acting in the child's best interest, who have experienced adults who are untrustworthy. A therapist might say to a new client, "I am here to help you. You can trust me!" The client may feel, "Yeah, sure. I've heard that before. That's never gonna happen!" It is especially difficult to establish the therapeutic alliance with these clients. However, as the client I referred to above, who opened up to me when he remained closed with a previous therapist, said when I asked him why he opened up to me but not to the previous therapist, "I saw the animals trusted you, so I thought I could trust you, too." The animals served as cues of safety for him, helping him to perceive me as a safe haven for him, also.

This psychological explanation is backed up by principles of neurobiology. At the very level of neuronal systems, our brain is constantly scanning the environment for cues of danger or safety. This process is called *neuroception* and does not involve conscious awareness, which would slow the process and prevent the quickest possible reaction in the case of danger. Should cues of danger be perceived, the hormonal reaction would prepare the body for fight or flight. The *polyvagal theory* explains the neural reaction to danger and safety and how it affects behaviour. In short, in the presence of cues of danger, the vagal nerve directs us to fight or flight. If this proves to be ineffective or impossible, then the vagal nerve directs us to freeze (also referred to as *immobilisation with fear*) and perhaps dissociation.[4] If however, there is a safe person in the area, the vagal nerve directs us to *social engagement*, affiliation with that person, for safety. This person serves as a safe haven in times of danger. Think of the small child who feels danger and runs to his or her mother as a first reaction. The effects of oxytocin reinforce the process of social engagement. That is, in the case of animals serving as cues of safety, the presence of the animals is likely to raise the client's oxytocin levels, encouraging the client to trust and want to affiliate with the therapist.

The polyvagal theory states that once one feels a sense of safety in the presence of another person, they may enter a state of immobilisation without fear. This state may also be related to the oxytocin system, which serves as a neuromodulator promoting connectedness, social bonds and calmness. We may assume that the oxytocin released by animal's presence aids this process, facilitating the ability of the client to be in a calm connection with the therapist and trust in him or her to be there for the client (thus the therapeutic alliance) when anxiety-producing content arises.

This process may be seen as an explanation for the therapist serving as a safe haven. Indeed, the conclusion of some research articles concerning therapy for clients with PTSD suggest administering intranasal oxytocin prior to therapy sessions in order to increase the building of the therapy alliance and enhance therapy outcome. However, the use of chronic exogenous oxytocin, or its use in exceptionally high doses, may lower the ability of the neural system to make use of the oxytocin. We have the animals to naturally supply the client with the oxytocin needed to facilitate social engagement system for the establishment of the therapeutic alliance and the ability of clients to enter into their inner world safely.

---

[4] Here I would like to emphasise that this is a very simplistic explanation of a very complicated and involved neurobiological reaction and does not go into the details of other reactions such as pleasing or fawning.

Even in cases in which a strong therapeutic alliance has been established, mistakes by the therapist or misunderstandings that occur between the client and therapist may cause a rupture in the alliance which can do serious damage to the therapy process if not repaired. There are numerous ways in which the presence of animals may prevent dropout from the therapy and facilitate the repair or resolution of the rupture. For instance, if the client is angry at the therapist due to lost trust in him or her, the client may recede to the animal as a safe haven. As the therapist attempts to process the problematic interactions that led to the rupture, the animal may serve as a secure base from which to explore the experience.

EXPANSION OF THE POTENTIAL SPACE IN PLAY THERAPY THROUGH THE INTEGRATION OF ANIMALS INTO THE PLAY THERAPY SETTING
A MECHANISM FACILITATING PLAY THERAPY PROCESSES

As mentioned earlier, the potential space is the place where the client's inner world and outer reality meet, allowing for imagination, thought processes and the ability to play. In the safe play therapy situation, various inanimate objects in the outer reality (dolls, toys, art supplies) can be used to expand the potential space and express the inner world. In AAP, however, animals serve as both a richer stimulus and mode of expression that even further expand the potential space in the client. A child may pretend to have a relationship and interact with a doll, but the relationship and interaction with an animal is real. The doll does not initiate, but an animal might. The client may move the doll around as if the doll is running around, but the animal actually runs around. The client may pretend the doll expresses emotions, but the animal really does express emotions.

Thus, the outer reality (the presence of the animals and interactions with them) is more than just a passive prop for the client, but rather is likely to actively stimulate associations from the inner world of clients, more than a doll to connect them at a conscious or unconscious level with their emotions and relational experiences with others that can then be played out in the therapy session, furthering the therapy process.

In a way unique to AAP, there is a loop that may occur during a client's interactions with the animals which further stimulates the client's inner world. A client may manipulate the movement of a doll, but the doll does not react back. However, as the client and animal continue to react to each other, there is a mutual stimulation back and forth that is likely to bring up more content for as long as the interaction continues. This may even occur in the case of one continuing to trying to interact while the other ignores the attempts or runs away, which might bring up content related to rejection or harassment.

At the base of this mechanism is the fact that while animals are not humans, they are reminiscent of humans. They act, react and interact with the client, with the therapist and with each other, similar to the way that the client does with those in his or her life. That is, the animals and the client's relationships with them are different from yet similar to relationships with other humans. In this way, the animals and the client's relationships with them represent reality, yet at a safe psychological distance from the client's experience with relationships outside of the therapy setting.

This distance serves to protect the client from threatening content arising from the inner world ("It's not real and it never happened. I'm only playing with the animals."), allowing the therapist to reflect on the actions and emotions arising during that play. Clients may or may not at a later time draw a connection between the play and their own real-life situation outside of therapy, yet the therapist can still help the client process the content and related emotions connected to that situation.

Further expanding the potential space in AAP with children is the integration of the animals' presence and ALIVENESS into the traditional play therapy setting, stimulating emotional expression and bringing up content in less threatening and more authentic ways while leaving much-needed defences intact. For instance, a client may place a hamster family in a doll house and watch them running around. This situation may bring out the child's experiences with their own family dynamics which previously the child had not been able to talk about. A mother hamster who runs out of the doll house may represent for the child, a divorce. The hamster parents might happen to be in the bedroom, and a young hamster wandering in might be seen as a child "catching the parents in the act". I might stop my dog Buffy from eating something she shouldn't. The client might then take a toy gun and say "Bang bang!" and "kill" me, or take the toy handcuffs and "put me in jail" for not letting Buffy eat what she wants, leading to a discussion of the anger the child feels when adults draw limits on the child's behaviour.

Now I will refer to specific mechanisms that explain the potential space in AAP as described above.

CONSCIOUS AND UNCONSCIOUS SYMBOLISATION IN AAP

As mentioned above, children (and not only children) may feel threatened by content arising from within the therapy session. They might deny the understandings of the therapist ("I see you are really angry" or "You did something that hurt someone else" or "Your parents sound like they don't understand you") or even suppress the content from arising in the first place. It is easier for them to observe and discuss issues in the animals, who serve as reality from a safe psychological distance. Furthermore, children who have experienced severe interpersonal trauma at an early age may have suffered from arrested neurological development, or damage of, areas of the brain which make the symbolisation, the cornerstone of play therapy, impossible for them. For these children, a doll is only a piece of material, plastic and yarn and cannot possibly have feelings or intentions. A toy gun is simply a piece of plastic that could never shoot. The aliveness of the animals, however, allows for an unconscious symbolisation, leading to a sort of unconscious play. There are certain psychological processes that come to play in a unique way through AAP which facilitate symbolism for the sake of expansion of the potential space, expression of important content, and emotional expression.

ANTHROPOMORPHISM

Anthropomorphism is the attribution of human characteristics (emotions, thoughts, intentions, etc.) to a non-human entity. Although this definition allows for a person to anthropomorphise an inanimate object such as a doll, the phenomenon will be stronger when applied to an animal due to their aliveness and social features that provide more external cues reminiscent of humans. Furthermore, there is evidence that oxytocin release facilitates the process of anthropomorphic attribution when the object of the attribution has social features, such as animals. The presence of the animals releases the oxytocin in the human, which further encourages them to anthropomorphise.

Thus, the human is more likely to infer internal states (such as intention and emotion), allowing for a type of unintentional play. This process can be very useful for the unconscious working through of content as part of the therapy process with children who find it difficult to play or to project through symbolisation. This unintentional play can be seen in the way that anthropomorphism serves as a basis for identification, projection and transference in the client's perceptions of and interactions with the animals.

IDENTIFICATION

Identification is a process of seeing one's qualities in another person (or seeing the other's qualities in oneself). This can be used by the client in therapy to understand oneself or the other better, or by the therapist to understand how the client perceives him or herself or where the client is in the therapy process. Clients may use the animals as objects of identification to explain themselves to the therapist. We often hear of clients who identify with the aggressor or identify with the victim. One client may admire and identify with a lab rat (who would eat a hamster, given half of a chance) as an aggressor, saying, "I'm just like the rat. I'll get anything I want, even if it means beating up another kid to get it." Another client may identify with the hamster as a (potential) victim. "I'm just like the hamster. He has no way of knowing if or when the rat is going to try to eat him. I'm scared of the kids at school, who love to bully me. They may do so at any time, but I never know when it's going to be."

I have had clients who perceive the complexity of an animal's personality and use that to describe themselves. A client may identify with a lab rat, who, despite the stereotype of a rat as aggressive and dangerous, is in reality playful and social with humans, saying, "It's just like what people think of Packrat [the rat present in therapy]. Everyone thinks I'm bad but inside I'm really nice. They only see me from the outside and don't even try to get to know the real me."

PROJECTION AND TRANSFERENCE

A client is likely to project his or her emotions, behaviour or characteristics, or transfer another person's emotions, behaviour or characteristics, onto an animal. This allows clients to talk about their issues while keeping their defences intact. Looking at a hamster family in which the parents sometimes squabble with each other, a child who lives in a family where the parents have violent arguments might

say, "The poor hamster babies! Their parents are fighting all the time. They must be so frightened! I'm so lucky, because my parents get along so well and NEVER fight. They love each other so much. We have to do something to make them feel better!"

Through this projection onto the baby hamsters, the child can express his fears and the predicament in which he finds himself. In this example, through the baby hamsters, the child is able to show empathy towards himself and even ask for help. The therapist might ask the child what might help the baby hamsters, and the child might talk about what he needs that might help him. Although this may be at first an unconscious process, with time and through gentle reflections and questions by the therapist, the child may then be able to open up and discuss with the therapist what is actually happening at home.

IDENTIFICATION THROUGH PROJECTION

I have had clients identify with a hamster, who by nature, is a solitary animal and in general is not interested in connection, saying, "Whenever I want to pat the hamster, she always runs away, even though she would like to be with me. I'm shy just like the hamster." In this way, clients are taking advantage of the hamster's behaviour to express their feelings about themselves and share these feelings with the therapist, as a sort of invitation to talk openly about these feelings.

It is very important here to remember that in the case of projection, transference and identification, the therapist should not correct the client and explain the animal's true characteristics. The client's statements are a window to his or her inner world and thus provide opportunities for the therapy process and for unobtrusive interventions by the therapist. AAP is not psychoeducation or a lesson in animal behaviour. I often say to my clients, "Wow! You're amazing that you are so perceptive! I didn't notice, and you are right! Kids understand an animal's behaviour much better than adults!" This allows children to flow with their associations and describe their own narrative, experiences and emotions, unconsciously, through the animals.

That being said, if these projections and transferences are in any way dangerous to the animal's welfare, then the therapist must immediately stop any behaviour on the part of the client towards the animal that would cause any harm to the animal — physically or emotionally. In certain situations, therapists may stop the behaviour but encourage the clients to continue expressing themselves through what they would like to do to the animal.

I have had clients try to let the rats out of the cage, while the hamsters were running around, in order to see what murder would look like. While not allowing the client to let the rats out, my reaction is to say, "You would really love to see the rat kill the hamster, wouldn't you? I wonder how the rat would feel killing the hamster. What do you think? Have you ever seen anyone hurt someone really badly? Have you even been so angry at anyone that you wanted to kill them?" It is very important to say all this in a nonjudgmental way, to show curiosity and to differentiate between thoughts/feelings and behaviour.

Often, once someone finds the words and can express their feelings and emotions to others in a way that critical content is brought up, they no longer have the need to act out the behaviour. Other times, the therapist may decide to reflect what the animal is experiencing in reality. For instance, if a client decides to play a game of tag with Buffy, my dog, and runs toward her at high speed, she might try to get out of his way out of fright. I have to immediately stop him and say that his action frightened Buffy. But instead of explaining what he had done that scared her and what in her behaviour showed us that she was scared, I would ask him if he was ever frightened just like Buffy. I have had many clients answer this question with content that proved to be a breakthrough in therapy. (At a later stage in therapy, when clients have reached insight and are showing interest in understanding and changing their behaviour, then I might explain the interaction in a more psychoeducational way.)

> *Often, once someone finds the words and can express their feelings and emotions to others in a way that critical content is brought up, they no longer have the need to act out the behaviour.*

Freud, the father of the terms projection, transference and identification, would have been excited to find that there is a neurological basis for these processes. The mirror neuron system allows for one person's actions to become messages understood by another, without the involvement of cognition, leading us to understand the intentions of others. That is, we observe the movement of others, whether it be large body movements or slight change in facial expression, and then attribute intention to that other based on what we would be intending (or feeling) if we made that movement, in that situation. This is a critical element in understanding others and is seen as the basis for empathy. These attributions are the basis for projection. "If I scrunched up my face that way, with tears coming out of my eyes like that, then I would be sad. Therefore, that person must be sad."

If there is no movement, the mirror neuron system will not be activated and unconscious and authentic projections will not be made. Dolls make no movements so will not activate the client's mirror neuron system. Clients' projections on them are intentional and they are aware that the therapist is listening and perhaps judging. Yet, like a human, an animal moves, breathes, eats, has facial expressions and other body language, approaches clients or hides from them.

Animals certainly do have intentions. The movement and behaviour of the animal will be likely to stimulate the mirror neurons to activity, likely causing clients to unconsciously calculate what they would do in a similar situation, and then ascribe intentions to the animal based on their own personal experience, emotions, needs, thoughts and sensations.

Of course, we may not always be correct in our projections, which is even more likely with animals since although they share some qualities with humans, they are also different. This difference may cause misunderstandings of their intentions. Yet we do not correct these misunderstandings. Rather, we allow and even encourage clients to project her own needs, emotions, feelings, and thoughts onto the animal, and to interpret animals' behaviour according to their needs, for we understand that actually, clients are referring to themselves. The activation of the mirror neurons provides the clients with opportunities to unconsciously project, allowing us a window into the inner world of the client while leaving defences intact.

It can be interesting to observe progress in the therapy process through the client's use of anthropomorphism towards the animals, or even the same animal, at different stages. For instance, at an earlier stage in therapy, a victim of rape may project onto a rat the helplessness she had felt during the rape, expressing how badly she feels for the rat for being "trapped in the cage with no way to escape to freedom". At a later stage, when she develops the ability to express anger, she may become angry at the rat for his violent wishes (to eat the hamster) and fantasise what punishments she would like to mete out to the rat and even play out those fantasies through play.

NEUROBIOLOGICAL PROCESSES IN AAP CONTRIBUTING TO THE EXPANSION OF THE POTENTIAL SPACE

The animals' presence preserves the potential space through the sense of safety they provide in the AAP environment. It has already been mentioned that animals supply a safe haven and a secure base for the client, both enabling the expansion of the potential space, and that lower cortisol levels in the client due to the presence of the animals is likely to lower anxiety, which might otherwise result in a collapse of the potential space.

However, due to the facilitation by the animals of the therapeutic alliance with the therapist, and during the state of calmness and immobilisation without fear, the therapist can also be perceived as secure base from which to explore one's inner world. Indeed, the polyvagal theory states that social engagement, together with immobilisation without fear, facilitate the ability to concentrate on inner processes. Together, these mechanisms further facilitate the expansion of the client's potential space.

Yet another contribution by the animals can be seen occurring through a possible influence they may have on the connectivity of the default mode network DMN. There are children who are likely to feel unsafe in the therapy setting and with the therapist due to prior maltreatment by other adults. These children are likely to suffer from a damaged oxytocin system, lowering their ability to connect with others. This damaged oxytocin system causes disruptions to DMN connectivity, making it more difficult for the child to form a potential space. It is logical to assume that the buffering effect of oxytocin, due to the animal's presence, on DMN connectivity might enable clients' entrance into their inner world in an imaginal space in the flow of time.

ANIMAL ASSISTED PSYCHOTHERAPISTS: WHAT IS IT ABOUT US?

For years, questions dealing with my identity as an AAP therapist have swirled in my head. Yes, I am a social worker, but when asked my profession, I automatically answer "Animal Assisted Psychotherapist." The field is not recognised by any official body — by law or otherwise. Yet we exist and we are sought after.

When I was doing my research comparing the therapeutic alliance in AAP with that of other therapies, in residential treatment homes, I of course had to explain my research to the director. I was usually told, "It's not the animals - it's HER. She's different from the rest of the therapists. She acts different. The kids are crazy about her." I would always explain the ways that it was the influence of her relationships with the animals. I have written of this extensively in my book, in articles and in chapters.

But what if we ARE different? I have often wondered if we are more open to relationships from the outset. Gee — we all grew up with animals, looking for more relationships with more animals. Somehow, relationships with the humans around us just were not enough for us. And for some of us, our relationships with our animals were simply safer than some of our relationships with humans.

As we psychotherapists know, one's emotional problems originated in problematic interactions and relationships with others in the past, so psychotherapists work with their clients on the client's emotional problems through the client-psychotherapist relationship. So, it was just natural for us to include relationships with animals in our work. In a recent conversation, a friend and colleague wondered if it works in the opposite direction. Maybe our relationships with our animals as children helped us develop our ability to participate in relationships, so we are then more open to relationships. Perhaps, since our relationships with animals, who even as children we cared for, towards whom we were sensitive and empathetic, developed our ability to be the same way towards our clients.

As mentioned earlier, there is evidence that oxytocin may be released during interactions with animals, raising one's ability to be social. It is possible that a chronic flow of endogenous oxytocin may even change certain structures of our brain, resulting in a higher tendency for sociability. Maybe our constant interactions with animals while growing up, or even now, make us more open to relationships in general?

There are other ways in which we are different. I will never forget a supervision meeting I had with my clinical supervisor while I was a student, during my field placement for my third year of studies in AAP, in an emergency shelter for maltreated children (where I then worked for the next 19 years). When I told her about a breakthrough I had with my client during a walk outside with my dog, Mushu (for we had learned that Boris Levinson talked of the opportunities for therapy provided

by such a walk in an AAP meeting), she was aghast!!! "What? You left the 4 walls of the therapy setting???" She was always saying that I went past accepted boundaries. I see it as thinking out of the box, taking advantage of the concrete situations provided by the interactions with the animals and their behaviour, for the sake of the therapy process. My AAP colleagues are always being "accused" of going past boundaries. So maybe, yes, we are different.

Finally, I often find myself reaching out to pat Buffy during a session. It is clear to me that the animals serving as a secure base and safe haven, as well as lowering cortisol levels (source of anxiety) and stimulating oxytocin levels (calming us and encouraging affiliation), also works on us in the therapy setting. That is, when a client brings up content that may be anxiety-producing for us, such as a small child telling us explicit details of having been raped, we may be more able than other therapists to handle our feelings and be there for the client whereas other therapists may shut down, show their anxiety, or even burst into tears while listening.

There have been sessions in which I handled such situations superbly, even able to laugh with the client "at the stupid rapist", allowing for a comfortable environment encouraging further disclosure and processing. After the client has left, I have picked up Buffy and hugged her, thanking her for witnessing together with me, being there with me and for me! The animals are there for us no less than there for the client.

WORKING WITH DOGS: A "THERAPY DOG" OR A DOG WITH ME IN THERAPY?

I am strongly against training dogs for obedience for the purpose of psychotherapy. I like to say that I don't want a therapy dog[5] with me, rather I want a dog with me in therapy. I do not expect my dog in therapy (or out of therapy, for that matter) to do tricks, to act or react according to commands, to be obedient. She may misbehave or resist my requests. She may sometimes be pushy in her demands. She does not have to "put up and shut up" with interactions or touch that she may not enjoy or that bother her, and is allowed to express her dislike of intrusive behaviour by the client by either moving away or coming to me for support. She is allowed to express her needs and she should always be respected. All these caveats make it more likely for the client to identify with her, to project onto her, to interact with her in ways that will raise content and help me understand the client even better.

That being said, there are two principles that I recommend for those psychotherapists who choose to integrate a dog into the therapy setting. Firstly, I pick my dog for her basic personality. I don't want her to be too rambunctious, too anxious, or at all aggressive, for I don't want the dog to "steal the show"; nor do I want to be constantly dealing with my dog if my client is in a process that will be dis-

---

[5] There are numerous organisations that run courses to train and license "therapy dogs". These dogs must be highly obedient and even have to behave in ways that are against their nature. These requirements may be as benign as answering to the command "Come", going against a dog's natural instinct such as not reacting to someone walking nearby with food, or even abusive as allowing people to grab their tail.

rupted by my dog's behaviour or by the need to focus mainly on my dog's needs. My main focus should always be the client, and our (mine and that of the client) focus on my dog should always be for the good of the client's processes. I want her to be friendly, generally cooperative, naturally know how to navigate social situations, and to enjoy coming to sessions. An assessment of the dog's inborn personality and successful socialisation, by a canine specialist who is aware of these expectations, is a must.

Secondly, as a friend and colleague of mine, Inbar Barel, says, instead of training a dog, we should educate the dog on how to get along in our therapy setting, in our home, and in society, similar to the way we educate our children. We should know what to expect of each other. Instead of giving commands, we should communicate in a sensitive and, yes, assertive way. I have never given my dogs treats to learn behaviours, yet they always understood certain requests such as come, stay, up and down. This approach leads to a sense of mutuality and positive emotional relationship instead of a hierarchical relationship based on obedience. This creates a relational environment that the client finds to be authentic and safe, one that can either be identified with or contrasted with, depending on the nature of the client's family atmosphere.

CONCLUSION

In the introduction to this chapter, I asked the questions about my ability to work with maltreated children: Is it something about me? Is it the animals? Is it me with the animals? I believe that it is all three.

In this chapter, I have tried to cover some of the mechanisms unique to Animal Assisted Psychotherapy that can reach and help our clients in ways that other fields of psychotherapy may have difficulty doing. Integrating the psychological and neurobiological effects of these mechanisms, it is interesting to note a fascinating phenomenon which has important implications for the therapy process. On the one hand, the presence of animals facilitates contact with difficult and even threatening content which is the basis for the client's emotional problems but is also difficult to be in touch with, raising the client's level of anxiety, potentially resulting in the client either shutting down or dropping out of therapy. Yet that very same presence of the animals lowers that anxiety, whether as a result of the animal serving as a safe base or as a result of the lowering of cortisol. The result is the client being able to be in contact with difficult and threatening content without suffering debilitating anxiety, and feeling safe enough to continue exploring that content and processing. That is, the very medium with brings up the anxiety-producing content that needs to be worked on also is responsible for the lowering of that anxiety, allowing the client to stay in contact with that content.

In addition, animals serve as the only psychotherapy medium with which we can have an interpersonal relationship. It is through their presence, the associations they stimulate, and the relationships that are present in the AAP setting, that the client's content can be raised, worked through, leading to insight, and through which new cognitions and behaviours can be practiced.

Don't be mechanical. Don't have the answers. Be curious. Expect the unexpected. The animals' aliveness ensures spontaneity in the therapy sessions, leading to the creation of authentic interactions and relationships of all types, so take advantage of the spontaneity and unexpected situations that they offer. Clients naturally and authentically join these situations and make them their own, bringing up content and creating process. Dare to join this process as opposed to leading it. This is the unique journey that AAP allows.

REFERENCES

Code of Ethics - IAAAP - Israeli Association of Animal-Assisted Psychotherapy. https://www.iaa-psytherapy.org/english

Parish-Plass, N. (2020). Animal-assisted psychotherapy for developmental trauma through the lens of interpersonal neurobiology of trauma: Creating connection with self and others. *Psychotherapy Integration*. Advance online publication.

Parish-Plass, N. & Bachi, K. (2020). Psychodynamic Animal-Assisted Psychotherapy: Processing and Healing through Relationships. In Driscoll, C. (Ed.), *Animal-assisted Interventions for health & human service professionals* (pp.361-405). Nova Science Publishers, New York.

Parish-Plass, N., & Pfeiffer, J. (2019). Implications of animal-assisted psychotherapy for the treatment of developmental trauma through the lens of interpersonal neurobiology. In P. Tedeschi, & M. Jenkins (Eds.), *Transforming trauma: Resilience and healing through our connections with animals* (pp. 123-187). Purdue University Press, Lafayette.

Tedeschi, P., Jenkins, M., Parish-Plass, N., Olmert, M., & Yount, R. (2019). Treating human trauma with the help of animals: Trauma informed intervention for child maltreatment and adult post-traumatic stress. In A. Fine (Ed.), *Handbook on animal-assisted therapy* (5th ed., pp. 363–380). Elsevier, San Diego.

Bachi, K. & Parish-Plass, N. (2017). Animal-assisted psychotherapy: A unique relational therapy for children and adolescents. *Clinical Child Psychology and Psychiatry*, 22(1),3-8.

Parish-Plass, N. (2016). Order out of chaos revised: A call for clear and agreed-Upon definitions differentiating between animal-assisted interventions article (English translation and revision of the original Hebrew article). DOI: 10.13140/RG.2.2.20631.57769

Tedeschi, P., Sisa, M., Olmert, M., Parish-Plass, N., & Yount, R. (2015). Treating human trauma with the help of animals: Trauma informed intervention for child maltreatment and adult post-traumatic stress. In A. Fine (Ed.), *Handbook on animal-assisted therapy* (4th ed., pp. 305–319). Elsevier, San Diego.

Oren, D. & Parish-Plass, N. (2013). The integration of animals into the therapy process and its implications as a unique medium in psychotherapy. In N. Parish-Plass (Ed.), *Animal-assisted psychotherapy: Theory, issues and practice* (pp. 3-45). Purdue University Press, West Lafayette.

Parish-Plass, N. & Oren, D. (2013). The animal as a relational medium: An object relations approach to the therapy triangle in animal-assisted psychotherapy. In N. Parish-Plass (Ed.), *Animal-assisted psychotherapy: Theory, issues and practice* (pp. 47–64). Purdue University Press, West Lafayette.

Parish-Plass, N. & Oren, D. (2013). Dilemmas, questions and issues concerning the integration of animals into the psychotherapy setting. In N. Parish-Plass (Ed.), *Animal-assisted psychotherapy: Theory, issues and practice* (pp. 245-260). Purdue University Press, West Lafayette.

Parish-Plass, N. (2013). The contribution of animal-assisted psychotherapy to the potential space in play therapy. In N. Parish-Plass (Ed.), *Animal-assisted psychotherapy: Theory, issues and practice* (pp. 79–109). Purdue University Press, West Lafayette.

Parish-Plass, N. (Ed.) (2013). *Animal-assisted psychotherapy: Theory, issues, and practice*. Purdue University Press, West Lafayette.

Parish-Plass, N. (2008). Animal-Assisted Therapy with children suffering from insecure attachment due to abuse and neglect: a method to lower the risk of intergenerational transmission of abuse? *Clinical Child Psychology and Psychiatry*, 13(1), pp. 7-30.

Winnicott, D. W. (1986). *Playing and reality*. Tavistock Publications, London.

Chapter 9:

A HORSE OF A DIFFERENT COLOUR

WORKING WITH CAMELS IN ANIMAL-ASSISTED INTERVENTIONS

MICHAEL KAUFMANN, MIYAKO KINOSHITA AND
SAMANTHA AREVALO OF GREEN CHIMNEYS

ABOUT MICHAEL KAUFFMAN

Farm and Wildlife Director at Green Chimneys and the Director of The Sam and Myra Ross Institute

Michael Kaufmann has been actively involved in Human-Animal Interaction Programs, Animal Welfare and in Humane Education for many years. He is the Farm and Wildlife Director at Green Chimneys and the Director of The Sam and Myra Ross Institute, dedicated to education and research on the human connection to animals and the natural world. He directs all aspects of Green Chimneys' nature-based activities to support the therapeutic and educational programs for children with special needs.

Michael began his career as a humane educator at the American Society for the Prevention of Cruelty to Animals (ASPCA) in New York City and continued at the American Humane Association (AHA), a national child and animal protection organisation that promotes the highest standards of competence among child welfare and animal care and control professionals. At AHA he served as a national spokesperson with a special focus on humane education program development, the correlation between animal cruelty, domestic violence and child abuse and equine welfare issues. Subsequently he represented the North American Riding for the Handicapped Association (NARHA) as Director of Education and Communication and editor of the national magazine STRIDES.

Today his focus is on Green Care, the concept of working with animals, plants and nature to enhance human environments and lives. He continues to lead and facilitate workshops and seminars internationally and edits and contributes to various defining publications in the field of nature-based education, therapy and activities. Michael currently serves on the board of trustees of the Professional Association of Therapeutic Horsemanship International.

ABOUT MIKAYO KINOSHITA

Farm Education Program Manager at the Green Chimneys Farm and Wildlife Center

Miyako Kinoshita is Farm Education Program Manager at the Green Chimneys Farm and Wildlife Center. Serving as the key facilitator for over 200 children with psycho-social challenges enrolled in Green Chimneys' therapeutic day school and residential treatment center, she co-supervises a wide range of animal-assisted and plant-based nature programs to support the students' special education and treatment. She is the liaison to the social work department, child care, and teaching staff, and advocates for the positive impacts of the farm environment at treatment team meetings, in administrative rounds, and during agency staff training.

Miyako holds a master's degree in Educational Studies and specialises in Animal-Assisted Activity and Animal-Assisted Education. She has over 20 years of working in direct service with children and animals as a Certified Advanced Therapeutic Riding Instructor through the Professional Association of Therapeutic Horsemanship International (PATH Int'l), an education program leader, and is the manager of The Sam and Myra Ross Institute Internship at Green Chimneys. Miyako is the former president of the Equine Facilitated Mental Health Association (EFMHA) and a board member of the PATH Int'l .

As a noted speaker on the incorporation of nature-based programs in a residential treatment setting, Miyako has lectured extensively in the United States and internationally at regional and national conferences. Her lectures have taken her to State University of New York at New Paltz, Asabu University and Teikyo University in Japan, among others. She is a former trainer for the Therapeutic Crisis Intervention Course (TCI) developed by Cornell University as a tool for child care professionals.

ABOUT SAMANTHA AREVALO

Equine Program Coordinator at Green Chimneys

As the Equine Program Coordinator at Green Chimneys in Brewster, New York, Samantha has created a professional and welcoming therapeutic program where children learn how to build relationships with both horses and camels.

After graduating in 2011 from Post University in Waterbury, Connecticut, with a degree in Equine Business Management, Samantha initially started her work managing the therapeutic riding program but quickly expanded her skills and responsibilities once camels arrived to the Green Chimneys campus. Samantha currently holds certification as a Therapeutic Riding Instructor through PATH Int'l and oversees the riding and groundwork program.

While working with horses has been her specialty for the last twenty years, developing and implementing a therapeutic camel program has been her growing passion over the last nine years. Her work incorporating camels into traditional therapeutic groundwork sessions has driven the image behind safe and educational camel interactions for children and adults. Samantha has been invited to speak about her work at a variety of conferences and workshops, most notably the Southwest Camel Conference happening annually in Texas. Now training a camel-specific team of staff at Green Chimneys, Samantha continues to expand the boundaries of what it means to have safe and profound connections with animals as a therapeutic relationship is established.

ABOUT GREEN CHIMNEYS

Green Chimneys is a renowned non-profit school and human services agency providing education, residential treatment, animal and nature-based therapeutic programs, community-based support for youth and families and public recreation and education programs.

As part of a special education school and residential treatment centre, Green Chimneys employs over 500 professional staff and is home to approximately 300 animals of many species including all types of farm animals, horses, birds of prey, reptiles, and dogs at its Farm and Wildlife Centre. Favourite activities of the nearly 250 students, ages 5-17, range from taking a goat for a walk, riding horses or gently holding snakes.

Students experiencing severe anxiety, depression or autism spectrum challenges participate in the everyday tasks of feeding, cleaning stalls, grooming animals and rehabilitating injured birds of prey. Traditional mental health support and a full academic curriculum round out the experience, but it is the interaction with animals under the guidance of trained professionals that helps to develop critical skills such as trust, self-esteem, empathy, emotional regulation, and responsibility. All the animals are treated as companions to be cared for and to build relationships with.

On a typical day at Green Chimneys, residential students arrive at the farm before breakfast to assist with animal-related duties, such as feeding. Later in the morning school classes rotate to spend time with the wildlife teacher, the riding instructor or a wildlife specialist. Social workers conduct individual therapy sessions in the presence of sheep or donkeys, while occupational therapists work with a dog as they support children to attain fine motor skills and hand-eye coordination. On a summer afternoon, some students might bathe the draft horses or take the camels for a long walk in the woods; a snowy winter day might include students playing catch with dogs. Interactions with animals are part of the regular day in all seasons and in all kinds of weather.

THE SAFE INCLUSION OF DIVERSE SPECIES INTO THERAPEUTIC INTERVENTIONS

Among Green Chimneys' animal residents are Phoenix and Sage, two Bactrian camels (*Camelus bactrianus*), a domesticated species native to the steppes of Central Asia. Phoenix and Sage bring a unique experience to students at the school, which is highlighted in this conversation with Shauna McWilliams, social worker/therapist at Green Chimneys. We hope this conversation will provide an insight into how the safe inclusion of diverse species into therapeutic interventions can support client outcomes.

Q: AS A THERAPIST WHAT MAKES CAMELS INTERESTING TO WORK WITH IN SESSION?

Camels are interesting animals to work with in therapy session because they are so unique. Camels are not common or well known to most people like dogs, guinea pigs, or horses are, and it is this uniqueness that clients often respond to. There is something very special about being able to work with a camel. They are big animals, far larger than most horses or other farm animals, and that impressive size certainly impacts our sessions. They can inspire a sense of awe, curiosity, and their impressive size can be significant.

Q: DO YOU CHOOSE WHICH CLIENTS HAVE SESSIONS ALONGSIDE CAMELS AND WHY?

I usually choose students who, overall, are well-regulated. I would not bring children who have a tendency toward outward aggression or even uncontrolled impulsiveness into a session with camels. Children who need help with attention, focus and building self-esteem tend to do very well in their presence. A skill that Phoenix and Sage really support is decision making — making choices and encouraging the students to express what they want. The camels' confident demeanour and size ensure that one cannot force Phoenix or Sage to do anything.

In order to build a relationship and engage with the camels, the client has to communicate, invite the animal and work with them in a dialogue, rather than through commands or force. During moments when the camels are not entirely cooperative, or if they challenge the student, opportunities arise for me to assist the child to process their anxiety and frustration, to help the child recognise those feelings and work through them.

For example, if while on a walk, Phoenix stops and will not move forward, we all have to stop. In that moment, I will prompt the student to notice how they are feeling, and what they are thinking. Often the client will describe feeling frustrated, anxious, and occasionally irritated or embarrassed, and will connect those feelings to the thoughts that they are having in the moment. This is a great way to get at the client's internal dialogue and is often an opportunity help them to shift their perspective and narrative to a healthier, more adaptive narrative by encouraging them to consider alternate possibilities and then move on.

I find that the camels are helpful to partner with when working with clients who struggle with attentional deficits, difficulty with social skills, low self-esteem, as well as developing self-awareness and coping skills.

I am currently working with the camels to help a student to develop his self-awareness, self-confidence, and social skills. Through working with Phoenix and Sage, the student is developing and practicing these skills in the moment. He is encouraged to observe what is happening with the camels, to express what they are doing and what the camels may want or need in the moment. In doing this, the student is learning to attune to others, which is a fundamental social skill. The student is then encouraged to reflect on his observations, and related thoughts and feelings (noticing within himself what is going on), make choices and move forward with a goal in mind of how to proceed.

Q: WHAT ARE SOME OF THE CONVERSATIONS YOU ENGAGE IN WHEN FACILITATING A SESSION INCLUDING CAMELS?

It honestly depends on what treatment goals I am working on with my client. However, we always start outside the paddock fence, looking in, talking about the camels. We establish a relationship, discuss how the camel might be feeling, what the student might feel at that moment, and we observe the fine cues that might give a clue as to the emotional states of Phoenix and Sage. How do the feelings of the animal compare to human feelings, and is there similarity? We talk about what is going on that may be impacting the camels, what they may need from us, and what is the best way to meet that need. Our discussion also includes what the client is working on, why we are doing what we are doing with the camels, and how it connects to their goals.

For example, our two camels are very personable and seek us out most days, but sometimes they don't and that is OK. The children must learn that the animals also have off days or may not feel like communicating all the time, even if we want them to. One of my students was working on social communication skills and attention. One of the tools we talked about to gauge another's mood is eye contact (e.g. attention and focus); what can you see in the eye of each camel, and what is the message that comes cross from those eyes? It was very effective to create the image of a "golden thread" between him and Sage and we imagined that this thread was the actual lead rope. The goal was to lead with eye contact and intention. The student experienced how easily distracted both he and Sage could get; and that in any relationship connection is so important.

Q: HOW DO YOU PLAN A THERAPY SESSION WITH THE CHILD AND CAMEL?

I try to have a plan, but it usually evolves as we work. Flexibility is key when working with children and animals alike. There is always an overall treatment plan in place that is connected to educational and therapeutic goals. On a given day, however, I might have set the goal to focus on self-care — therefore grooming the camel might be an activity I offer to support a discussion around that topic. Quite often my beautiful ideas and plans go out the window and we adapt. If the student is not totally focused on grooming that day, we may end up taking a walk with the camel and discuss issues of leadership, or I find a way to weave in the subject of self-care into our walk.

Q: DO YOU HAVE ONE MOMENT THAT STANDS OUT TO YOU DURING A SESSION WITH A CLIENT AND CAMEL?

I was working with Brian, an 18-year-old student and the topic was "challenges he was facing" and how to recognise them and overcome them. We worked together to create an obstacle course with four elements for him and Sage to navigate. Brian designated a feed pan, a tarp on the ground, a wooden pole and some cones as the obstacles for the camel. Each obstacle would present Sage with some anxious moments and would not be all that easy to walk past or over without good leadership from Brian. We talked about goals and obstacles that get in our way, and how those obstacles are really just other goals.

We then symbolically connected each obstacle to something that Brian was viewing as a difficulty in his own life, attending school, doing coursework, his upcoming high school graduation and a driving test he wanted to complete. As he was guiding Sage around the course successfully, we focused on what support Brian was able to give Sage. We then discussed what support he himself needed to be successful and from whom — specifically the kind of help he wanted from his parents, teachers and therapist to reach his goals.

It is at moments like these, standing there with a huge camel between the student and myself; that I really appreciate what these large animals offer, the doors they open, and in their presence, we can turn seemingly ambiguous concepts into lasting tools and life skills for the student.

PHOENIX AND SAGE

The journey of bringing Phoenix and Sage to our campus at Green Chimneys has, like the journeys of our students, been one of immense learning and growth. At the point of adopting the duo, we made an unwavering promise to their former stewards to always respect the camels and to work with them in a non-coercive, positive and relationship-based model.

Our contract states: "Green Chimneys understands and agrees that the camels' training will be approached as a process in relationship, not to merely accomplish control nor gain a fixed result. Ongoing training of the camels will be developed on the premise of relationship, mutual knowing, trust, patience, cooperation and respect, with the camels regarded as participants in the relationship." This is a promise we have remained committed to, despite challenges we have faced along the way.

None of our experienced animal care staff had ever worked with camels prior to Phoenix and Sage entering our care. Whilst we had familiarity with equine and farm animals, including llamas, camels were new to us. The day Phoenix and Sage stepped off the oversized horse trailer after a long cross-country drive was Day One in every respect. With both camels being young, and well socialised but largely untrained, we should have anticipated a multi-year learning curve for all concerned. We were blissfully naïve.

Even half-grown, their physical power could be intimidating. On the other hand, gaining moments of trust with them or having a training success were immensely motivating. Their previous caregiver had suggested we just sit in the paddock with the camels for hours, not to directly interact with them but to acknowledge the presence of each other, based on our natural behaviour with each other. We did that. We got to know each other by being with each other; simply "sharing space". Gradually we learned, they learned, and our interactions became more steady. It is not lost on us how, in many ways, our own journey of learning, experimenting and relationship-building with the camels is similar to the experiences of students as they participate in our programs and experience the social and emotional learning, growth and healing benefits it provides.

Phoenix and Sage have brought a vast amount of learning — not only to our students but to the team at Green Chimneys. The camels require our staff to invest in them and ourselves in an ongoing basis as partners and professionals. We had to learn and glean information from others, including:

- National experts in camel training;
- Reading about indigenous cultures who have worked with camels for centuries; and
- Learning from our own success and mistakes.

Whether it is a question of proper animal husbandry, medical management, debates about training approach, or personality conflicts over what to try next, the camels have brought our team together as people.

The overall impact of Phoenix and Sage on our students during their time at Green Chimneys has been unexpected and profound. Being a unique species, our camels have touched the hearts of staff, students and the public who visit our farm. Adding camels to the therapeutic, educational and recreational programs at Green Chimneys offers anyone who visits a chance to connect with this unique species, and build a healthy and meaningful relationship.

By introducing Phoenix and Sage to the students, our clinical and educational staff find opportunities for motivational, educational, recreational, and/or therapeutic benefits to enhance quality of life. Caring for and working with the camels allows the staff team to teach and promote humane attitudes toward people, animals and the environment. Providing the camels with a caring home illustrates our philosophy behind involving students with unique and slightly unusual animals; to show others that we care about all living beings, and to make the point that camels can be caring partners that show their displeasure (e.g. spitting) only if treated harshly. The delightful authenticity of Sage and Phoenix simply being themselves and encouraging others to meet them on their terms is powerful.

Chapter 10:

VOLUNTARY PARTICIPATION OF ANIMALS IN THERAPY

BUILDING RECIPROCAL RELATIONSHIPS WITH ANIMAL THERAPY PARTNERS

DR RISË VANFLEET

ABOUT DR RISË VANFLEET

Dr VanFleet is a licensed psychologist, registered play therapist-supervisor, certified dog behaviour consultant, and certified ethology and behaviour consultant-instructor from Boiling Springs, Pennsylvania, USA. She has over 45 years of clinical, leadership, and program development experience in mental health.

Dr VanFleet is a co-founder with Tracie Faa-Thompson of the field of Animal Assisted Play Therapy® (AAPT) and author of 14 books on psychotherapy with children and families, including the Maxwell Award-winning *Animal Assisted Play Therapy*, named the best book of the year on the human-animal bond (2017, cowritten with Faa-Thompson). The AAPT approach emphasises reciprocal human-animal relationships and voluntary participation of animals.

Dr VanFleet is known internationally for her fun skill-building training workshops for professionals as well as her advocacy for animal agency and well-being within Animal Assisted Interventions. She is an acclaimed speaker who has been recognised with 15 national and international awards for her teaching and writing. Dr VanFleet has conducted AAPT work with individuals, families, and groups involving dogs, horses, goats, and cats, and also works with a variety of feral, unsocialised, and traumatised animals. She participates periodically in studies of Alaskan brown bears in the wild. Risë currently lives with four dogs and one husband.

INTRODUCTION

This contribution is drawn in part from a presentation by Dr Risë VanFleet for the Nourished Virtual Conference in early 2021. It is based on the approach used in Animal Assisted Play Therapy® (AAPT) as conceived and created by the author and co-creator of AAPT Tracie Faa-Thompson.

When 8-year-old Brian arrived for his second Animal Assisted Play Therapy (AAPT) session with me and my dog Kirrie, he appeared more dysregulated than usual. He had experienced considerable trauma in his young life prior to being placed with an experienced foster mother, and periods of dysregulation appeared from time to time. After several months of play therapy and Filial Therapy (VanFleet, 2014), a trial of AAPT had begun with goals of building his coping skills, strengthening his empathy for others, and working on other trauma-related challenges. The first session had gone well as he learned how to meet dogs safely and to do some simple consent testing with the dog.

Midway through the second session, however, Brian became frustrated when Kirrie would not do something he wanted. As the therapist, I reflected, "It's frustrating when she won't do what you want. I'm not sure she knows that trick, though. Do you remember how we checked to see if she was okay last time?"

He nodded and turned his attention back to the dog. When Kirrie still would not do the behaviour he asked, he raised his hand in a fist over his head. It was clear to me that he intended to hit Kirrie in his frustration. I saw Kirrie back away, and I stepped between Brian and Kirrie, saying, "Brian, I know you're frustrated, but one of the things you may not do is to try to hit Kirrie. You can do just about anything else, though."

Brian sighed and said he didn't want to play with her anymore because she was walking away from him. Again, I reflected, "You feel mad and sad when she won't do what you want and walks away." Again, he nodded, this time emphatically. He continued the play session but no longer included Kirrie, who had seen his raised arm and continued to keep her distance, eventually retiring to her off-limits bed under a table.

During his third session with Kirrie, Brian was better regulated, and he eagerly participated in some activities with Kirrie. He helped teach her to get into her bed and lie down, and with some simple prompting remembered to ask her permission and gain consent when petting her. The session ended with a game of fetch designed to help both Brian and Kirrie alternate between short periods of excitement and relaxation. Kirrie eagerly returned to him each time for another toss of her favourite ball, and Brian smiled throughout. At the end, Brian commented, "She really likes playing with me!" I reflected, "You're happy that she is connecting so well with you and wants to play with you!"

When Brian arrived for his fourth session with Kirrie, she met him with full relaxed tail wag and a lick on his arm. He was immensely pleased. "Kirrie is my best friend!" he said, to which I replied, "That makes you so happy. You can see that she is very happy to see you!" This led to a very brief conversation about how friends feel when we look out for them, and how Brian and Kirrie were working well together now, just like friends do. This was a turning point in Brian's entire therapeutic program, and his interest and initiative in caring for Kirrie transferred to his daily life.

Each of the final six sessions included a variety of playful activities with Kirrie to help him achieve his goals and then ended with Brian choosing to pour fresh water for Kirrie. Each time he watched her lap it up with his eyes and mouth wide open, in amazement that he could have that impact on the dog.

BACKGROUND

The field of Animal Assisted Interventions (AAI), which includes many different species working alongside humans to assist with their professional work or visitation programs, has blossomed in recent years. Its popularity has soared with almost daily reports featuring animals and humans interacting in the news, on social media, and in blogs and magazine articles. This chapter focuses upon the involvement of animals in the work of professionals — mental health, allied health, and education — which are substantially different in terms of structure, goals, and competencies from volunteer visitation programs where animals cheer up people in hospitals, nursing facilities, and hospice programs while offering social support. Both types of programs, animals involved in professional endeavours to help clients meet goals and social support programs, are valuable, but there are different purposes, requirements, and ways of working (VanFleet & Faa-Thompson, 2017; VanFleet, Fine, & Faa-Thompson, 2019).

In addition to the media attention given to AAI, there has been more research scrutiny. Articles in peer-reviewed journals are now quite common (e.g. the Human-Animal Interaction Bulletin, or Anthrozoos), and conferences feature studies conducted as graduate theses and dissertations. It has been noted that much of the current attention focuses on the benefits to humans with relatively less attention paid to benefits or impact on the animals. This is true in the clinical literature as well. Media reports often extol the value of animal involvement whilst being illustrated with cringe-worthy photos of animals who appear to be stressed or objectified.

For example, in the past two weeks, there was a widely circulated photo of a child "hugging" a dog who is displaying clear signs of distress — whale eye (where the white of the eye shows prominently), furrowed brow, tightly closed jaw, pulling backwards from the firm grip around his neck, and tail tucked up under his belly. By actual count in two very large Facebook groups about pets and people, comments such as "I love this!" and "Adorable!" and "What a sweet relationship!" appear from 94 percent of respondents with comments from remaining 6% from people raising some awareness and concern about how the animal might be feeling. Perhaps this reflects our generally anthropocentric way of viewing our relationships with animals.

This contribution provides an overview of the field of Animal Assisted Play Therapy® (AAPT) and then explores one key aspect of AAPT work: attention to the needs of animals and the benefits of their completely voluntary engagement in professional work, not only for the animals but also for clients.

ANIMAL ASSISTED PLAY THERAPY˚

Since the voluntary involvement of animals requires a substantial and complex set of skills that are not ordinarily included in many AAI programs, a brief description of AAPT is included here to help readers see the elements needed and the context required to incorporate voluntary behaviour safely and sensibly. Ultimately, when therapists choose to forego the use of equipment on the animals most of the time and encourage animals' freely-chosen behaviours, it can greatly enhance the experience for the animals and clients alike. At the same time, it requires high-level animal-related skills in the therapist to ensure the safety of and benefit to both the humans and animals involved.

Animal Assisted Play Therapy® (AAPT) is the creation of Dr Risë VanFleet (USA, author) and Tracie Faa-Thompson (UK). It has evolved over several decades, with more systematic application in the past 17 years. The unique origins are covered in their Maxwell Award-winning book, *Animal Assisted Play Therapy®* (VanFleet & Faa-Thompson, 2017). AAPT represents the full integration of Animal Assisted Therapy and Play Therapy as well as ethology, animal behaviour, and several other animal-related fields.

AAPT is defined as "the integrated involvement of animals in the context of play therapy in which appropriately trained therapists and animals engage with clients primarily through systematic playful interventions, with the goal of improving clients' developmental and psychosocial health, while simultaneously ensuring the animal's well-being and voluntary engagement. Play and playfulness are essential ingredients of the interactions and the relationships" (VanFleet, 2004; VanFleet & Faa-Thompson, 2017).

AAPT can be used to achieve many different types of client and student goals, and it can be applied with individuals of all ages, families, and groups. It requires well-developed competencies of the practitioners who engage in it for clinical or educational purposes. Certifications for clinicians, educators, and animal professionals are based on demonstrated competencies evaluated by AAPT International Certification Board members who have neither trained nor supervised them (VanFleet, 2020a). The competencies are described in VanFleet and Faa-Thompson (2017) and focus not only on intervention skills, but also on the abilities to read animal body language fluently, split attention between client and animal, use peripheral vision well, use proactive attention, advocate for animal well-being, demonstrate reciprocity in the human-animal relationship, consider the animal point of view at all times, and integrate all of this within excellent practice. Most people take 2 years to complete training, supervision, and assessment of these competencies (VanFleet, 2013, 2018; VanFleet, 2020a).

From both the client and animal points of view, AAPT can be an enjoyable experience, as the therapeutic powers of play (Drewes & Schaefer, 2013) are applied to create the context of emotional safety in which change most readily occurs. It is a requirement that the animals involved in AAPT actually enjoy their involvement rather than merely tolerate it. Therapists learn to discern the difference through their ability to read body language fluently and in the moment. The climate of AAPT sessions is often light and playful, even though serious, difficult material is being covered.

THE GOODNESS OF FIT CONCEPT

AAPT uses a "goodness of fit" concept drawn from the child development literature (Lerner, 1983; Thomas & Chess, 1977; VanFleet, 2020b, 2021; VanFleet, Fine, & Faa-Thompson, 2019). This differs from many other AAI program approaches in that the non-stress-based assessment looks at the animal's unique personality, choices, and preferences and honours them at all times. The interventions are built around those features of the animal rather than the prominent AAI model of selecting animals by testing their behaviours to determine if they are appropriate for specific and fairly standard roles. Goodness of fit ensures that the animals feel comfortable in the roles they are invited to play. For example, one dog might be well matched to participate in nondirective play therapy whereas a dog with lots of initiative and who prefers "action" might work better in more directive or structured forms of play therapy.

AAPT is a diverse field with many options for animals, therapists, and clients. It can be used in a trans-theoretical manner, as its values and principles allow for flexible application by clinicians who conceptualise and offer their services according to different theoretical frameworks. While a techniques manual is available to those who have had initial training in it (VanFleet & Faa-Thompson, 2019), the field is focused far more heavily on relationships, starting with the relationship between therapist and animal which then serves as a model and metaphor for the therapeutic process and relationships (VanFleet, 2008; VanFleet & Faa-Thompson, 2010, 2017). The reciprocal nature of the human-animal relationship is paramount for ensuring the best results from the process. Both clients and the animals in the therapy can decline to participate at any moment, and they are not pushed to continue.

For example, if child clients are yelling loudly and the horses they were working with move away to graze on the far end of the field, the children might become upset, feeling rejected or that the horses "don't like them". The job of the therapist is not to "fix" this situation (unless intervention is needed to protect the animals, of course) but to help the clients process it to increase their understanding of the horses, themselves, and their relationship. The therapist might initially empathically reflect their feelings ("You're really disappointed that the horses moved away" or "When the horses moved to the

other side away from here, you thought they did not like you, and you feel bad about that"). Depending on the type of therapy being conducted with the horses, that might be all that is said. In other cases, the therapist might help the clients think further about the situation, "I wonder what caused them to move so far away." The children might be able to reflect on the cause (their noisiness), and the therapist might further prompt them to think how to apply their empathy, "Perhaps you can think of a way to help the horses feel safe with you again."

These are simple examples, as each situation might require a different response, given the child's goals and reactions. In each case, the horses are not blocked from leaving, they are not led back to the clients, and their departure is not seen as a problem. In fact, it might represent their honest reaction to the children's behaviours which may parallel similar situations in "real life". This provides an opportunity for the clients to develop and apply empathy in ways that might eventually be applied to their problematic human relationships.

One aspect of the goodness-of-fit model and the emphasis on reciprocal, mutually beneficial relationships is natural and voluntary animal behaviour. Animals are not "used" in therapy; the practitioners "work with" or "involve" the animals. The animals, for their part, are usually free to come and go. Most of the time, dogs and cats work off leash and horses and goats are at liberty. Voluntary participation of the animals offers benefits for the animals, but also for the clients, and ultimately, for the therapeutic process. The next section looks at what this means.

RECIPROCAL RELATIONSHIPS

The voluntary participation approach places value on the animal's ability to be themselves without undue influence by humans except to ensure safety. A focus on natural behaviours in natural environments is combined with attempts to maximise animals' agency and free choice whenever possible. Reciprocal relationships are developed through mutually enjoyable activities, play, use of animal-friendly training and preparation, avoidance of over-training, simple hanging out together, and fluency in the animals' own languages. An appreciation of the individual animal is critical to the process along with, clear-eyed and exceptional knowledge of each unique animal. Therapists distinguish observation from interpretation and know that context is critical in generating tentative understanding of what behaviours might mean from the animal's point of view. This type of relationship is detailed in VanFleet and Faa-Thompson (2017) and is the focus of a forthcoming, as yet untitled book, by Risë VanFleet, Tracie Faa-Thompson, and Patricia Tagg that explores relationships with dogs, horses, cats, sheep, and goats, among others.

Features of therapist relationships with their animals include the following: (a) mutually respectful (considerate), (b) accepting, (c) empathic (attuned), (d) attentive, (e) nurturing, (f) proactive, (g) securely attached, (h) interconnected, (i) flexible, (j) playful (fun), (k) developmentally appropriate, (l) autonomous (voluntary, with freedom of choice), and (m) humane (nonaversive). The therapist relationship must embody these features at home as well as at work, and this provides both a model and a "living laboratory" for clients to learn about their own relationships with others. In the *Animal Assisted Play Therapy* book, pages 158-159 include a series of questions therapists can ask themselves that help them focus more fully on the needs of their animals in this type of reciprocal relationship (VanFleet & Faa-Thompson, 2017).

Since AAI practitioners, for all intents and purposes, conscript animals into our work, it seems only fair that we learn their language and pay close attention to their communications about what the experience is like for them. In essence, practitioners must learn how to think like their dog, their horse, or their cat, both in terms of the species of that animal as well as each individual animal.

Therapists' competencies in terms of animal behaviour are reflected in their abilities to:

- Select animals and activities that "fit" both animal and client goals
- Communicate and build relationship with their animals
- Read body language fluently in real time
- Show proactive attention (anticipate and avoid conflicts)
- Split their attention effectively among client, animal, and environment
- Engage in positive training embedded with a clear understanding of learning theory
- Demonstrate animal-friendly handling skills
- Understand the ethology of the species and its implications for behaviour and interaction
- Separate their observations from interpretations of animal behaviour
- Apply profound knowledge of each individual animal with whom they work in a wide range of circumstances

All of these competencies must become like "second nature" to the therapist in order to seamlessly integrate them with the therapeutic methods and relationships involved with any client. "When we conduct any type of Animal Assisted Intervention, our relationship with our animals is on display as a model and metaphor for all relationships. There is no room for any aversive equipment or handling. Only mutually respectful and beneficial relationships should be brought into any therapeutic setting" (VanFleet, 2004, 2008; VanFleet & Faa-Thompson, 2017).

One of our workshops was held in Alaska a couple years ago, and the woman hosting the training had two Nigerian Dwarf Goats. When the dogs in attendance needed to rest, the group interacted with the goats, who ran free during the day on a large grassy area. At first, the goats seemed uninterested in the workshop people. To enhance this ability to see the perspective of the goats, I asked the group to use materials on the property (with permission, of course) to create some new goat-friendly spaces in the large lawn area.

The group built a structure suitable for jumping and leaping, and stuck apricots to short branches on the side of nearby spruce trees to create browsing opportunities. The goats had been jumping on some large rocks next to a wooded area on their own, but immediately came to the new structure created by these unfamiliar people. In no time, they were jumping onto the structure, exploring underneath it, and eventually reaching to eat the apricots nearby. Later in the day, I asked the group of therapists to develop a family therapy intervention using this goat-friendly environment that ensured the goats enjoyed it. They found it was quite easy to consider the metaphors of the situation and the goats' behaviours and create a useful intervention.

The story did not end there. I learned the next day that after a day of romping around the lawn and their new structure, the goats' owners had great difficulty getting them to go into their bear-safe enclosure for the night. The group was tasked once again with "thinking like goats" and solving this problem of moving the goats from their day of fun and freedom into the bear-proofed enclosure.

The group, thinking in terms of behavioural principles, ethology, and what they had learned about these particular goats decided to hold a "party" for the goats in the enclosure. The group took some novel items to capture the goats' curiosity, and entered the enclosure exhibiting playful sounds and behaviours as they had done in the lawn area. The goats trotted along with their "new people" and entered the enclosure without hesitation. The owners continued this practice using novelty, fun, and the occasional apricot to help the goats easily change venues for the night.

> *The goats trotted along with their 'new people' and entered the enclosure without hesitation. The owners continued this practice using novelty, fun, and the occasional apricot to help the goats easily change venues for the night.*

Animal behaviour is inextricably linked with environment, as is our own. More natural environments for the animals yield more natural behaviour. Animals feel safer in familiar surroundings. Furthermore, it is important to remember that the "environment" includes the humans involved, and animals will respond to them in a variety of ways, depending on their mood, their choices in that moment, and their perception of humans in general and the specific humans in front of them as being safe or questionable. When given agency to act within their environment as they see fit, animals can exhibit unexpected behaviours. These unexpected behaviours are likely a natural reaction of the animal, and they need not be a problem in therapy. Part of excellent practice includes preparation for unexpected behaviour and maximising it in terms of therapeutic goals.

For example, when a large stinging insect landed on a horse's back during a session, the horse was free to run away from it. This led to useful processing with the small group of clients present about how we respond when something or someone hurts us, physically or emotionally. Whatever choices the animal makes freely can be viewed from the animal's point of view: What does that tell us about the animal? What does that reaction do for the animal? In any AAI work, what does the animal get out of it?

ANIMALS' VOLUNTARY PARTICIPATION

To consider mostly unfettered voluntary participation by the animals, one must first understand the concept of agency. Agency refers to the "capability of humans and animals to act within their environment, usually by choosing (unconsciously or purposefully) a set of behaviours that help accomplish a goal. People (and animals) are said to 'have agency' when they take the environment into account and then decide on some goal-directed action over which they have some control" (VanFleet, 2020). Animals have intelligences of their own which are often overlooked (de Waal, 2016; Gardner, 2011; VanFleet, 2020c), but the savvy practitioner learns about these and maximises them, allowing animals to solve many of their own problems in their own ways while remaining cautious to avoid "overtraining" their animals.

While some training and preparation for therapy work is absolutely necessary, the goal is to retain as much agency for the animals and permit them as many open choices and as much freedom as possible. When therapists step back from directing virtually all behaviours of their animals during sessions, a far more valuable experience is had, both for animals and the human clients. We advocate working according to this ethos. We train our animals, and on occasion might use a leash or rope, but most of the time, the animals are "naked" (no equipment) and free to have both choice and voice in the sessions. We, as the therapists, are responsible for ensuring that the interactions that occur are processed in such a way as to become therapeutic for the clients.

In order to enable voluntary participation by the animals, practitioners must always ensure that the animals have ample room to leave the immediate vicinity of clients (i.e. an exit route). Animals need space, just as humans do, and the therapist watches to see that the animals have space at all times. If animals feel uncomfortable, they will remove themselves from the situation, as long as they have this space and a history of permission to do so. This means that we never encircle or crowd an animal.

Providing agency and structuring for voluntary participation against the backdrop of reciprocal relationship means that animals are more likely to approach clients when they arrive and eagerly engage with them while they are present, including initiating some activities with the clients themselves. Therapists, in turn, must be flexible and spontaneously able to tie whatever happens back to clients' therapeutic goals. Therapists certainly can plan certain activities that are enjoyable for the animals and geared toward achieving client goals, but they stand ready to allow spontaneity in the client-animal relationship and see the relevance of that for client goals and animal well-being at the same time.

When animals are involved in the therapeutic process in this voluntary manner, and when their choices are respected and incorporated, they appear to enjoy themselves. Dogs check in with their therapist-owners, but they focus mostly on the client with numerous signs of relaxation and playfulness. Horses run to see who has arrived and remain at the gate watching the clients depart. Cats swirl around clients' legs and engage in activities chosen not only for the client's needs, but for their own interests and abilities. There are relatively few studies of the impact of AAIs on animals, and most of them fail to describe what happens within the session for the animals or this principle of willing participation and voluntary behaviour within sessions. Clinical findings suggest that the animals truly enjoy themselves within this model, in part because AAPT-trained therapists know that this is a requirement and therefore attend to it, but it would be a valuable research study to tease out the "voluntariness factor" and the degree to which it makes a difference.

The animals are not the only ones who benefit from having agency, however. We believe that it adds to the authenticity of the client-animal relationship. When clients can see with their own eyes that the animal approaches them, stays with them, cooperates during activities with them, and responds to them without being instructed or held in place by the therapist, they can believe it is "real".

When horses move away to graze and then return with interest and curiosity to see what the clients are doing, the clients can begin to understand that sometimes others have needs of their own, but they also come back to spend time with them. When a dog plays hide-and-seek by searching for a client hiding in the playroom or outdoors, the client's needs relating to attachment relationships begin to be met. This is what it feels like when someone knows you're missing and cares enough to come looking for you.

When animals have a history of reciprocal, positive, relaxed, and fun interactions with the therapist, they typically choose to participate in the therapeutic process even though they have full choice to decline. When they choose not to participate, the therapist works with the clients to help them understand, adjust, cope, adapt, and accept. When animals choose to engage, however, the clients see the actual change in the animals and their decisions to interact.

There simply is no substitute for this type of authentic experience. It is the job of therapists in Animal Assisted Interventions (AAI) to give their animals this type of positive life experience and to help our clients experience this type of connection and incorporate it into their lives. A wide range of therapeutic goals can be met in the context of this authentic and safe relationship.

CONCLUSION

When animals have reciprocal and mutually beneficial relationships with their therapist-owners/ guardians, they learn to expect that from other humans as long as they are protected from negative interactions. When therapists then facilitate the client-animal relationship throughout their sessions, clients learn how to treat animals with respect and kindness while the animals learn that interactions with the clients can be fun and stimulating. When clients see that animals get to make choices and have a voice in sessions and that the therapist listens to the animals, clients learn that they, too, can expect that type of acceptance and genuineness from the therapist. When animals are free to move as they see fit during sessions, their choices can help clients learn about others' perspectives and to develop empathy when the therapist facilitates the interactions well. Clients also learn that animals respond in relationship-affirming ways when they treat them kindly.

Some children and adults with histories of trauma and attachment disruptions harm animals. There are a number of possible causes for this, but the power of play and relationship-building in which animals have agency and serve as partners in the therapeutic process help them see the animals as sentient beings with feelings and reactions like their own. I have worked successfully with dozens of children and young people who have harmed animals to varying degrees by encouraging and permitting the authentic, accepting, and playful relationships to emerge that help the clients see the animals as themselves — beings with ideas, choices, and motives of their own who respond to kindness and empathy.

As James Garbarino wrote in his book, Lost Boys (1999), and which applies to girls as well as boys, "Because we know that empathy is the enemy of aggression and that depersonalisation is the ally, all efforts at moral rehabilitation of violent and troubled boys hinge upon cultivating empathy and fighting against their tendency to depersonalise others."

Even for this challenging work, the first step starts with the therapist-animal relationship. When that relationship shows reciprocity, mutuality, and authenticity, it can then be brought into the therapeutic environment to help clients learn about how it feels when someone else cares, what it means to have empathy for another, and how good healthy and secure relationships can feel. Ensuring that animals have agency and are voluntary participants in the therapeutic process benefits all involved.

An adolescent client from an abusive environment summed it up as follows:

"I know that Kirrie really values me. She trots to greet me every time, and wags her tail so much that her whole back end swings back and forth. She remembers me even when I don't come for a while. When I walk around, she stays with me, and she likes it when I give her shoulder massages. She has helped me understand what friendship is really all about — something I never knew before. I make sure she is having fun, and she makes sure I pay attention. And we both have fun together. I don't take advantage of her, and she doesn't take advantage of me. We just like being together. I think it's the first time I ever truly loved somebody."

REFERENCES

de Waal, F. (2016). *Are We Smart Enough to Know How Smart Animals Are?* New York, NY: W.W. Norton and Company.

Garbarino, J. (1999). *Lost Boys: Why Our Sons Turn Violent and How We Can Save Them.* New York, NY: Free Press.

Gardner, H. (2011). *Frames of Mind: The Theory of Multiple Intelligences* (3rd ed). New York, NY: Basic Books.

Lerner, R. (Ed.). (1983). *Developmental Psychology: Historical and Philosophical Perspectives.* Hillsdale: Erlbaum.

Schaefer, C.E., & Drewes, A.A. (2013). *The Therapeutic Powers of Play: 20 Core Agents of Change* (2nd ed.). Hoboken, NJ: Wiley.

Thomas, A., & Chess, S. (1977). *Temperament and Development.* New York: Brunner-Mazel.

VanFleet, R. (2004). *Animal Assisted Play Therapy Manual.* Boiling Springs, PA: Play Therapy Press.

VanFleet, R. (2008). *Play Therapy with Kids & Canines.* Sarasota, FL: Professional Resource Press.

VanFleet, R. (2013, 2018). *Certification Manual for Animal Assisted Play Therapists.* Boiling Springs, PA: Play Therapy Press.

VanFleet, R. (2014). *Filial Therapy: Strengthening Parent-Child Relationships Through Play.* Sarasota, FL: Professional Resource Press.

VanFleet, R. (2020a). AAPT Certification Board: Information on the Process. Accessed from https://iiaapt.org/aapt-certification-board-information-on-the-process/ July 10, 2021.

VanFleet, R. (2020b). Assessment of Therapy Animals: Using a Goodness-of-Fit Conceptualization. Accessed from http://iiaapt.org/assessment-of-therapy-animals-using-a-goodness-of-fit-conceptualization/ July 10, 2021.

VanFleet, R. (2020c). Do We Sell Them Short? Supporting "Agency" in Animals. Accessed from https://iiaapt.org/do-we-sell-them-short-supporting-agency-in-animals/ July 10, 2021.

VanFleet, R. (2021). The Goodness of Fit Concept. Handout from conference presentation for the International Animal Assisted Play Therapy® Online Conference, March 9.

VanFleet, R., & Faa-Thompson, T. (2010). The case for using Animal Assisted Play Therapy®. *The British Journal of Play Therapy*, 6, 4-18.

VanFleet, R., & Faa-Thompson, T. (2014). Including animals in play therapy with young children and families. In M.R. Jalongo (Ed.), *Teaching Compassion: Humane Education in Early Childhood* (pp. 89-107). New York, NY: Springer.

VanFleet, R. & Faa-Thompson, T. (2017). *Animal Assisted Play Therapy®.* Sarasota, FL: Professional Resource Press.

VanFleet, R., Fine, A.H., & Faa-Thompson, T. (2019). Application of animal-assisted interventions in professional mental health settings: An overview of practice considerations. In A.H. Fine (Ed.), *Handbook on Animal-Assisted Therapy: Foundations and Guidelines for Animal-Assisted Interventions* (5th ed.) (pp. 225-248). San Diego, CA: Academic Press.

Chapter 11:

HORSE PLAY AND CANINE CAPERS

THE IMPORTANCE OF PLAY TO FACILITATE LEARNING AND HEALING

TRACIE FAA-THOMPSON

ABOUT TRACIE FAA-THOMPSON

BA Social Work, MA Crim, AASW, PG NDPT, Clin Hypno, Cert EAGALA, Certified Non-directive Play Therapist; Filial Therapist, Cert Animal Ethology and Behaviour Consultant and Instructor, Dip Consultant AHC, Supervisor and Filial Therapy Instructor. IIAAPT Instructor, Supervisor, international trainer and speaker.

Tracie has worked for 26 years as a specialist social worker in adoption working with traumatised children and their adoptive and foster families. She is a British Association of Play Therapists registered play therapist who uses a mix of individual play therapy, filial therapy, and group filial methods. A practice teacher of social work students and newly qualified social workers, and a trainer in Life Story Work, Attachment Theory, and resilience in adversity.

As a clinical hypnotherapist, she incorporates EMDR, Eye Movement Integration with Emotional Freedom Technique (EFT) as an effective approach to trauma. Tracie's passion is working outdoors in nature and since 2004, has been amalgamating Nature family therapy with Equine Assisted Family Therapy. As a lover of the natural world, Tracie trained as an Applied Herbal Choices animal health professional consultant. Believing only in positive approaches to animal welfare, she is a Certified Animal Ethology and Behaviour Consultant and Instructor. Tracie also has a unique approach to therapeutic life story work using nature to plot adopted and fostered children and adults' journeys in 3D!

Hailing from a Scottish/Romany Traveller family, Tracie grew up with multiple dogs and horses as integral to her native culture. She is the Founder of Turn About Pegasus, an Equine Assisted Programme for a range of client issues. Tracie believes that even when clients have endured terrible traumatic events that the power of play and laughter is as cathartic as tears. She is an EAGALA (Equine Assisted Growth and Learning Association since 2005) certified, dual approved as both mental health and horse specialist. Positive reinforcement works for humans and animals alike.

Tracie is the author of numerous manuals, articles, and training programmes on attachment and resilience, life story work, sibling contact in adoption, introductions of adoptive families and children,

EAL/EAP, and Animal Assisted Play Therapy®. She is the co-author of the book Animal Assisted Play Therapy which won the coveted Maxwell Award 2018 under the Category Human Animal Bond.

Dr Risë Van Fleet and Tracie have been collaborating since 2006 to bring together the modalities of play therapy and animal assisted therapies into a positive, cohesive ethical and playful way of working. And they founded the International Institute of Animal Assisted Play Therapy®.

Tracie is one of only three certified Filial Therapy Instructors in the UK and Ireland approved by the Original Family Enhancement and Play Therapy Centre. Training as a Filial Therapy Instructor is by invite only and is a three-year process to train as an Instructor.

INTRODUCTION

The objective of this chapter is to highlight the importance of playfulness, not just in Animal Assisted Play Therapy® (AAPT), but in other animal assisted interventions. Play is highlighted for its role in facilitating engagement, safety, affective expression, exploration, problem solving and mastery.

How can we use play and playfulness as tools for building a relationship? Have you ever experienced a moment when you have shared laughter with someone, made eye contact, and shared a smile? Did you feel more connected with them? Laughter is just as cathartic as tears can be; it is very healing across all age ranges. We all like to play, even as adults, but possibly as adults our play is less free play and more focused or integrated into team games.

SCIENTIFIC INTEREST IN PLAY HAS GROWN

For many years, biologists and other scientists simply didn't study play, they didn't seem to think play was important. Recently, Lorenz and Friberg observed that though play behaviours are more prevalent in the wild, we also see our young, domesticated animals, our dog, cat, and horse co-workers playing, and enjoying play. Play in children and play in young animals assists with practice for later life, building skills through play for real life situations.

From a survival point of view, animals will conserve energy for finding food and keeping themselves safe. They won't indulge in playing unless they have enough food, water, and have a sense of safety. If animals know they don't have to flee from anything, and they are not hungry or thirsty, and are not in pain, then we'll see more play. Aligned to that, when animals are fit and well, fed and watered and don't have to worry about predators but are kept in environments which are either too stimulating or not stimulating enough, they will go from allostasis to allostatic load. We need a little stress (allostasis-good stress) in our lives to learn and challenge ourselves. When we are overloaded (allostatic load) we are either in Fight or Flight mode or we shut down and become depressed. We don't see play in stressed children; we don't see play in stressed animals.

When we ourselves are stressed, in distress, or thinking about other things, we're unlikely to engage in play. It doesn't matter how wonderful or playful the other person is, we just don't feel playful. Free play uses a huge amount of energy, and it serves the important purpose of practice for adult life. All healthy young animals, young and older children, and some adults, use play as a way to practice different skills. Play makes it safe to practice those skills because it's pretend and not real life.

We all had childhood dreams and then we get told to grow up. But being an adult doesn't mean we cannot dream and fantasise about how life could be.

Since our animals don't know that they're doing interventions with us, they bring elements to the experience that we humans cannot. And so, to integrate the playfulness of the animals in our work allows us to let loose in a safe way. Our animals' natural behaviours provide the link between childhood and adulthood — which frees us up to become that child again. One of the most wonderful things I've seen is when the horses and dogs are running free and the humans start to run free with them, freeing them to become less uptight.

For all these noted reasons, play is critical. Reciprocity is important too. If we are playing outside or engaging with others (other than on an electronic device) we are getting exercise without knowing it. Intellectually we learn when we are playing, someone might do something that you are curious about (animal or human) and it sparks a debate or a desire to learn more, rather than having information fed to us. We learn about values and morality by experimenting and playing things through, either physically or sometimes in our minds. Doing these things with a playful demeanour doesn't make them any less valid or real and the physical and emotional health benefits are immediate.

PLAY AND DEVELOPMENT

Grow up. Be responsible. Who has been told that before? All of us no matter what our age, use different forms of play — imaginative, creative, comprehensive, and therapeutic play to name a few. Sometimes we play more than our grown-up world would like to admit. It would be even more beneficial if we could recognise when spontaneous play comes to our aid and could lead us towards a higher degree of awareness and self-knowledge.

The main type of play that animals and children engage in, is rough and tumble play. Physical play is fun; playing games is fun. If we didn't have a play instinct, maybe neither kind of play would exist. Playing a game that's focused on a goal, an outcome or specific rules, however, is not a primary play process.

The most primitive parts of the brain generate various primary-process emotions, including physical play. Playing games is likely to be a secondary process, dependent on learning and memories. Few people are studying the primary processes. To do that, you must think in a very Darwinian way, and understand that emotions emerge first from very ancient regions of the brain, which connect to more recent, higher brain regions that control learning and thought. This is a very important principle. Mother Nature built some important things into ancient regions of the brain.

Children are designed, by natural selection, to play, wrote Peter Gray, Ph.D., Professor of Psychology at Boston College and author, in 2011 in the *American Journal of Play*: Wherever children are free to play, they do. Gray argues that, without play, young people fail to acquire the social and emotional skills necessary for healthy psychological development.

PLAY HAS ITS OWN LANGUAGE

When two horses play, they might handicap each other to carry on with the play, and it will be reciprocal. They might be open mouthed, and nipping at each other, but not making contact at all. Play in all of us is loose limbed, fluid and joyful. Watch your animals and children play. There might be a lot of noise and movement but it rarely (if the players are feeling safe) goes over into aggression. My Shetland pony and Pintabian love to play. The Shetland nips his knees, and he falls down on them and they start mouthing at each other with snaky heads and open snapping mouths. It would seem on the surface that the game was unequal, the Pintabian is so much taller, heavier and faster. However, by getting down on his knees he is making himself equal height to the Shetland, he handicaps himself and so the game continues longer.

CURIOSITY IS A WONDERFUL THING

No creature animal or human will engage in free play if they don't feel safe. Play takes a lot of energy. If the feeling is that the energy is needed for fight or flight that leaves little time for playing.

The emotional release of cutting loose and just being in the moment of play is vital. In play therapy, children and adults work through their issues by experimenting or perhaps playing out the scenario and changing the outcome to something that is more healing for the player. I see it time and time again in therapy. When a client plays out a scenario where they've been hurt in the past, they play it out and they play it out until they have a different outcome. If we try out something in play and it works out, we are more likely to try it again and reinforce that behaviour. We learn through play and each learned experimentation can serve to reinforce or extinguish that behaviour. Although it's great to have solitary play, the huge benefits of playing together, turn taking, making up rules and just feeling part of something, promotes pro-social behaviour and inclusivity.

In our program, we work with a lot of family groups, especially during this COVID time. And it's quite a shock to them sometimes because they think that the child of focus is the only one that needs therapy. When we say no, we're working with the whole family, it feels strange for them, because it is unfamiliar, and they want their child "fixed" but were not expecting to be a part of the process. Having a session as a family is a fully systemic, integrative way to work, because everybody has their own self-defined role. Because our horses and our dogs live in groups and they have different friendships and different relationships, we can use observations of their natural interactions with each other as metaphors for familial groups. Families will make connections with the horses and relate that one of them is just like them, then they will come out with a reason why they and the horse are similar.

One caveat when working with family groups is that working with Family Systems is a skilled area of work. Therapists need experience and good working knowledge of family systems and systemic practice without animals involved before you think about working with animals in your practice in Family Therapy.

The huge benefits of playing together, turn-taking, making up rules, feeling part of something, promotes pro-social behaviour and inclusivity. We learn about values and morality by experiencing things through, either physically or sometimes in our minds. Who has gone through scenarios in your mind about what you're going to say to a certain person or people, **we practice the scenarios in our heads and fantasize about how you might want things to play out for real**. Although it might not look like play to anyone else, you're playing it through with your mind to prepare you for when the real-life situation comes up.

A playful demeanour when we're doing therapeutic work doesn't make it any less valid or real. In animal assisted play therapy, we adopt quite a playful, light approach. Some of the things that we're discussing with our clients can be very emotionally and physically difficult to discuss. Death, trauma, abuse, loss, complex trauma, ill health, etc. are hard subjects. We don't dismiss them or make light of the client's distress. We don't dismiss the validity of what people have gone through but it's really draining when things are so heavy inside all the time. So, if we can bring a bit of lightness in, even just for a short while, we have found that it helps clients in feeling hopeful for some future joy in their lives.

CREATING SAFETY WITH PLAYFULNESS

In the UK, there's a lot of emphasis on what you shouldn't do, and lots of safety information given out by riding instructors and even in AAI sessions regarding how to approach a horse. We have children who've had years of riding lessons at local riding schools, and they're actually more frightened of the horses than people who have never had any interaction with horses because they're taught that the front-end bites and the back-end kicks. Children don't get the opportunity to learn any body language, they just get put on the horse, the horse gets dragged around and that's it, no hanging out, no getting to know them or even thinking about what the horse is getting out of being ridden by them. So, in our sessions we spend a lot of time observing the animals, getting to know them without being intrusive (we are good at that as humans — being intrusive to an animal's space) and seeing what they're like. Hanging out with them and finding out what's on the animal's agenda, what they like and dislike, individual differences. In other words, we want to know who these animals are.

We have found that with any type of therapeutic intervention, that if you go in with a whole list of safety protocols before you even start the sessions, you can heighten anxiety and both children and families feel unsafe from the outset. We strive to keep our manner light-hearted and curious.

Creating safety or creating physical and emotional safety, is a delicate balance. If there's too much emphasis on safety, it creates anxiety. We only set limits and we only draw attention when there's potential for something unsafe that will need our intervention. So, as all we know, traumatised children need emotional safety to play out their feelings and to explore. None of us can explore our feelings or be curious when we're in allostatic load.

THE POWER OF PLAY

Play builds connections and friendships; it can overcome some problem areas. For those of us who work in play therapy, play is our core medium. Play also helps create a positive association and helps build connections with our clients.

The sessions must be carefully titrated to the animal's reactions and communications. We have a lot of emphasis on reading body language. We teach our children and families to read the animal's body language and to read the animal that they are working with body language — because they all have subtly different body language. Just as we humans do. What means something to one person might appear to be something very different to the next person. We all have our individual differences.

An example of this was Huck, a dog we met on Vancouver Island at the Bed and Breakfast where Dr Risë VanFleet and I were staying. He was a rescue dog and lived with the B&B owner's daughter on the grounds. Huck was curious but a bit afraid and he certainly didn't want any human-initiated touch and would have thought that was very rude had I attempted to do that.

So how do you make the connection? Through play. Huck was a mixed herding breed, so he liked to chase. But even better, by just observing him and not intruding, he showed us that he liked to be chased. Huck and I played chase every day and when we were done, he would come and lie down next to me. I never touched him, although as a human I would have loved to. We had a good connection and the play started it. If I'd gone in, all heavy and rude and touched this dog — which I wanted to — as humans we like touch, that would have been really, really rude and it would have broken our relationship before it had even started. I think it's important to remember that. Every day we played hide and seek. Huck was always the hider. I had no idea what the B&B owner thought, this middle-aged woman running around with her daughter's dog, but we both had fun. And I guess it doesn't really matter what anyone else thought of us as the building of the relationship was the important piece.

Life is too important to be taken seriously.

OSCAR WILDE

TAKING PLAY SERIOUSLY

Lightness, humour and laughter within a therapeutic relationship is cathartic and a wonderful way of releasing pent up emotions. A lighter tone creates emotional safety for clients of all ages. In our sessions, we engage in lots of storytelling activities with animals at the centre. The focus is taken away from the client and placed onto the animal.

GAMES THAT ARE FUN FOR BOTH DOGS AND PEOPLE

It's important when we're working with animals in our work to remember they are conscripts to the work. We decided that's what we want to do, and we want to involve them. So, it's important that it's fun for all involved. It's important that both enjoy the process. The more we utilise what animals are naturally inclined to do, the more everyone gets out of the interactions.

THE FREEDOM OF PLAY

For all of us, the sheer joy of playing is therapeutic, not therapy but it is therapeutic. That's where we come in, to help it become active therapy as qualified therapists.

PLAY HAPPENS WITHIN STRONG RELATIONSHIPS

Characteristics of Good Relationships:

- Respect: acceptance of who each sentient being is
- Understanding and empathy
- Mutuality, reciprocity, collaboration
- Flexibility: give and take
- Each person's input is considered
- Empowerment: each one's growth is encouraged
- Choices: shared problem-solving
- Hanging in there during tough times
- Playfulness and humour

We cannot play if we don't feel safe and if we don't act with respectful acceptance of each sentient being involved, human or animal. Sometimes we'll see when we're working with our clients and our children, one might be playing and the other person might not be enjoying that play, and they don't recognise that that the other is not having as much fun as they are or feeling uncomfortable or is even a little scared.

So, when we're working through our animals, we do a lot of work, as already stated, with body language. We might be asking clients to wonder and say something like, "I'm curious what you think the horses are doing." Or, "When you shouted loudly did you notice what Buster (an Arabian) did?" Often clients are unaware of their impact on others and it's too shaming to discuss it from a human-to-human impact so doing it through noticing the animals' reactions in a gentle way is non shaming and solution focused. We can then go on to wonder how they could help Buster when he reacts to shouty voices, for example. It's really, important that we spend this time building these relationships up in sessions as it is through sentience and connectedness in a playful, safe environment that true healing can happen.

You can have flexibility in free play; there are no set "game rules", give and take and everyone is considered. It helps us to understand problems and feelings better when you're playing out things, it helps with sharing and problem solving.

Allowing as many natural behaviours in their natural environment is what assists with therapeutic changes. Animals need to be well behaved, like humans, but not be so controlled that they aren't free to behave naturally. Therapy happens regardless of whether the animals do what we or the clients want. Animals, whilst being therapeutic are not therapists themselves, they're a bridge.

PLAY AND ANIMAL ASSISTED INTERVENTIONS

Many programs focus only on what the animal can do for us, and clients. People might say, "The animal did this for me, this is what I got out of it." But you rarely hear, "The horse really enjoyed it," or, "I noticed that he wanted to carry on and he didn't want this activity to end."

People might expect the animals to tolerate what we asked them — however, when we are working with an animal, if a client wants to dress them up, and they put something on the horse and the horse then shakes it off, it stays shaken off. We don't expect them to tolerate something they don't like. It's an important lesson, when you're working in therapy and when you have clients who have been expected to tolerate things that they really do not like, who have been used and abused in different ways that, just like our animals involved in the sessions, clients have a choice to say NO to something they don't like.

If we allowed clients to interact with our animals in a way they did not enjoy and if we also did that with our animals, it would be a poor metaphor and message that we as therapists are conveying to our clients. We would be implying that it's okay to do things to others that they don't like. I just say, "my horses like to choose their own clothes."

When the horses are curious like this, and the dogs are curious like this, clients (and therapists too) enjoy and get a lot of fun out of seeing them picking things out of the box and flinging them around, that's all part of it. What's really important is not to over train your animals, or as the example with Buster, train a behaviour just because you can because it's the dog in the dog and the horse in the horse that's the fundamental power and wonder of Animal Assisted Play Therapy — it's why we engage and believe in this amazing intervention. If you've got an animal that's over trained, and there's no spontaneity anymore we believe it detracts from the whole purpose.

Lincoln University has recently released a paper looking at working with dogs, showing how much training therapists had received on animal body language, or even how much training they have had with their animals in a classroom setting or in different settings. There was quite a disparity regarding how much training people have actually had. Currently in the UK, there's a big movement of taking dogs into schools with very little or any training in canine communication, ethology, individual dog breeds etc. and what dogs have evolved to do.

The internet is strewn with images of some of these situations, where the animal is displaying many stress signals, which are ignored or overlooked or not recognised as stress signals. These images often get many, many likes and positive comments on how therapeutic it is for the humans involved, whilst not seeing how miserable the animals are. This is one reason why it is so important to try and learn the body language of the animal you are working with.

It's a requirement of anyone trained in AAPT that the animals have a real choice about whether to participate or not. We try to work on grass as much as possible, so the horses have access to food and water at all times. We ensure that our gates are open, so an animal can leave the session at any time, and we use that as a physical metaphor for freedom to choose.

WHAT IS ANIMAL ASSISTED PLAY THERAPY®?

- Complete integration of Animal Assisted Interventions with many forms of play therapy
- Relationship-centred, play based, process-oriented
- Nondirective, directive, individual, family & group forms
- All ages — works really well with family and groups
- Strong emphasis on animal welfare; animal must ENJOY, not merely tolerate the majority of interactions
- Therapist-animal relationship is metaphor for therapeutic relationship
- Focus of client-animal relationship through play, in service of therapeutic goals

THE "PLAY" IN ANIMAL ASSISTED PLAY THERAPY®

It's important, as stated earlier, that we create a light, playful, emotionally safe climate and accept the naturally occurring play that clients and animals exhibit. My horses live outside on lush, grassy fields 24 hours a day, seven days a week, so they often have a lot of flatulence, which is really a great icebreaker when you've got nervous or anxious clients, or most clients really. Their flatulence is really loud, and as most of the clients haven't been around animals very much, it's sort of like shock horror and wide-eyed disbelief at what they are hearing. Once over the shock they invariably think it's hilarious.

FIGURE 1: THE "PLAY" IN ANIMAL ASSISTED THERAPY

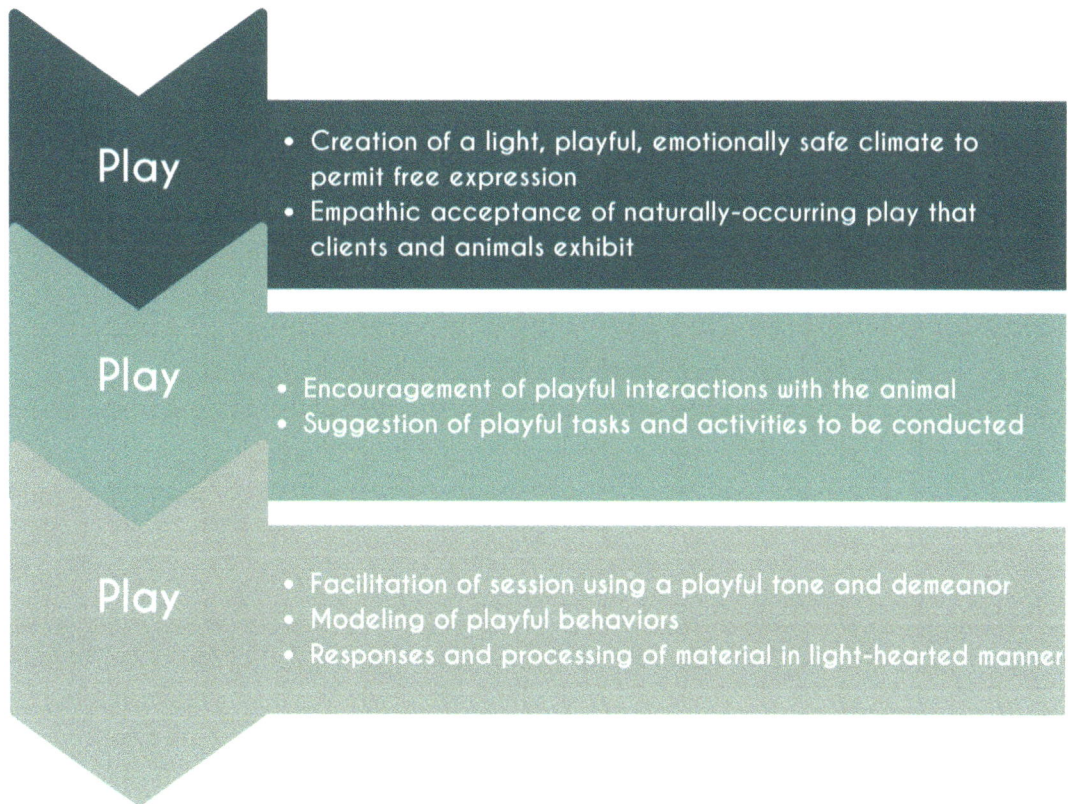

Play
- Creation of a light, playful, emotionally safe climate to permit free expression
- Empathic acceptance of naturally-occurring play that clients and animals exhibit

Play
- Encouragement of playful interactions with the animal
- Suggestion of playful tasks and activities to be conducted

Play
- Facilitation of session using a playful tone and demeanor
- Modeling of playful behaviors
- Responses and processing of material in light-hearted manner

Equine Flatulence can be a great icebreaker or mood breaker when situations get tense. Some clients have asked if we train them to do that at really difficult moments. If only! If we broke wind as therapists, I think there would be something to say and probably some complaints, not to mention how unprofessional it would be! The encouragement of playful interactions, as I said, and suggestion of playful tasks is encouraged by the therapists in a light manner and tone. For example, "*Your task for today should you choose to accept it is………*" If we're invited by clients, we'll get involved in the play and in the session too and we'll model playful behaviours. We are not averse to helping the clients break loose. When we are processing the material that people come up with, what their thoughts are, we don't focus on that very long, otherwise it can turn into a talking therapy.

DIFFERENT SPECIES IN ANIMAL ASSISTED PLAY THERAPY®

We build our work around the natural behaviours of animals. Animals with different likes and dislikes will work with different clients. Natural behaviours occur in natural settings. The animals we work with in our sessions are free to come and go as they please. The more space animals have, the more space they have to escape, explore and feel safe. We always provide escape routes. It is very difficult to have escape routes, to allow the animals to show their natural behaviours and have choices if they are being held or taken to environments where it is unsafe for humans and animals for them to be loose or 'at liberty.'

Recently we were working with two brothers. It was mid-winter. We spent the whole session breaking frozen puddles for the horses to ensure the horses got a drink. It was a metaphorical dream for us. For example, when you fall down you pick yourself up again. Some of the puddles were huge and would ice up again before we even got around them, which was a metaphor about trying and not giving up, back to square one, having fun. We made a joke about IS this was what is meant by breaking the ice. The whole 90-minute session was basically playing in puddles.

You can utilise anything in nature that is naturally available, as long as you respect the natural environment you are in. Our therapeutic skills and expertise utilise the tools we have available to work towards healing for our families wherever we are working. It wasn't the breaking of the puddles that was therapy, otherwise every winter people could go out and break puddles, but the therapeutic alliance between family and therapists. The horses were in the field and hung around nearby. The power of this session was multidimensional in the fact the brothers were working together, having fun, getting physically active and, most importantly, they were breaking the ice as an empathetic response to helping the horses out so they could easily have a drink.

I've seen over the years animals who are overly trained and I'm not sure who the animal is anymore. They don't do anything spontaneous but wait for the cue from the client or the owner. That makes me really, really sad. It's like, the animal is an automaton. If we saw a human acting that way and waiting for another human being to give them a cue before they could respond or wait until they were told what to do, it would raise alarm bells. We must ask ourselves why is it different for animals? Our animals do need good behaviour, but the more spontaneity, the better the relationship - and the better the outcomes over the years, the better the therapy intervention, because its naturally occurring, not forced or set up to achieve a particular outcome of result.

We are so grateful that many of our students have gone on to further study AAPT. Over the years we've been building up a rigorous research base. We want to be inclusive, not exclusive. We recognise that people come to AAPT from different backgrounds, and with different skills and experiences. Therefore, over the years we've developed levels of professional certification. We've often had people who are educators or occupational therapists, and they've decided to train to be a Play Therapist.

Chapter 12:

HOW ANIMALS CAN NOURISH WHEN WE DON'T KNOW WE'RE STARVING

ANIMAL ASSISTED PSYCHOTHERAPY FOR THE "RESISTANT" CLIENT

DR LINDA CHASSMAN CRADDOCK

ABOUT LINDA CHASSMAN CRADDOCK

Co-Founder and Executive Director, AATPC, USA.

Dr Linda Chassman is a licensed Marriage, Family Therapist in Colorado and California and has been working with clients since 1986. Before starting Animal Assisted Therapy Programs of Colorado (AATPC), she had a successful private practice for over 20 years as well as directing several agencies treating severe trauma and chemical addiction.

Dr Chassman is also an educator, having taught at California State University at Fullerton and CU Denver for 14 years, and consulted to residential treatment programs throughout the United Sates. She and her first animal partner, Norman, provided animal assisted therapy for more than 15 years with a variety of clients, including children, adolescents, adults and couples.

Dr Chassman opened Animal Assisted Therapy Programs of Colorado with the inspiration and assistance of Mazey, her former feral kitten that she raised after Mazey and her siblings were found outside in freezing weather. Sadly, Mazey passed away at only 17 months, but made a strong impact on those she helped.

In addition to holding a Doctoral degree in Counselling, and a Master's Degree in Clinical/Community Psychology, Dr Chassman has advanced certificates in Animal Assisted Psychotherapy, Animals and Human Health, Animal Assisted Therapy Activities and Learning, Treatment of Child Abuse, and Treatment of Adult Children of Alcoholics. She and Rupert have been Certified as a therapy team from Professional Therapy Dogs of Colorado since 2011. She has lectured around the world and has several professional publications to her credit.

In her private life, Dr Chassman is married with two children and several adopted animals. She volunteers weekly socialising challenging cats at Cat Care Society. in Lakewood, Colorado.

I met Norman in 1985. He was a little boy with red hair and a friendly disposition. I was seeing clients at my home at the time, and Norman would spend time with them in the waiting room before sessions. It didn't take long for Norman to work his way into the office with the clients, and inevitably became my co-therapist. Norman wasn't formally trained; he was a kitten. But he had natural empathy and a keen sense of when he was needed for a snuggle or to demonstrate boundaries in a polite but assertive manner. Norman started coming to work with me at the group home where I worked, and we found even more ways to help pre-teens with issues around boundaries, relationships, trust and a myriad of other issues. For the adolescents who had been in therapy for years, he was a welcome change and his charm won them over. They would relax and disclose more than when it was just me. Norman changed my life and my future, and I know he changed others' lives as well.

Fifteen years later, a formerly feral kitten, Mazey, inspired me to co-found Animal Assisted Therapy Programs of Colorado (AATPC) with another clinician, Ellen Winston, and her dog Sasha. What started with two animals and two mental health clinicians is now a large non-profit mental health organisation in Colorado with 35 animals and 14 clinicians. Our centre fills a much-needed niche for our 200 weekly clients who have experienced limited benefits from traditional counselling.

Though there are countless ways that our therapy animals help clients, the focus of this chapter is how animals can play a special role in helping those clients who are so hungry that they are no longer in touch with their hunger pangs. These clients need nourishment but have shut down the alert mechanism after being hungry for so long. We often call these clients "resistant to treatment", "mandated clients", or just downright frustrating. We may still find them challenging, but our animals have found ways to make contact with these clients when we cannot. In this chapter, I will refer to these clients as Malnourished.

These Malnourished clients may struggle with addiction, legal problems, attachment disorders, Oppositional Defiant Disorder or Conduct Disorder, personality disorders, and those whose "problem" has become their identity. Other clients may include those teens dropped at our door for therapy without explanation, those who have had unsatisfactory experiences with therapy in the past or have even been hurt by a therapist. Some have trust issues in general.

Some clients have had so much previous therapy that they could be "professional clients". This is often the most difficult group of clients to work with because they know the therapy game and play it well. They have "tried everything" and "nothing works." Professional clients can talk about their trauma, their history, and may even have good insights, but no matter how much talk therapy they try, nothing changes. After three decades in mental health, I am convinced that for some clients, their problems feel like all they have; their identities are so intertwined with their problems that unconsciously they are afraid to be any different. They seek help with the best of intentions and aim for a better life yet sabotage their own healing.

These are the clients that need nourishment the most yet have been hungry and empty for so long that they can't see a life beyond their hunger. I recently adopted a cat named Cleopatra. For the first two months she would bite me when I came into the room, then she'd settle down, then bite me again when I was getting ready to leave. I had the distinct feeling that she was so afraid I would never come back that she rejected me before I could leave her. She was terrified. Something must have happened to Cleo that taught her to anticipate being abandoned; her aggressive behaviour became her default self, always self-protective. Cleo clearly was starving for love and safety yet afraid to allow herself to have it.

In Cleo, I saw many of the clients we see at AATPC who resist the very love and safety they seek and make it difficult for anyone to give it to them. After months of working with her, Cleo and I have a strong, positive bond but she still tests everyone else she meets. I healed my relationship with Cleo because I kept coming back to her, no matter how many times she hurt me. I knew she needed me and so I showed her what stability looked like. Eventually, she accepted that I would continue to be there, and she trusted me. Just like with Cleo, the most challenging clients need us the most, yet will make it hard for us to care for them.

How do we "make" someone change when they don't want to or don't think they need to? Moreover, is it even ethical to try to change someone who is afraid to be different? To answer that question, I go back to the fact that they came to us so that their life could be better, therefore I think we have a responsibility to try to help nourish them even if they reject what we have to offer. Rather than getting into a power struggle with the client over making changes in their life, we invite them into a relationship triad with the animals and let them experiment what it is like to care for, and be cared for, by an animal.

This is attachment therapy at its most basic. The animals help with the initial relationship by building a sense of safety through their unconditional acceptance, as well as the neurochemical changes that come along with interacting with an animal. Dogs are excellent animals for this initial phase of treatment since they are often the most familiar animals for clients and tend to be the most accepting and nonjudgmental. Developing a sense of trust is just the initial step; the real work begins with other animals who will challenge the client to act differently. In this way, we partner with the client to experience what it is like to be in a relationship with an animal and be challenged to behave and believe differently.

The clinician's job is to create animal assisted interventions that most challenge the client into change. At our Barking C.A.A.T. Ranch (Center for Animal Assisted Therapy) we have over 35 rescued or rehomed animals of 10 different species. These include horses, donkeys, alpacas, goats, chickens, dogs, cats, rabbits, guinea pigs, and rats. Each species has something different to offer and each indi-

vidual animal chooses how to interact with each individual client in varied ways. Depending on the client's goals and where they are in their treatment, the clinician may create an activity or environment with a particular animal or group of animals that challenge the client in a new way. Therapy is always relationship-based and relies on the premise that people, including this group of clients, are motivated to establish close, accepting, mutual relationships. The animals at our farm have been chosen as therapy animals because they also want and benefit from the relationships built with the humans. Our motto is: Rescued Animals Rescuing People, but truly it is a reciprocal helping process.

The most powerful means of affecting change in this group of malnourished clients is through "Sideways Interventions". I call them "Sideways" because they nudge the client with impact without the client seeing it coming. Animals, especially those that are novel to the client, can act in ways that are unpredictable to the client, but ideally not surprising to the clinician. These novel and unexpected behaviours can metaphorically, knock clients off balance enough to require a slight correction through a new way of thinking, feeling, or acting (or all three!). Like tiny muscle tears needed to build muscles, humans grow not through comfort but through change and stress. The key is to present just enough "press" to encourage the client to try something new, without too much stress that causes the client to run.

Michael came to me while trying to end a destructive multi-year relationship with a woman upon whom he was emotionally dependent. One session, in the middle of treatment, we went out to work with the herd of horses and goats. I asked him to identify who each animal reminded him of and then interact with them in any way that felt natural (and safe). The first horse Michael identified was our full-sized horse Cody, who reminded him of his mother, and then our miniature horse, Misty, as his girlfriend. His "mother" walked into a stall while Michael was trying to talk to and brush her. He followed her and continued to talk to her, with him on one side of the fence and his mother on the other. His "mother" tossed her head about, showing displeasure and impatience with Michael. Michael found some hay and offered it, but again, the horse "mother" rejected his efforts. Misty, his "girlfriend" was off in the other direction, basically ignoring him. When I asked Michael, "what's happening?" he shared feeling dumbfounded at how the horses were behaving towards him. He talked about how rejecting his mother was, but how he was still trying to earn her acceptance and love, just like he did with his girlfriend. Michael was able to see and feel his desperate efforts for their love and accepting their rejection in return. I asked Michael, "Is there something else you'd like to do?" After a few moments of thought, he put down the hay, and said, "I'm done. Goodbye Cody ("mum")."

In this example, Michael had the powerful insight about how his relationship with his girlfriend was a repetition of his relationship with his mother. More importantly, he was able to feel the hunger, fatigue, and futility of his compulsive efforts to get nourished by her. He also was able to feel what it was like to create a different ending to the interaction — walking away on his own terms with his head up, instead of slinking away, feeling hurt. Michael had been in years of therapy without being able to change the pattern of destructive relationships. This may have been the first step in feeling what it was like to choose differently, and then see himself being a different person. This type of intervention can help Michael create a new self-image that includes powerful statements of self-care and action. It was the first glimpse of the kind of man Michael could be and it gave him hope to continue to practice behaviours that were nourishing to him.

Another client example was Sue, a 12-year-old who came to us after being sexually abused by a neighbours' father. She didn't have the language and was too fearful to put her experience into words. Previous therapies focused on the effects of the abuse, including deteriorating trust, feeling vulnerable, a loss of safety in the world, splitting off the childlike part of herself, and being uncertain about the boundaries around her body. Our therapy cat, Clementine, who was rescued from a cat hoarder's home, demonstrated the physiological effects of Post-Traumatic Stress Disorder (PTSD). Clementine's safe space was a tall cat tree with a view of the entrances and a quick route to the basement where she could hide when needed. She was hypervigilant, showed signs of stress even when relaxed, yet over time, purred and drooled when enjoying being pet by humans. Clementine demonstrated the ambivalence of wanting connection yet was physiologically stressed by it. Sue could see her own PTSD reactions mirrored in Clementine, which helped to "normalise" them. Interventions such as wrestling with our pygmy goat Dahlia, showed her how to let go and enjoy the moment; walking Cody, our large, elderly horse taught her how to project confidence and communicate assertively; grooming our temperamental, miniature horse Misty, taught her to watch for subtle cues, set boundaries and monitor for her safety. Sue was able to complete therapy without having to talk about her abuse experience, yet still work through the damage that the abuse created.

By building empathy for the animals, clients build empathy and acceptance for themselves and their symptoms.

Many of our prey animals, such as the rabbits and alpacas, demonstrate the flight or freeze response when meeting new people (unlike Cleo, mentioned earlier, who has the fight response when afraid). Developing a relationship with one of these animals takes empathy, being able to understand and appreciate the animals' worldview, and then enacting behaviours that demonstrate safety and trustworthiness. By building empathy for the animals, clients build empathy and acceptance for themselves and their symptoms. By furthering a relationship with a prey animal, the client practices trust, vulnerability, and safety, as they are demonstrating those qualities for the animals.

Clients use their bodies, minds, and emotions when interacting and practicing with the animals. One of the ways that clients can help themselves is through finding ways that help others. Sue was a client who demonstrated a strong motivation to help the animals. She wanted to help the animals feel safe, secure, and content in their environments. Through practicing behaviours that made the animals feel comfortable, Sue practiced and felt what it was like to do the same for herself. Through nourishing the animals, she learned how to nourish herself. Sue didn't feel or see herself as a victim any longer, but a young girl with strength and inner knowledge.

A key to a Sideways Intervention is that it is not explained in advance to the client. Because animal assisted psychotherapy consists of a series of intentional, relationship-based actions, the focus is on the animal, not the client. This focus on the animal allows the client to avoid the unconscious need to resist, yet they still participate in nourishing activities. A clinician may simply say, "let's go play with the guinea pigs today!", or "the alpacas need to learn how to better walk on a leash, let's go help them practice". The clients are willing and eager to "help the animals" when in reality, they are healing themselves.

If you notice in these examples, I did not ask the client if they wanted to interact with an animal, or with that animal in a particular way. Making a request of the client to help the animal appeals to a different part of the client where empathy and altruism can be (or develop). Asking a malnourished client if they want to eat, or participate in a nourishing activity, gives them room to activate their ability to deny comfort, for whatever reason they need to do that.

Another benefit to a Sideways Intervention is that it does not require language or communication skills. Trauma is difficult to talk about. Children, adolescents, and even some adults, find it difficult to put their experiences into words. Like play therapy for children, which relies on metaphor for change, the animals also act as a medium for metaphor. By focusing not on the trauma itself, but the effects and/or outcomes of the trauma, the client can have experiences in therapy that show them that they can be different, and they experience what it feels like to be different. Each animal intervention can provide a little morsel of hope that builds into a network of new experiences from which to build a new, nourished identity.

Therapy with animals can look very different from traditional therapy, which offers another advantage for therapy-savvy clients. It is hard to know how to resist treatment while bathing a goat. Clients are caught-up in the experience; language and talking are secondary to the actions, feelings and thoughts occurring as new behaviours and beliefs are encouraged, coached and practiced. Children find animal assisted psychotherapy fun and even adults enjoy therapy more when the animals are present.

Most clients are not aware of the power of the relationships they are building with the animals, but they return because something feels good. It is not uncommon to hear that changes are occurring outside therapy, as clients are more willing to try new behaviours and challenge old assumptions and beliefs. As they walk a 1500-pound horse, a domestic violence victim may see themselves as strong and brave, instead of small and vulnerable. Experiencing themselves differently is how they move towards being different. Permanent change will occur when they experience themselves act in ways that are compatible with the person they want to be.

Animal assisted psychotherapy allows clients to build relationships with animals that show them how to live differently and experience what that difference feels like in their body. The novelty of the treatment allows for the Sideways Intervention effect of being knocked off balance enough to trigger small change. Through interventions that nourish the animals, the client experiences change in their own behaviours, thoughts, and feelings, which ultimately helps them to feel differently and see themselves differently. As a client's self-image changes in a positive way through these new experiences, positive actions will follow.

Chapter 13:
A CONCEPTUAL FRAMEWORK FOR UNDERSTANDING ANIMAL-ASSISTED INTERACTIONS

TANYA BAILEY

ABOUT TANYA K. BAILEY

PhD, LICSW, Animal-Assisted Interactions (AAI) Program Coordinator at the University of Minnesota (UMN), and the PI of a seven-year longitudinal study on campus-based AAI programs for college student wellbeing

Tanya brings over 25 years' experience in AAI focused on mental health, wellness, and education for youth, families, adults, and human-service organisations. For over 10 years, Tanya was a licensed therapy animal team evaluator with Pet Partners®, and is an equine specialist in mental health and learning with the Professional Association of Therapeutic Horsemanship International (PATH Int'l).

She directed one of the first therapeutic farms in the Twin Cities, co-authored AAI education, activity, and curriculum manuals to fill a need when the AAI field was expanding, and developed and taught several graduate courses in AAI at UMN. In 2013, she established UMN's Pet Away Worry and Stress (PAWS) program, a multi-species AAI program offered four days per week that is delivered by over 100 volunteer therapy animal teams. As part of the Health Promotion department of UMN's Boynton Health, PAWS contributes to the overall public health initiative for college student mental health, the number one public health concern on campus.

Tanya is a multi-species practitioner – dogs, cats, rabbits, horses, chickens, goats, sheep, guinea pigs, llamas – and currently works with four registered therapy chickens – Tilly, Layla, Henley, and Hennifer.

INTRODUCTION

Over the course of the past five decades, some animals have become part of purposeful, facilitated, and active human health experiences so that a specific modality has been developed known as *Animal-Assisted Interactions* or AAI. I define AAI as a professional practice whereby a person and animal are trained and then work in partnership with each other to provide the purposeful delivery of direct and measurable therapeutic and educational services for human learning and well-being (A. H. Fine, 2019). Terminology, theoretical frameworks, scope of practice, and research agendas have further helped to establish this field (Hines, 2003); however, practitioners, educators, researchers, and scholars have also had to grapple with a lack of mutual consensus as to what constitutes an AAI experience. Similar to the parable of the blind men who feel different parts of an elephant and respectively think they are touching a snake, a tree trunk, or a wall, AAI can mean having a one-time or multiple-session encounter with a dog, horse, rabbit, or cat for physical, emotional, social, or cognitive outcomes.

As a social worker, educator, and researcher, I have had the unique opportunity to be a part of the AAI field for over 25 years as it has moved from an experience heavily-driven in the United States by volunteers and non-profit organisations to one that is now receiving gradual recognition as a reputable human health modality. I am a multi-species practitioner and primarily work with dogs, horses, and chickens, in addition to other domestic animal species. Each one of my animal partners has served as a teacher and mentor as I strive to continually grow in my understanding of the depth and breadth of the AAI field. I have also had the fortunate position to learn from many AAI pioneers and highly skilled and gifted animal trainers and instructors.

However, it was through my work with college students and teaching graduate courses in AAI that I noticed a disconnect between the way many of them thought AAI was facilitated and the actual reality of the incredibly rich nuances that must be present and then occur to have a successful AAI session. I often use a phrase, In the simplicity is the power, when I talk about AAI with other people. Animal-Assisted Interactions can appear to be as basic as humans and animals coming together in a facilitated fashion, yet when this outer layer is pulled away, what is revealed is much deeper and complex. To that end, I have developed a way of teaching the foundational and critical concepts that are a part of the broad application of AAI, and the purpose of this chapter is to present a conceptual model of practice I created called the Practitioner, Animal, Client, and Environment (PACE) Model for AAI. Depicted in Figure 1, the PACE Model is a synthesis of how I relate with and think about AAI on a practical as well as philosophical level. To illustrate the application of the PACE Model, a case example of an AAI program for college student mental health is provided; however, the PACE Model is applicable across all manner and types of AAI services.

FIGURE 1: THE PACE MODEL FOR ANIMAL-ASSISTED INTERACTIONS (AAI)

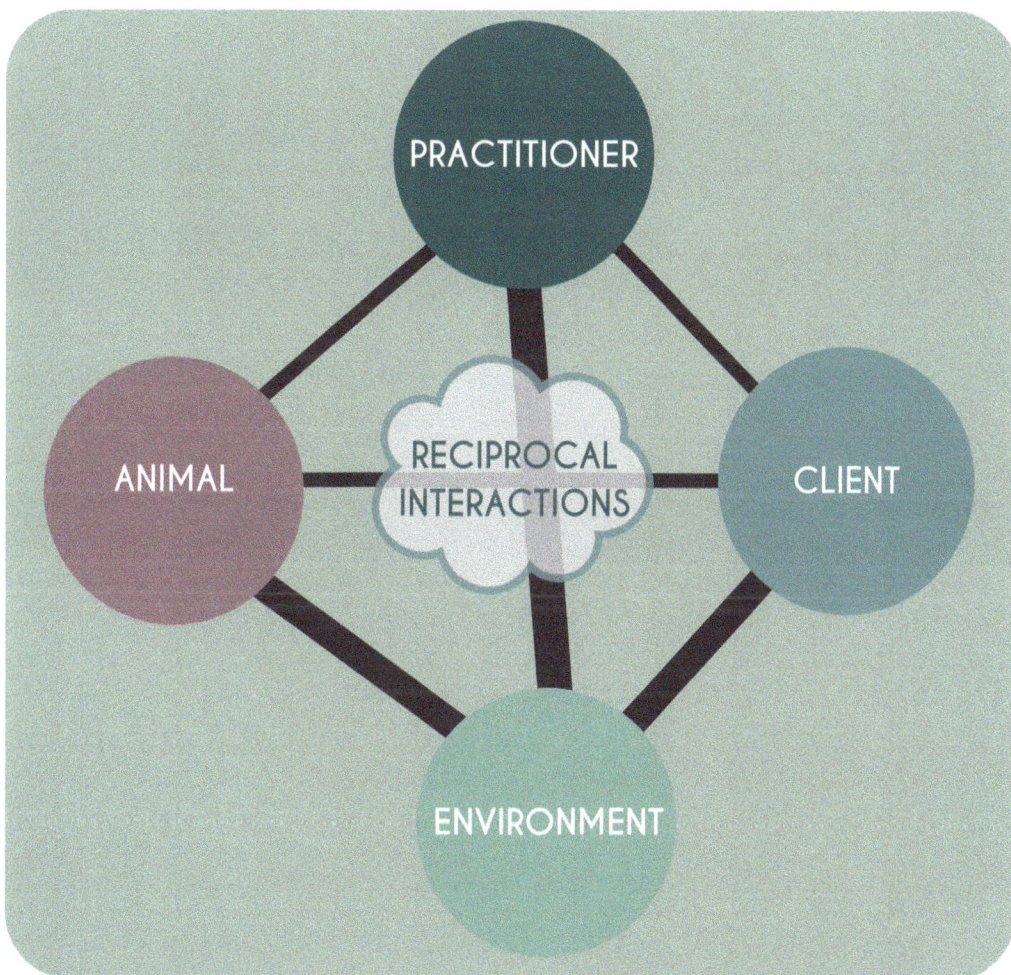

OVERVIEW OF THE PACE MODEL FOR AAI

The PACE Model for AAI defines four essential components — practitioner, animal, client, and environment — that exist and are consistent in every AAI session. This comprehensive and encompassing framework is meant to provide "the clear display of complexity" that is AAI (2013) due to the fact that the practice of AAI includes a wide range and variability of programs and services across the world. Depending on the audience, AAI can almost seem like speaking or living out another language because working with a horse and a group of teenagers differs profoundly in program planning, application, and appearance than a person visiting an eldercare facility with a rabbit. Using the PACE Model helps to optimise an intervention like AAI because each piece of the experience can be independently examined, all interactions can be assessed, and the most ideal or safest combination to produce the highest possible outcomes can be selected (Collins, 2018).

PACE MODEL COMPONENTS

Drawing on the underpinnings of socio-ecological systems theory (1977), the PACE Model emphasises an ecosystem that is bi-directional, and it overtly and equitably represents the living experience every practitioner, animal, client, and environment produces at AAI sessions. I maintain two primary tenets as essential guides when using this model: (1) all beings involved in AAI are autonomous and have an inherent right to be treated with dignity and respect, and (2) the dynamic interplay that happens during an AAI session produces an alchemy greater than the sum of the four components on their own.

Using a three-dimensional image helps to demonstrate that the PACE components are independent, yet interrelated, and form a network of reciprocal relationships that ultimately influence AAI outcomes regardless of a session's structure or personnel experience.

The four key mechanisms of practitioner, animal, client, and environment distinguish this modality from other human well-being experiences, and while AAI outcomes focus on influencing change in human well-being, a significant strength of the model is the inclusion of the environment. When combined, these four components set the pace for all AAI programs and are discussed in more detail in the following sections.

PRACTITIONER

The first component in the PACE Model is the practitioner who is the identified individual responsible for the delivery of AAI services. This person may or may not work with an animal depending on the level of program oversight and supervision required to manage the needs of the identified client, animal, and environment in an AAI session. Individuals providing AAI sessions may also include more than one person from more than one professional discipline, such as a psychologist and a physical

therapist. All support staff are also included in this category as they add additional structure to the overall program implementation.

A practitioner who delivers AAI services should work within the scope of their profession and also possess advanced skills and training such as the example in Table 1 to demonstrate their competence for working with such a complex modality (Fine, 2019). Many programs feature a human-animal team approach in which one person works with an animal, usually their own, or two people work together with an animal such as in many equine programs (Stern & Chur-Hansen, 2019). Often overlooked in the AAI literature, by partnering with one's own pet and sharing considerable familiarity with each other (e.g. this animal lives with the practitioner), the ethical concern of a dual relationship in a therapeutic setting is introduced. It is a delicate process of assessment and management for a practitioner to intellectually and psychologically separate from the personal relationship they have with their animal and establish boundaries in a working environment where they must determine that this animal has requisite skills to match a session's goals and objectives (Boland-Prom & Anderson, 2005).

Of primary consideration for any AAI program is if the outcomes are beneficial for all beings involved. Only recently has the AAI field explicitly acknowledged and included in codes of training and practice the importance of an animal's welfare when engaged in these programs (A. H. Fine & Ferrell, 2021; Howie, 2015). No longer is it appropriate to say, "I use a horse in my work with children" or "I use a dog to help counsel people with addictions issues". Instead, practitioners are encouraged to work with or partner with the animal in the same way they would with a human co-therapist and not use the animal as an inanimate tool.

For AAI programs that serve a large group of people, multiple practitioners may work together and either be partnered with their individual, assigned animals or engage with a group of animals such as a herd of horses to simultaneously provide interactions to several people. In the case of a campus-based AAI program, the practitioner is also responsible for upholding the values and objectives of this large group program, always advocating for the health and safety of all beings while balancing program quality with quantity. The varying environments for each session, both in terms of physical locations and natural conditions, coupled with the kaleidoscope of students who may range from frequent to first-time attendees, can increase the factor of variability at each program session to infinity. Other terms for practitioner include provider, therapist, teacher, instructor, educator, and facilitator.

ANIMAL

The second component in the PACE Model is the animal which can be one individual or several animals working together. Based on best practices in the field of AAI (Pet Partners, 2021), this animal is ideally a domestic species no less than six months of age for animals like rabbits, guinea pigs, and fancy rats, and at least one year of age for dogs, cats, horses, birds, etc. Animals that are directly involved in AAI sessions should have a natural temperament suited to a program's goals, objectives, and setting (Butler, 2013). For example, a cat that remains calm and seeks out interactions when introduced to a group of people is a potential candidate to work in a large, heavily attended campus-based AAI program. Another cat that tends to stay close to one person may be better suited for a less complex setting like individual therapy sessions. To prepare them for the multifaceted work in AAI programs and services, animals also need specific training beyond basic obedience (Butler, 2013) and should receive some level of assessment as to their skills and aptitude for working with people through national organisations such as the Alliance of Therapy Dogs (2017) or Pet Partners (2021).

Occasionally, animals that are not identified or trained become part of AAI sessions and are considered ad hoc program animals. When taking in the larger milieu of a session, these ad hoc program animals could include songbirds, squirrels, or another dog going for a walk with a student on campus. Adding ad hoc animals often occurs when AAI programs take place outdoors or in settings where multiple other animals already reside, like a horse barn or dog training centre (Bokkers, 2006). A chicken working outdoors during an AAI session will be attuned to its surroundings in a much more vigilant way than one working indoors or a less dynamic environment and may therefore be less present in its interaction with people than if the session was held in a covered space that provided protection from predators (Fischer & Milburn, 2019). While these additional animals are not the intended program animal for AAI sessions, they can have minimal to very significant influence on the other three components of the PACE Model.

CLIENT

The client is the third component in the PACE Model and is the identified and intended recipient of an AAI service. All sessions start and end with the client in mind, and better rapport with the client leads to better outcomes (American Psychological Association, 2019). If the goal of a campus-based AAI program is to address college student mental health, then the "client" could reasonably include all students on campus or it could mean a specific roster of students who are receiving mental health services focused on conditions such as anxiety, depression, or disordered eating (Binfet, 2017; Engel, 2011; Pendry et al., 2020). Animal-Assisted Interactions was developed and exists for human well-being and therefore, sessions must also adapt and conform to human health outcomes.

The feedback loops that result any time there is interaction between two or more components serve to create meaning and inform future transactions (e.g. "Was that a pleasant and empowering experience I was to repeat or a traumatic and destructive experience I want to avoid?"), and there may be some clients who are inappropriate for AAI programs and services. Just because a person might view or experience interactions with animals as enjoyable does not always mean those experiences will be therapeutic or help to accomplish specific treatment goals.

Some common precautions and counter-indications for AAI include a person's physical ability (e.g. whether they are they ambulatory or able to move around safely with staff support); their sensitivity to allergens such as fur, dander, and pollen; and their mental status such that they are not actively psychotic, violent, or have phobias and fears about animals (A. H. Fine, 2019). Thorough preparation on

the part of the client as a consumer and by the practitioner who is responsible and ultimately liable is just as critical as the selection and training of an animal to help ensure that AAI sessions are effective as well as safe for all involved.

As with the animal component of the model, the client includes all people present in an AAI session who are not program staff or support personnel. Simply put, each person present at an AAI session, whether active or passive during a session's interaction, has a sphere of relational influence on a program's operations and must be considered integral to the process (Arnold et al., 2012; Kivlighan III & Narvaez, 2020). Other terms for the client are participant, student, group, family, and individual.

ENVIRONMENT

The fourth component in the PACE Model is the environment and is defined as the identified location where the AAI program occurs; it includes the greater milieu of one's "everyday geographies" that are natural, created, and negotiated (Mossabir et al., 2021). The environment can be the most complex and often overlooked factor in the PACE Model due to common assumption that AAI sessions that take place in commercial buildings or spaces are more focused, predictable, and less impacted by natural elements compared to those that occur in outdoor capacities such as barns or farmyards.

For example, the environment of programs that occur inside can include such factors as room temperature, floor surfaces that may pose a slipping hazard, lighting that is too bright or dim, the scent of hand sanitiser or cleaning supplies that have left a residue on tables and chairs, loud or unpredictable noises and sounds, and spatial set-up which could constrict interactions or result in a lack of accessibility for all participants. Furthermore, natural weather patterns are influential regardless of session location as evidenced by many dogs that display fearful behaviours like shaking or vocalising when there is a loud thunderstorm.

Regardless of whether or not an AAI program's activities are sheltered from the elements, the physical surroundings invoke all the senses and can have a major impact on how a session progresses (Guite et al., 2006).

APPLYING THE PACE MODEL

When I set out to create an AAI program or get ready for an individual AAI session, I first consider the four PACE Model components as individuals, and then as collaborators, in a shared experience to create some type of human health or education. Typically, I am the practitioner and so I check in with myself as to my overall emotional, physical, cognitive, and spiritual disposition. The myriad of ways my whole being can be influenced is limitless and changes with time. For example, now cancer-free, I was treated with radiation and chemotherapy which altered my cognitive processing and some of my physical abilities. The goal of my personal assessment is to check my fatigue, arrange for ample opportunities to drink water, and review my program and client notes so that I am fully prepared and able to be responsible for each of my AAI sessions.

Next, I decide which animal or animals fit best for the upcoming sessions, and this selection is also balanced with the client and the environment in mind. I spend time with my animal partner, check them out physically, and observe important behaviours like eating, drinking, and how they interact with me and any other animals. Numerous times, the animal I plan to work with will change because of what an animal might demonstrate during this preliminary check-in or because of an intuitive impression I get as to how they are feeling.

For example, I typically work with chickens in many of my sessions and as they age, their natural egg production declines and becomes sporadic so that in the middle of a session, they can become agitated and seek out their kennel to lay an egg. It is my responsibility to provide an appropriate place for the chicken to lay her egg and also to allow her to leave a session to do this. Furthermore, I may need to have a second chicken with me and consider how I might have to prepare the client for a possible change in an animal's program participation.

Third, the client in an AAI session is likely the most common component for practitioners to assess because a provider's human health or education training, certification, or licensure is structured around the optimal care of this participant. As with the practitioner and the animal, a client's physical, emotional, cognitive, and spiritual disposition can significantly impact any point of an AAI session. A clear interplay is evident at this point in the PACE Model because now there is the factor of who I am and how am I showing up combined with the connection and interaction I have with my animal partner, the independence of this animal to behave and engage as they are able, and then the impact I and my animal experience from the client in each session who also is having their own internal reaction and response to me and the animal.

Using the PACE Model helps to instil an overt mindfulness and recognition that AAI is not a one-way activity whereby an animal gives and a person receives. Ultimately, AAI is a modality meant to positively impact another human being which means constant attention and attunement is required in order for an AAI session to support a client's goals and objectives, remain safe and enjoyable for the animal, and adapt to the surrounding impacts of the environment.

The fourth component in the PACE Model is the environment and is a factor that is overlooked, underestimated, and rarely brought into AAI programs and services as an active participant because the animal and the client are given the majority of attention in each AAI session. The environment takes what is often seen as a three-dimensional activity and adds a fourth sphere of influence, and with this additional awareness, practitioners have an opportunity to further enhance the power of their AAI services.

Typically, my AAI practice is one that occurs inside buildings that are built and regulated for human comfort. As with the earlier description of the chickens who are often my animal partners, these environments tend to be too warm and if they lack natural light, produce a setting that can cause a chicken to become quiet and less inclined to engage with people. If this type of chicken behaviour is a poor fit for the goals of the AAI session, then I am responsible for making a change to some part of the PACE

Model and while this alteration could be to work with another animal, in this case, I need to adjust the environment. Some examples for how to change the environment for this chicken-client session could be to create a more natural surrounding for the chicken to experience, such as a large tray of soil and a roll of sod. Or if the chicken could not walk about freely, then a cooling pack could be added to its basket so that when the chicken was sitting in this carrier, the room's temperature would decrease and the chicken would physically feel more comfortable as it interacted with the client.

The PACE Model encapsulates what makes AAI programs and services unique—a practitioner, an animal, and a client come together in a shared environment to accomplish a human health or well-being objective. However, as demonstrated in the previous example of an AAI session with a chicken, each of these four components brings a wide range of attributes and distinguishing features that when combined, creates a fifth concept called Reciprocal Interaction. In this next section, I add some metaphorical movement to the PACE Model given that the intersectionality of these four components creates outcomes that are multi-dimensional and greater than the sum of each part.

RECIPROCAL INTERACTION

Conceptual models help to visually identify the key or most important features of an area of interest or phenomenon, especially one comprised of many subtleties like AAI where a component's presentation and meaning are constantly evolving (Britt & Chen, 2013). Furthermore, conceptual models also help define the causal nature of relationships between and among concepts (Soulliere et al., 2001). In addition to the individual merits of each PACE component and how they uniquely behave and evolve at every session, the term Reciprocal Interaction describes the process and results created when the four components converge and form a separate yet similarly changing unit (Eriksson et al., 2018). Because the components have relationships that operate with and independent of one another that may modify over time, a constant give-and-take occurs throughout an AAI session to find balance.

For example, a registered therapy rabbit will have a relationship divergent from that with a student who attends an AAI program once versus with another student who comes every week, regularly sits on the floor, and engages with the rabbit. Including reciprocal interactions in the PACE Model is a specific way to demonstrate how the four components interact and also provides a means to consider the mechanisms that impact AAI outcomes.

The reciprocity between each of the four components is represented by the bars shown in Figure 1. Adapted from Mostwin's Family Life Space Drawing (1980), these bars are dynamic and reflect the strength or health (narrow or wide) of each connection as well as the familiarity (close or distant) between them. In Figure 2, the bar connecting the animal with the practitioner is wide and short. This human-animal team may be one that has worked solidly and successfully together for many years, has a strong relationship (wide bar) and knows each other well (short bar). In Figure 3, this same short bar could signify that the practitioner is well-versed in working with a particular species, but because this individual animal is a fairly new partner in AAI programming and their relationship is still forming, the bar is narrower. Another example in Figure 4, shows a thin and long bar between the animal and the client. This could indicate that the client is not yet socially or emotionally connected to this animal (narrow bar) and may be new to receiving AAI services, so the whole context of participating in therapy this way is unfamiliar (long bar).

FIGURE 2: EXAMPLES OF RECIPROCAL RELATIONSHIPS IN THE PACE MODEL FOR ANIMAL-ASSISTED INTERACTIONS (AAI)

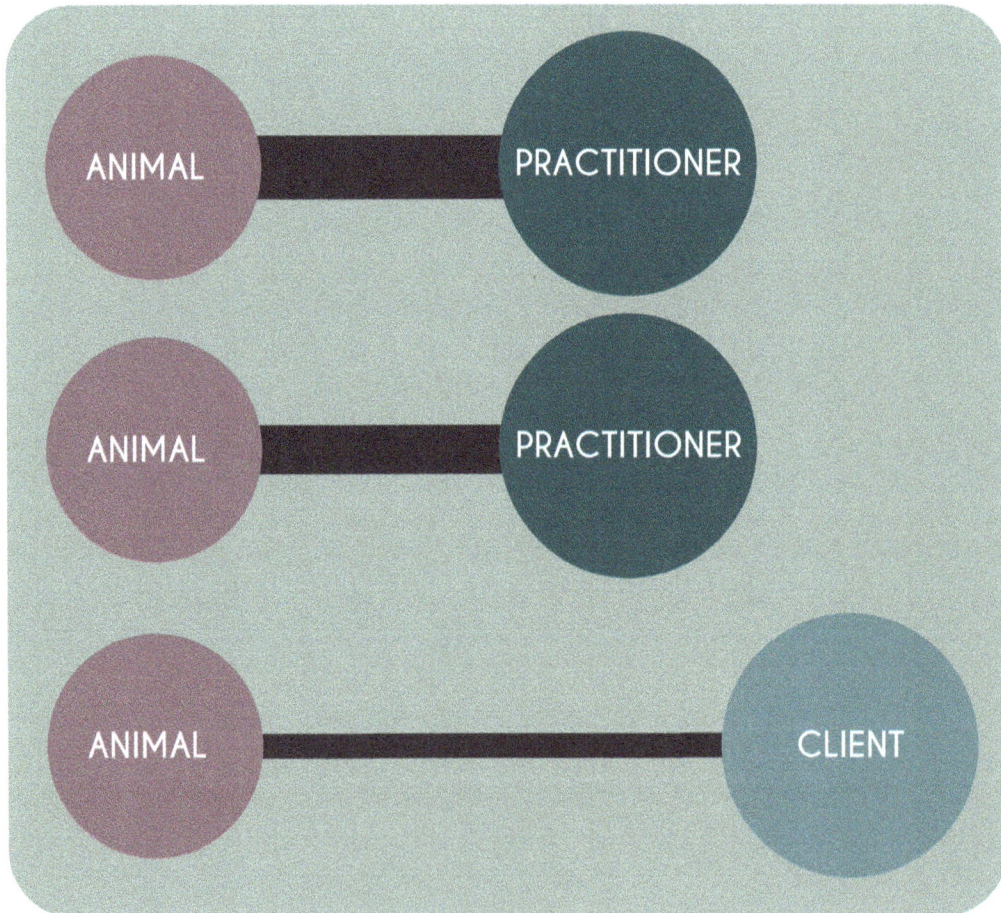

Using socio-ecological theory, each PACE Model component represents a context that is impacted biologically, socially, and culturally (Eriksson et al., 2018), and because these four components interact individually yet collectively with one another, their varying relationships create outcomes that are multi-dimensional and greater than the sum of each part. Much like baking bread, the finesse of planning, combining the four PACE components, and conducting AAI programs is both an art and a science (Van den Brink et al., 2019). A recipe may call for combining different amounts of ingredients and although there is an exact measurement of how much water to use, an intuitive baker also knows when the bread dough they are making requires more or less liquid to be successful. Similarly, the therapeutic and skilled use of self (Harris & White, 2013) prompts an AAI practitioner to thoughtfully examine the strengths and weaknesses that each program element could bring to a session, known as *Quality of Competence*, and then plan what permutations of the model are most appropriate to maintain safety, ensure animal welfare, and effectively address therapeutic goals and objectives (Soulliere et al., 2001).

QUALITY OF COMPETENCE

Each PACE Model component brings a level of skill, aptitude, and capability to an AAI session that I define as *Quality of Competence* (QOC). As with the recognition of four main components comprising every AAI session, this consideration of each component's aptitude for program engagement is generally a process that happens innately. An experienced clinician knows to conduct a mental health status exam (Forrest & Shortridge, 2020) each time they meet with their client, yet using a similar process to assess their animal partner and an AAI session's environment may not be at the fore of that day's program planning. The QOC is dependent on context and individuality, and involves quantitative attributes like one's age, animal breed, species, and facility layout as well as qualitative elements like experience, formal education or training, and a person's mental health status or cognitive ability.

When using this model and considering the reciprocal interactions of a session, the goal is to create balance by recognising the shortcomings and strengths of each component and adjusting accordingly. Where one component may have less skill or ability (low QOC), the other three can be examined for higher levels of skill or ability (medium and high QOCs) so that shortcomings in one area of a session can be compensated for and balanced by strengths in other areas. Equality is not a goal of balance (Evans, 2020). Instead, the model endeavours for equity, stability, and congruence in AAI sessions. Furthermore, the PACE Model provides ways of evaluating program components so that objectivity is added to an otherwise very experiential process (Van den Brink et al., 2019).

The PACE Model in Figure 3 illustrates the QOC by using a gauge or meter with a "minus" end and a "plus" end. The greater the competence each component brings to the AAI session, the higher that component is listed on the gauge. For example, a car can have a full tank of gas (high QOC) or be almost empty (low QOC) and the car will still run so long as gas is present in the tank. Similarly, a young dog that has recently started working in AAI programs will have a lower QOC when compared to a dog that has been coming to campus for four years. While the older dog knows the ropes a bit more than the younger one, the QOC for both will continue to evolve as they age and gather more experience. This gauge does not assign meaning to a component's QOC (e.g. a bad animal or a good practitioner) and is only one way of attributing a quantifying marker to a living entity at one moment in time.

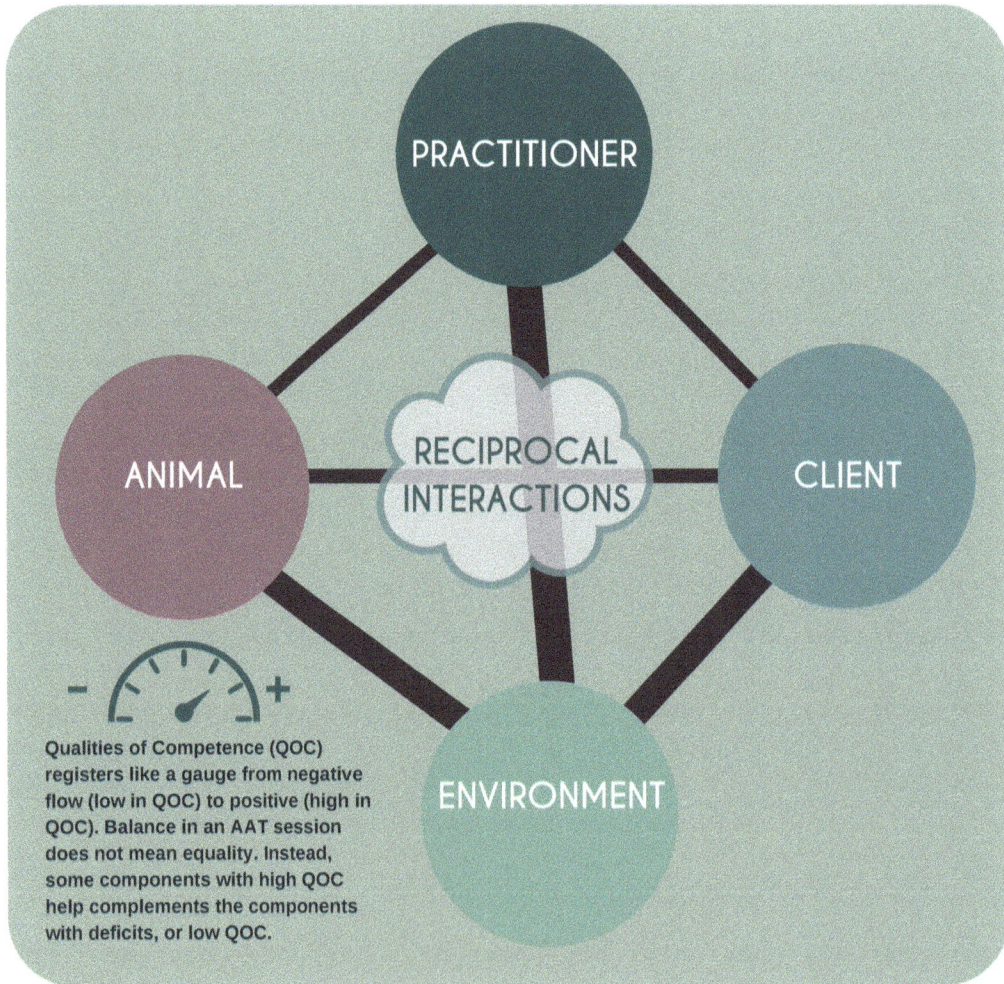

Another tool to conduct a PACE Model assessment is demonstrated in Figure 6 which is a table of QOC rubric and uses the first three stages of Howell's Conscious Competence Learning Model (Howell, 1986) — *unconscious incompetence, conscious incompetence,* and *conscious competence.* As shown in the hypothetical example in Figure 4 a component's QOC can move from low to high competence during a session, and as one connection changes, the entire model constantly evolves. That same rabbit visiting with a student could be calm and have a high QOC one moment and then quickly experience a low QOC because the sound of a slamming door has startled it (Gewirtz & Radke, 2016; nidirect, 2015). I do not include Howell's fourth stage, *unconscious competence,* because I believe the practitioner must maintain active and purposeful attention during a session. Considering that the three other components in the model have an ability to function at a high level of independence, these dynamics require constant monitoring to assess and reassess the total interplay of the experience and this cannot be left to an unconscious, albeit competent, practitioner.

FIGURE 4: EXAMPLE OF COMBINED RECIPROCAL RELATIONSHIPS IN THE PACE MODEL FOR ANIMAL-ASSISTED INTERACTIONS (AAI)

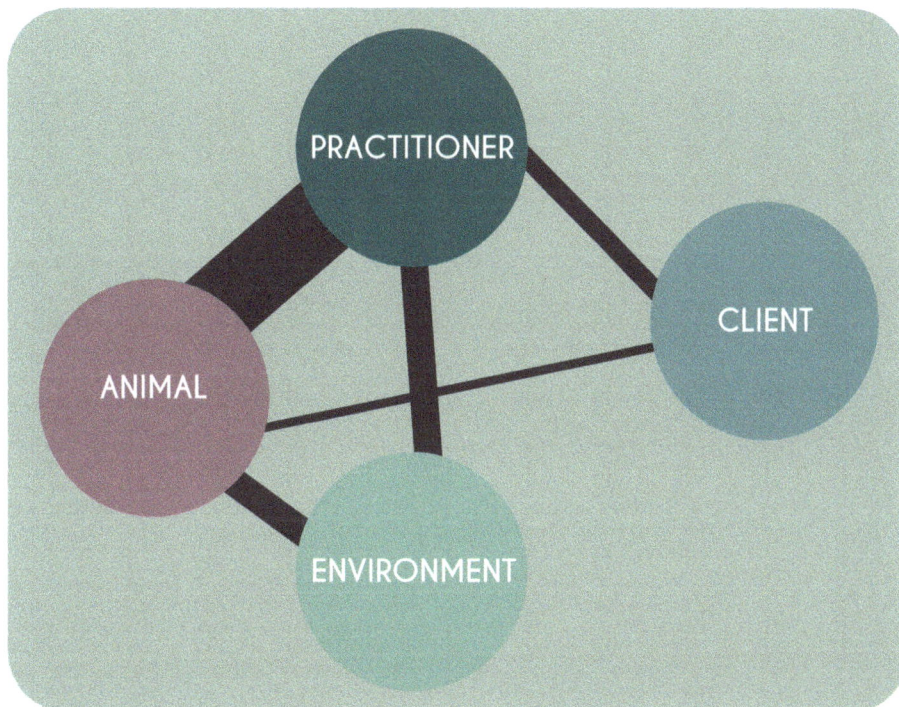

For example, conducting an AAI session on a very hot day could result in an environment with a low enough QOC that the other three components do not have a combined QOC high enough to create balance. Instead, if the environment can be changed to help increase the session's QOC (e.g. relocated to an indoor facility with air conditioning), it can now complement the QOCs of the other three components.

In another example, a standard poodle that is a registered therapy dog demonstrates much trepidation when walking on slick or polished surfaces. While the dog has been working in AAI programming for more than five years, its QOC increases or decreases depending on the location (environment) of each session. The handler may not be able to provide enough of their own QOC to appropriately support their canine partner because this standard poodle weighs 70 pounds and is too heavy to carry over a long length of tiled flooring. Therefore, the handler could decide to only work with their dog at facility environments that have anti-skid concrete or carpeted floors. This decision would help the handler and the dog maintain high QOCs and thereby contribute to the safety of the session. The handler is not distracted and worried about where the dog is walking and the dog maintains its confidence and ease while moving about the AAI session. Furthermore, because the practitioner and animal have high QOCs in this instance, the environment or the client could have lower QOCs and still produce an AAI session that demonstrates high standards of practice.

FIGURE 5: THE QUALITY OF COMPETENCE (QOC) RUBRIC FOR AAI ASSESSMENT

PACE MODEL COMPONENT	QOC: LOW	QOC: MEDIUM	QOC: HIGH
PRACTITIONER	• New to the AAI field and 0 to 3 years experience with: ◦ Animal species ◦ Client population ◦ Presenting problem ◦ Environment • Animal partner is a new relationship. • Works alone or within an agency this is not proficient in the AAI modality.	• Moderately new to the AAI field and 4 to 7 year experience with: ◦ Animal species ◦ Client population ◦ Presenting problem ◦ Environment • Animal partner is moderately familiar. • Has access to a few others in the AAI field, uninvolved employer.	• Established in the AAI field and 8+ years experience with: ◦ Animal species in general ◦ Client population ◦ Presenting problem ◦ Environment • Animal partner is highly familiar. • Access to AAI mentors and collegues, supportive and engaged employer.
ANIMAL	• New to the AAI field and depending on species, 0 to 4 years experience or familiarity with: ◦ Session environment ◦ Session activities ◦ Client population • Basic animal/obedience training. • First successful passing of therapy animal evaluation (assuming every 2 years).	• Moderately new to the AAI field and depending on species, 2 to 8 years experience or familiarity with: ◦ Session environment ◦ Session activities ◦ Client population • Continued training specific to AAI skills. • Second successful passing of therapy animal evaluation.	• Established in the AAI field and depending on species, 4 to 10+ years experience or familiarity with: ◦ Session environment ◦ Session activities ◦ Client population • Advanced training specific to AAI skills. • Third successful passing of therapy animal evaluation.
CLIENT	• New to receiving AAI services. • Working with a new/unfamiliar: ◦ Practitioner ◦ Animal or animal species ◦ Environment • Apprehensive, fearful, overly excited, aggressive, severely depressed. • Recent change in any biopsychosocial abilities, i.e., new medication dosage.	• Some past experience with AAI or based on current experience, can identify and describe session protocols and activities. • Starts to identify areas of understanding or knowledge about the animal or the environment. • Fairly stable biopsychosocial condition or any challenges are easily predictable and identifiable.	• Extensive past or current experience with AAI, can distinguish and execute interactions with independence, can mentor other clients in session activities. • Aware of and accepting of program boundaries as well as personal limitations, able to ask for assistance. • Demonstrates an awareness for changes in animal's behavior or the environment.
ENVIRONMENT	• Unpredictable weather, barometer rising. • Open, large, heavily trafficked area. • Extremes in noise, light, odors, or temperature that create a distraction, require additional support/intervention for comfort, or are a safety hazard. • Inconsistent or new location for each AAI session.	• Weather is slightly disruptive but predictable, minimal change or intervention is needed for comfort. • Aesthetics are adjustable-lighting, tables, windows, etc.-and with enough prep time to not impact the session. • Location is conducive to diverse groups of people and a wide variety of animals and that will occupy the space.	• Calm, stable weather patterns that are mild and comfortable for all participants. • Location is accessible and designed for specific practitioner, animal, and clients' needs. • Easy and effective access to consistent program materials and safety equipment. • Can maintain confidentiality.

CASE EXAMPLE USING THE PACE MODEL FOR AAI PROGRAMMING

The importance of having a conceptual model of practice in AAI is demonstrated by exploring the recent surge in campus-based AAI programs for college student mental health, and the following case example of a campus-based AAI program provides a high-level summary of how to use the PACE Model for program planning, implementation, and assessment. Similar to how the overall field of AAI continues to rapidly evolve, campus-based AAI programs as a whole do not follow an established course of implementation and based on a recent scoping review (Bailey, in progress), remain highly variable in numerous ways.

First, some programs are facilitated by college staff or community volunteers, both of whom may or may not have training in some associated discipline such as health promotion or mental health.

Second, while it is commonly perceived that these programs work with animals trained and registered as therapy animals, such standards are not always the case. Some animals may be less than a year of age which means they have received minimal formalised training. Animals may come directly from an animal shelter and are only assessed for their friendliness and general willingness to engage with people, or animals may include exotic species so as to run a greater risk of zoonotic disease (Lefebvre et al., 2008).

Third, some AAI sessions are open to all students while others specifically target students to support their mental health outcomes (Grajfoner et al., 2017).

Fourth, AAI sessions can range in frequency from operating only during finals and midterms (House et al., 2018) to occurring weekly or monthly throughout the academic year (Bailey, 2020; Stewart et al., 2014).

Fifth, AAI is naturally a spatially diverse modality; it can be practiced via an intimate, one-to-one interaction in a small space (Engel, 2011) or occur in large open areas that provide accessibility to all students (Camaioni, 2013).

While extensive descriptions of each of the four components are limited, the intention is to provide the reader with an exercise in awareness or conscious competence. Having great animals or a space to hold an AAI session are important and are only part of what is required to have a safe, ethical, and successful AAI program.

PROGRAM BACKGROUND

In the fall of 2013, I developed a weekly AAI program called PAWS — Pet Away Worry and Stress — through Boynton Health, the campus health service on the University of Minnesota's Twin Cities (UMTC) campus. PAWS is a program within the Health Promotion department of Boynton Health and its objective is to provide social support, stress reduction, and enjoyment to college students by leveraging the many health benefits of relationships with animals (Bailey, 2021).

Staffed by a licensed social worker and three to five student support workers, PAWS regularly receives over 11,000 visits each year. Multiple species work in the PAWS program including dogs, cats, rabbits, miniature horses, chickens, and in the past, fancy rats, llamas, and guinea pigs. During the academic year, PAWS sessions are held every Monday through Thursday and once a month in the evenings as well as once a month in the summer. Based on anticipated attendance at each of eight loca-

tions, an average of four to ten PAWS teams from a roster of over one hundred teams are present, and along with dogs, usually every session is comprised of an additional animal species. Students can come as often as they want during the week and stay for a short visit or the entire two hours. PAWS teams are also not limited to how often they can participate and can work one or both hours at each session.

Confirming the current research on college student mental health, students at UMTC report depression and anxiety as the two most common mental health concerns (Lust, 2021). On an annual survey given from 2014-2020 to participants at PAWS (Bailey, 2021), students also shared that attending PAWS was a bridge to additional mental health support. Students were asked, "In the last month, how often have you felt nervous and stressed?", and consistently, approximately two-thirds of respondents have selected above average stress or high stress. Respondents were then asked, "I believe PAWS helped me manage my stress" and nine out of 10 participants agreed or strongly agreed with that statement. Students found PAWS to be a "safe" place for them to show up and be authentic in their thoughts and feelings, and a place where they felt accepted and important to others. Many students also shared that they selected UMTC, or stayed at UMTC if they were a transfer, because of the PAWS program which helped them find community and a sense of belonging in an environment that often produced feelings of overwhelm, stress, and loneliness (Bailey, 2021).

APPLYING THE PACE MODEL
PRACTITIONER

There is a micro and macro method to using the PACE Model with the PAWS program. On an individual level, each volunteer brings a wide range of experience and perspective to their AAI work. The practitioner's QOC can be influenced by such things as their overall health on any particular day, their ability to navigate a large and potentially confusing campus layout, their confidence in working with college students or being in big groups of people, their relationship with their animal partner, and their adaptability to an ever-changing program environment that includes other dogs and animal species.

In contrast, the program director of PAWS could use the model in a much broader fashion and take into account a pooled QOC for each of the four components. First, the group of human-animal teams that work each session, including the potential dynamics and conditions of multiple species working together, creates many layers that exponentially impact program operations. It is rarely sufficient to only rely on national therapy animal evaluation standards (International Association of Human-Animal Interaction Organizations (IAHAIO), 2018) as a marker for a subsequent fit into a unique culture such as a college campus where diversity, equity, and inclusion are core institutional values (Office for Equity and Diversity, 2021). Not every practitioner who is interested in joining PAWS is also adept at understanding and respecting student differences, beliefs, and mental health challenges or maintaining clear boundaries between the animals when they are working at sessions. Furthermore, the "overall" practitioner is also responsible for upholding the values and objectives of this large group program, always advocating for the health and safety of all beings while balancing program quality with quantity.

To continuously build and increase the practitioner's QOC, mentoring, training, building community, and recognition are successful strategies used in PAWS. First, the human member of each team must be registered with a national therapy animal organisation such as Alliance of Therapy Dogs (2017) or Pet Partners (2021) as they provide a strong QOC baseline consisting of a written exam and an in-person AAI evaluation. Adding to that foundational QOC, all prospective volunteers must complete a program application, attend a two-hour orientation, and pass a background check.

During the orientation session, attendees are provided with a thorough description of the complexity and unpredictability that is inherent in the PAWS program. The current state of being a college student in the United States, the delivery of PAWS in collaboration with other PAWS teams and non-canine species, and that sessions are also in a group format instead of one-to-one with students is vastly different than other AAI programs which are delivered in a much more managed fashion. It is at this point that some practitioners may decide their or their animal's QOC needs to be balanced by a high environment or client QOC and may wait until their QOC increases, (e.g., they complete a major life transition so as to have more focus and time), or forego joining PAWS altogether. Before signing up for their first PAWS session, the practitioner helps to enhance their QOC further by attending at least once without their animal. At this observation session, they are paired with an active PAWS team so they can ask questions, receive another handler's perspective about program delivery, and witness how students experience the program.

ANIMAL

Just like the practitioners, the animals that work in PAWS programs are very diverse and cover a wide range of domestic species as well as breeds. Each animal's QOC evolves when working with groups of college students and can even be parsed into distinct QOCs for each animal-student interaction. Collectively, all the animals at each program session also create a group QOC that describes how they function together. In order to set each animal up for success and increase their QOC, some may have to work in ways that help minimise distractions. For example, a rabbit may be on a table at one end of the room while at the other end is a dog that also hunts with its owner, even though this dog has never shown any interest in the rabbit. Another example that often happens is that two dogs know each other well outside of being in the program so at times, cannot work next to each other during a session because they want to engage in play behaviours.

Each practitioner is responsible for monitoring their animal's stress signals, bathroom and watering needs, and assessing their animal's capacity before, during, and after each session. All PAWS handlers are empowered to advocate for their animal and can leave a session should there be such a need. Likewise, the program director also attends to each animal's fit with the program and documents cases where an animal had an accident, excessively vocalised, or exhibited other uneasy or distressed behaviours during a session. The program director has the overall responsibility of dismissing an animal that in the moment, or over time, displays behaviours that are dangerous, go unchecked by the human partner, or do not support the program's goals and objectives.

While animals are not human-animal, they act, react and interact with the client, with the therapist and with each other, in similar ways to the way that the client does with those in his or her life...this is a wonderful opportunity for new learning within the safe container of the client-therapist-animal-environment.

As part of being a registered therapy team with the practitioner, all animals have completed some level of training, veterinary screening, and an in-person evaluation of their appropriateness for AAI work (Pet Partners, 2021). And while there are some differences between national therapy animal organisations through which a team can become registered, there is an overall and broad enough consistency between them so as to provide a fairly level baseline of competence when that animal joins the program. When an animal is new to AAI work, they can receive support for the development of their QOC by only working for a maximum of one hour and starting at one of the eight program locations that receives fewer visitors and has a quieter environment. Limits may also be placed on how many people can engage with a PAWS animal so that the animal gains experience and confidence in a more controlled experience while also exposed to the larger, dynamic milieu. Consistency, structure, familiarity, and love are four other principles that help animals thrive, go from good to great, and exhibit ease and confidence when they are at a PAWS session.

CLIENT

The clients who attend PAWS are primarily college students who range in age, experience, overall well-being, and motivation for coming to an AAI session. Because dogs are so prevalent in AAI programs in general (Pendry & Vandagriff, 2019), PAWS was particularly designed as a multi-species program so as to respect student diversity and provide a space that is inclusive and equitable. Students may have cultural or religious traditions that discourage interactions with dogs (Hanif, 2015; Nasrullah, n.d.), violent or traumatic experiences with dogs as symbols of white supremacy (Lawson, n.d.), or little experience with dogs as pets which can manifest into fears or disinterest in attending a program like PAWS (Herzog, 2019; Ma, 2013). A campus-based AAI program like PAWS that allows for and actively recruits other appropriate registered human-animal teams like birds, llamas, and rabbits is one way of also helping a student maintain a higher QOC when they attend a session.

Like the practitioners and animals in the PAWS program, each student who attends on any given day brings their own QOC while at the same time contributing to an overall group client QOC. People are active participants and spheres of influence when engaging with their surroundings because all beings in an environment, through their agency and capability, are constantly changing and impacting each other (Arnold et al., 2012). The feedback loops that result any time there is interaction between two or more people serve to create meaning and inform future transactions (e.g. "Was that a pleasant and empowering experience I was to repeat or a traumatic and destructive experience I want to avoid?"). However, it can be easy for a student to arrive at the program with a high QOC that quickly drops to a low QOC due to many factors they are not aware of or have not considered.

For example, some students may experience a feeling of overwhelm or anxiety when they come to PAWS because a large number of people in one space could stimulate a feeling of social phobia. One way to support all students before they come to PAWS is to have images or "day in the life" videos showing what a session looks like at the different program sites. Another common concern is that students may be unaware that they have animal allergies. Even if a student knows they are sensitive to dogs or cats, hypoallergenic animals do not exist and their reactions to the other species in the program may be untested and result in a dismal experience (National Institute of Environmental Health Sciences, n.d.).

Many students learn that coming to the program provides added value to their self-care routine and some have admitted that they will schedule their classes around the PAWS calendar. Most participants share the experience of feeling stressed about school which creates a form of QOC that practitioners and other attendees know will be a part of conversations at each session. In the small circles that form around each team, it is fairly common for students to reveal their own journeys with their mental health and what supports they have found to be helpful. If a student arrives at a session with a low QOC because they are struggling with their mental health or have failed an exam, it is possible to increase their QOC while they are at the program. The peer-to-peer exchange can be one important factor to help elevate a student's QOC. PAWS is often a place students have come to trust, where they can engage with a responsive and accepting animal, and where they feel a sense of belonging and community. A source of support and the feeling of "mattering" to others are critical factors that help a person move through and adjust to change and stressful experiences with healthy versus harmful behaviours (Schlossberg, 1989).

ENVIRONMENT

The QOC varies among each of the eight PAWS program sites; however, optimal well-being is fostered through encounters that create a safe space for discovery because these places are reliably consistent and frequent enough to foster a sense of belonging (Hoffman et al., 2005). PAWS sessions are consistently held in the same location and at the same time each day of the week, for example Monday sessions are always held at the recreation centre from noon to 2:00 pm in room MP7 on the fourth floor. Each session is two hours in length, does not require an appointment, and while targeted to students, is free and open to all who are part of the UMTC community.

For some of the same reasons PAWS was developed as a multi-species program, each setting is structured so that it respects all people on campus and not just those who are coming to PAWS. With few exceptions, PAWS is conducted in an enclosed space so that anyone entering the building that is hosting that day's session has a choice as to how they want to engage with PAWS. For each session location, there is a balance between finding a room that is accessible for students and PAWS teams while also having a high environmental QOC such as even lighting, pleasant acoustics, comfortable seating, clean flooring, and regulated temperature. Ample signage inside and outside each building helps provide direction, and PAWS sessions are ideally located as close as possible to an external door for animal bathroom needs and to restrooms for handwashing and drinking water. Once at the program, students have multiple ways to interact with the animals such as having some of the animals on tables versus the floor, and any extra chairs or tables are typically removed or stacked to the side of the room to increase traffic flow and accessibility.

Overall, the environment's QOC for each PAWS session is in a middle to high range because an indoor facility is usually easier to manage and control than outdoor settings. If or when a new PAWS session site is added, significant preparation is invested in site visits and meetings with facility management and a contact person at each location. Prior to every session, staff arrive early to set up the space and attend to any logistics such as missing tables or food on the floor. Finally, the environment for each PAWS session is also mapped for emergencies such as a fire or tornado alarm, and for security should there be a need to shelter in place or to secure the space in response to an active threat on campus or in the community.

SUMMARY

The fundamental purpose of this chapter was to present a conceptual model of practice for AAI called the PACE Model — practitioner, animal, client, and environment — and to provide an example of its application with a campus-based AAI program for college student mental health called PAWS. The PACE Model provides an exercise in awareness, or conscious competence, and a tangible way to assess the practical development and facilitation of each AAI session by considering every component's QOC and, subsequently, the reciprocal relationships that are possible once all four components converge. If a practitioner has yet to established proficiency in a human health or educational condition, working in a predictable and calm setting with an animal partner they know well becomes one strategy that would help them balance their current low QOC and contribute to an intended outcome that benefits their client. The model also strives for a holistic and broad perspec-

tive of AAI practice by overtly naming the four essential components present in every AAI session and contextualising them in relation to socio-ecological theories and current empirical literature (Eriksson et al., 2018; A. H. Fine, 2019).

AAI's growth in popularity and expansion as a modality, especially in health care and education, is apparent despite lacking a robust body of empirical support (Rodriguez et al., 2018; Serpell et al., 2017). On the one hand, a 2018 survey with 300 mental health practitioners revealed that 91.7% perceived AAI as a valid modality and more than half were interested in practitioner and program training (Hartwig & Smelser, 2018). In contrast, scholars recognise that existing research contains limitations such as constructs with inconsistent definitions, assessment tools that lack reliability and validity, and unrefined results (Herzog, 2015). The current state of AAI sits at a unique junction. It can be argued that the most important direction must provide further study on the impact and outcomes of these programs. However, without full understanding of the processes and mechanisms that drive the implementation of AAI sessions, the field ignores another course and opportunity to clarify what, how, and to what extent various factors interact and collaborate to generate optimal learning and healing.

The PACE Model contributes to and addresses a way for all AAI methods to come together under one common understanding which ultimately adds integrity, accountability, and efficacy to all facets of the field. Assessing an AAI experience is complex because it requires measuring multiple living entities who and that are constantly evolving at every moment of that session. Naming the four concepts that are critical to any AAI session helps foster shared principles, language, and behaviour among people who develop, implement, or evaluate AAI programs and services (Delcambre et al., 2018). Regardless of a practitioner's training or style, the animal involved, the client who is receiving services, or the location of the program, the PACE Model can serve as a high-level framework for all permutations of AAI. A social worker who works with her registered therapy chickens to support college student mental health can connect and have immediate familiarity with a registered nurse who oversees a group of human-dog AAI teams that visit a paediatric oncology department. The PACE Model supports the continued evolution of AAI because it provides a unified way of knowing, a universal language that can be used and understood around the world and unite the intentional and mighty practice that is animal-assisted interactions.

∞

REFERENCES

Alliance of Therapy Dogs, Inc. (2017, March 23). Certified therapy dog: Get your therapy dog certification. Alliance of Therapy Dogs Inc. https://www.therapydogs.com/therapy-dog-certification/

American Pet Products Association. (2019). 2019-2020 APPA National Pet Owners Survey. APPA.

American Psychological Association. (2019). What the evidence shows. *Monitor on Psychology, 50*(10), 42.

Arnold, K. D., Lu, E. C., & Armstrong, K. J. (2012). The ecology of college readiness. *ASHE Higher Education Report, 38*(5), 1–138.

Bailey, T. K. (n.d.). A scoping review of campus-based animal-assisted interactions programs for college student mental health. In Progress.

Bailey, T. K. (2021). PAWS annual report 2013-2021. Boynton Health, University of Minnesota.

Binfet, J.-T. (2017). The effects of group-administered canine therapy on university students' well-being: A randomized controlled trial. *Anthrozoös, 30*(3), 397–414.

Blazina, C., Shen-Miller, D., & Boyraz, G. (Eds.). (2011). Introduction: Using context to inform clinical practice. In *The psychology of the human-animal bond: A resource for clinicians and researchers* (pp. 3–24). Springer.

Bokkers, E. A. M. (2006). Effects of interactions between humans and domesticated animals. In J. Hassink & M. Van Dijk (Eds.), *Farming for health: Green-care farming across Europe and the United States of America* (pp. 31–41). Springer.

Boland-Prom, K., & Anderson, S. C. (2005). Teaching ethical decision making using dual relationship principles as a case example. *Journal of Social Work Education, 41*(3), 495–510.

Bossard, J. H. S. (1944). The mental hygiene of owning a dog. *Mental Hygiene, 28*, 408–413.

Britt, D., & Chen, Y.-C. (2013). Increasing the capacity of conceptual diagrams to embrace contextual complexity. *Quality & Quantity: International Journal of Methodology, 47*(1), 567–576.

Bronfenbrenner, U. (1977). Toward an experimental ecology of human development. *American Psychologist, 32*, 513–531.

Butler, K. (2013). *Therapy dogs today: Their gifts, our obligation* (2nd ed.). Funpuddle Publishing Associates.

Camaioni, N. (2013). *Creating social connections in higher education: Insights from the Campus Canines Program at the University of Pittsburgh*. ProQuest LLC.

Charles, N. (2014). "Animals just love you as you are": Experiencing kinship across the species barrier. *Sociology, 48*(4), 715–730.

Collins, L. M. (2018). *Optimization of behavioural, biobehavioral, and biomedical interventions: The Multiphase Optimization Strategy (MOST)*. Springer.

Crawford, E. K., Worsham, N. L., & Swinehart, E. R. (2006). Benefits derived from companion animals, and the use of the term "attachment." *Anthrozoös, 19*(2), 98–112.

Delcambre, L. M. L., Liddle, S. W., Pastor, O., & Storey, V. C. (2018). A reference framework for conceptual modeling. In J. C. Trujillo, K. C. Davis, X. Du, Z. Li, T. W. Ling, G. Li, & M. L. Lee (Eds.), *Conceptual modeling* (pp. 27–42). Springer International Publishing.

Engel, S. E. (2011). An animal-assisted intervention with college students with Asperger's syndrome. *Dissertation Abstracts International: Section B: The Sciences and Engineering, 72*(5-B), 3092.

Eriksson, M., Ghazinour, M., & Hammarström, A. (2018). Different uses of Bronfenbrenner's ecological theory in public mental health research: What is their value for guiding public mental health policy and practice? *Social Theory & Health*, 16(4), 414–433.

Evans, M. K. (2020). Health equity: Are we finally on the edge of a new frontier? *New England Journal of Medicine*, 383(11), 997–999.

Fine, A. H. (Ed.). (2019). *Handbook on animal-assisted therapy: Foundations and guidelines for animal-assisted interventions* (5th ed.). Academic Press.

Fine, A. H., & Ferrell, J. (2021). Conceptualizing the human–animal bond and animal-assisted interventions. In J. M. Peralta & A. H. Fine (Eds.), *The welfare of animals in animal-assisted interventions: Foundations and best practice methods* (pp. 21–41). Springer International Publishing.

Fischer, B., & Milburn, J. (2019). In defense of backyard chickens. *Journal of Applied Philosophy*, 36(1), 108–123.

Forrest, J. S., & Shortridge, A. B. (2020). History and mental status examination. Medscape - EMedicine. https://emedicine.medscape.com/article/293402-overview

Gewirtz, J. C., & Radke, A. K. (2016). Potentiation of the startle reflex as a behavioral measure of anxiety. In Animal models of behavior genetics (pp. 333–357). Springer Science + Business Media.

Grajfoner, D., Harte, E., Potter, L. M., & McGuigan, N. (2017). The effect of dog-assisted intervention on student well-being, mood, and anxiety. *International Journal of Environmental Research and Public Health*, 14(5), 483–491.

Guite, H. F., Clark, C., & Ackrill, G. (2006). The impact of the physical and urban environment on mental well-being. Public Health, 120(12), 1117–1126.

Harris, J., & White, V. (2013). *A dictionary of social work and social care*. Oxford University Press.

Hart, L. (2000). Psychological benefits of animal companionship. In A. Fine (Ed.), *Handbook on animal-assisted therapy: Theoretical foundation and guidelines for practice* (pp. 59–76). Academic Press.

Hartwig, E., & Smelser, Q. (2018). Practitioner perspectives on animal-assisted counselling. *Journal of Mental Health Counselling*, 40, 43–57.

Herzog, H. (2015). The research challenge: Threats to the validity of animal-assisted therapy studies and suggestions for improvement. In A. H. Fine (Ed.), *Handbook on animal- assisted therapy: Foundations and guidelines for animal-assisted interventions* (4th ed., pp. 402–407). Academic Press.

Hines, L. M. (2003). Historical perspectives on the human-animal bond. *American Behavioral Scientist*, 47(1), 7–15.

House, L. A., Neal, C., & Backels, K. (2018). A doggone way to reduce stress: An animal assisted intervention with college students. *College Student Journal*, 52(2), 199–204.

Howell, W. S. (1986). *The empathic communicator*. Waveland Press.

Howie, A. (2015). *Teaming with your therapy dog.* Purdue University Press.

Kivlighan III, D. M., & Narvaez, R. C. (2020). Mutual influence in group psychotherapy: A review and application to group psychology. In C. D. Parks & G. A. Tasca (Eds.), *The psychology of groups: The intersection of social psychology and psychotherapy research* (pp. 191–206). American Psychological Association.

Lefebvre, S. L., Golab, G. C., Christensen, E., Castrodale, L., Aureden, K., Bialachowski, A., Gumley, N., Robinson, J., Peregrine, A., Benoit, M., Card, M. L., Van Horne, L., & Weese, J. S. (2008). Guidelines for animal-assisted interventions in health care facilities. *American Journal of Infection Control, 36*(2), 78–85.

Lust, K. (2021). 2021 College Student Health Survey report: Health and health-related behaviors. Boynton Health, University of Minnesota.

Mossabir, R., Milligan, C., & Froggatt, K. (2021). Therapeutic landscape experiences of everyday geographies within the wider community: A scoping review. *Social Science & Medicine, 279*, 113980.

Mostwin, D. (1980). *Life space approach to the study and treatment of a family.* The Catholic University of America.

Nidirect. (2015). Rabbits should show normal behaviour patterns. Nidirect. https://www.nidirect.gov.uk/articles/rabbits-should-show-normal-behaviour-patterns

Office for Equity and Diversity. (2021). Mission, vision, & values. University of Minnesota. https://diversity.umn.edu/

Pendry, P., Kuzara, S., & Gee, N. R. (2020). Characteristics of student-dog interaction during a meet-and-greet activity in a university-based animal visitation program. *Anthrozoös, 33*(1), 53–69.

Pet Partners. (2021). Program requirements. Pet Partners. https://petpartners.org/volunteer/become-a-handler/program-requirements/

Rodriguez, K. E., Guerin, N. A., Gabriels, R. L., Serpell, J. A., Schreiner, P. A., & O'Haire, M. E. (2018). The state of assessment in human-animal interaction research. *Human Resource Development Review, 6*, 63–81.

Serpell, J. A. (2000). Creatures of the unconscious: Companion animals as mediators. In A. L. Podberscek, E. S. Paul, & J. A. Serpell (Eds.), *Companion animals and us: Exploring the relationships between people and pets* (pp. 108–121). Cambridge University Press.

Serpell, J. A., McCune, S., Gee, N. R., & Griffin, J. A. (2017). Current challenges to research on animal-assisted interventions. *Applied Developmental Science, 21*(3), 223–233.

Shannon-Missal, L. (2015). More than ever, pets are members of the family. The Harris Poll, Survey no. 41.

Soulliere, D., Britt, D. W., & Maines, D. R. (2001). Conceptual modeling as a toolbox for grounded theorists. *The Sociological Quarterly, 42*(2), 253–269.

Stern, C., & Chur-Hansen, A. (2019). An umbrella review of the evidence for equine-assisted interventions. *Australian Journal of Psychology, 71*(4), 361–374.

Stewart, L. A., Dispenza, F., Parker, L., Chang, C. Y., & Cunnien, T. (2014). A pilot study assessing the effectiveness of an animal-assisted outreach program. *Journal of Creativity in Mental Health*, 9(3), 332–345.

University of Minnesota. (2021). Student data. Office of Institutional Research. https://oir.umn.edu/student

Van den Brink, N., Holbrechts, B., Brand, P. L. P., Stolper, E. C. F., & Van Royen, P. (2019). Role of intuitive knowledge in the diagnostic reasoning of hospital specialists: A focus group study. BMJ Open, 9(1), e022724.

Wood, L., Martin, K., Christian, H., Nathan, A., Lauritsen, C., Houghton, S., Kawachi, I., & McCune, S. (2015). The pet factor: Companion animals as a conduit for getting to know people, friendship formation and social support. Plos One, 10(4), e0122085.

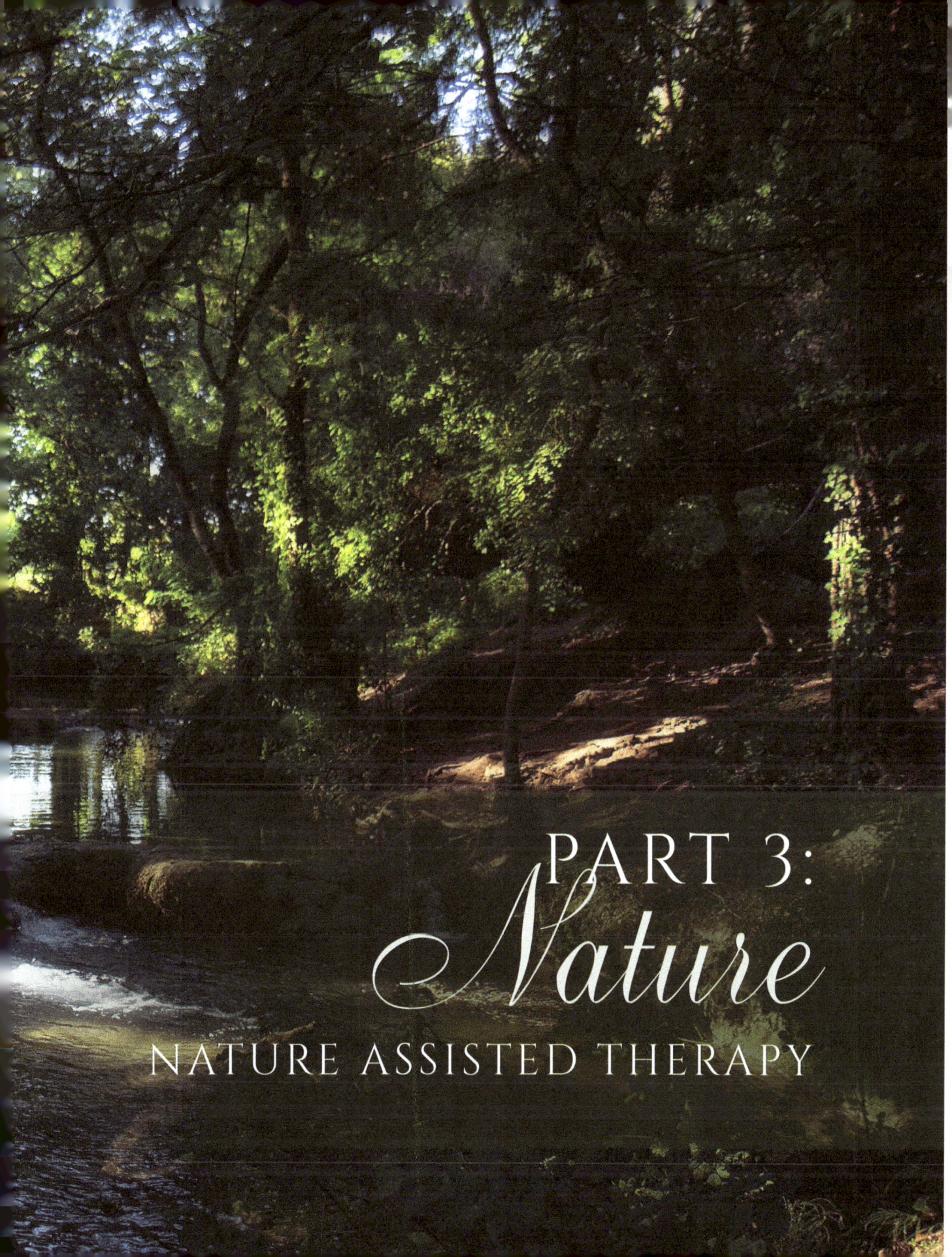

PART 3:
Nature
NATURE ASSISTED THERAPY

Chapter 14:

DEEPENING YOUR RELATIONSHIP WITH NATURE

NOEL HAARBURGER

ABOUT NOEL HAARBURGER

B.B.SC, B.Ed (Counselling), Adv Dip Gestalt Therapy, Somatic Experiencing Practitioner (SEP), MAPS. ClinGANZ, Senior Trainer at The Equine Psychotherapy Institute, Victoria, Australia

Noel Haarburger has been a faculty member and trainer at GTA (Gestalt Therapy Australia) since 2001, and now works in full time private practice as a Psychologist and Psychotherapist working with individuals and couples, as well as offering supervision to allied health professionals. He also practices and trains Equine Assisted Psychotherapy, Animal Assisted Psychotherapy (canine) and Nature Assisted Therapy.

He has worked extensively in a wide variety of counselling and psychological services since 1995, including most recently the role of Senior Psychologist at Malmsbury Youth Justice Centre for 4 years. Previous to this he has worked in family counselling, drug and alcohol, sexual assault, problematic gambling, men's behavioural change programs, and the mental health fields.

Noel has a special interest in Trauma and Body Work, as well as integrating developmental/attachment perspectives, Buddhist psychology and non-dual spiritual approaches into his work. He is a certified "Somatic Experiencing" practitioner, who utilises highly effective and safe body awareness methods for negotiating and releasing trauma, developed by Peter Levine. Noel is also an ongoing student of the "Diamond Heart approach", a western psycho-spiritual school that integrates mindfulness, western depth psychology, Sufism and Buddhist approaches to personal and spiritual development.

Noel is excited about the human-animal connection and the power of animal assisted psychotherapy and nature assisted therapy. He co-facilitates with Meg Kirby offering the Foundation and Advanced Trauma training at The Equine Psychotherapy Institute.

INTRODUCTION

This chapter is about how to understand and deepen our relationship to nature through nature assisted therapeutic processes. Before I open this up, I would like to begin with a reflection on the bigger picture causes of our individual and collective suffering and the implications for how this impacts our relationship with nature. I will share with you some of the research on the benefits of spending time in nature, and then finally will articulate a variety of inquiries and interventions that I have found helpful in supporting clients to engage with and deepen their relationship with nature. I will outline some of my thoughts on how nature can be a resource, a source of wisdom and guidance, and a way to help symbolise and work with client's inner world as well as the parts of self they may have trouble integrating.

THE RELATIONSHIP BETWEEN NATURE AND SUFFERING

LOST IN THOUGHT

In the eco-psychotherapy and eco-psychology literature, it has been understood for a while that human suffering is not only caused by the disconnection from ourselves, our bodies and others but also from the natural world around us (Rozsac, Gomes and Kanner,1995). Our all-too-common alienation from ourselves has a lot to do with our disconnection from knowing we are intrinsically part of and born of this planet and natural world! But how did we become so alienated?

From my perspective, one big cause of this suffering and alienation is a result of being lost in, over-identified or over-blended with our thoughts. I often wonder if our over emphasis on our narrative dominated sense of self is driven by a need to distract from deeper, split off, unmetabolised feelings of sadness, loneliness, anger, shame, and fear that is often the result of the accumulated trauma over our life span. The impact of being overly identified with our thoughts (and our left brain) is that we become unnecessarily stressed, over activated in our sympathetic nervous systems, and more and more dis-connected from our embodied life, our senses and the here and now.

As Eckhart Tolle (2011) reminds us, living in the here and now can nurture a sense of presence, nourishment and a deep inner sense of fundamental wellbeing. When lost in thought and our narrative self, we end up living above our eyebrows, constantly preoccupied with trying to tick off our to-do list, problem finding and problem solving, planning or worrying about our future, or ruminating about the past. This moment becomes a means to an end, not an end in itself! This often leaves us in a state of low-grade sympathetic activation, with very little time to truly slow down and become present with our sense perceptions. Being lost in thought, not only gets in the way of us being present to ourselves and others, but also to being available and receptive to the sensory nourishment of the natural world.

Nature can, when immersed in it, support a sense of mindfulness and become a portal to presence. Presence is a word, as often used in many spiritual traditions across the world, that refers to the part of us that is most unconditioned, immediate, open, spacious, naturally accepting, knowing and in touch with our existence prior to thought and concepts. Presence is strongly associated with a sense of fundamental wellbeing and a feeling that everything is OK, even when it's not. (Almaas, 2008; Eckhart Tolle, 2011).

DIFFICULTY WITH EMOTIONAL REGULATION

Closely related to this, is the individual suffering that comes from having difficulty regulating our emotions. Ultimately this means having the capacity to identify what we're feeling and to then listen to, value, allow, contain, soothe, and or express those feelings in healthy ways. When we are not able to be present to our emotions, we lose the capacity to listen to the wisdom of what they're communicating and we become vulnerable to becoming disconnected, disembodied, reactive, depressed, anxious, lost, and without an inner navigation system. Our categorical emotions drive us to take wise action.

It also seems apparent to me from years of clinical practice that the more disconnected we become from our bodies and our feelings, the more we attempt to control and manipulate our experience, often wanting our inner or outer reality to be better or different than what it is and engaging in compulsive self-soothing behaviours (often socially sanctioned) to distract and numb ourselves.

In my experience there is often an interesting parallel between how we relate to our body and feelings and how we relate to nature! When we tend to relate to our vulnerable or uncomfortable feelings from the position of wanting them to be fixed or different (aversion), and we grasp onto the states that we interpret as pleasurable, we often end up relating to our more than human world; the natural world in the same way, as an object to be manipulated and used rather than as a sacred form to be honoured and listened to.

THE IMPACT OF STRESS AND DEVELOPMENTAL TRAUMA

There's a definition of stress you may be familiar with. *Stress is the gap between what is and how we want things to be!* The wider that gap, the deeper our suffering! From a Buddhist psychology perspective

(Pema Chodron, 2005), unnecessary suffering is often caused by the desire for things to be different and an aversion to how our experience is actually unfolding in the moment. Pain is inevitable, but suffering is optional! Suffering is that extra layer we add through the way we interpret, judge and relate to our pain! Buddha called this the 2nd arrow, which is the arrow of pain we inflict upon ourselves! When we're really attached to the outcome of things and wanting things to be a certain way or not wanting things to be a certain way, we go to war with reality and what is, which inevitably creates more suffering on top of the daily pain and ordinary existential challenges (the first arrow!) we already face by being human.

Many of you would know that the impact of trauma and accumulated stress can also cause enormous suffering. Unresolved acute or developmental trauma without ensuing support sets us up for becoming chronically alone and activated into either the hyper-aroused states of fight, flight or freeze states within the nervous system, or the hypo-aroused states of para-sympathetic shut down and energy conservation (Steven Porges & Deb Dana, 2018), or flipping between both.

Polyvagal theory beautifully helps us understand what happens to the nervous system as a result of trauma. It goes on to explicate how early and chronic unresolved trauma can activate deep states of fear, overwhelm and impending dread. In the face of this experience without relational support, the nervous system eventually learns to shut down, leaving us feeling chronically deadened, numb, disconnected, and depressed. A lot of people that experience chronic stress or who have histories of developmental and relational trauma will spend most of their time stuck in these states and robbed of the ability to experience feelings of safety and connection.

Such states of safety and connection are mediated by what polyvagal theory calls the ventral vagal complex, the part of the vagus nerve (the largest of the cranial nerves in the body) that helps us socially engage, feel safe, be curious and present to this moment. When we are stuck on "on" or "off" in our nervous system as a result of unresolved relational trauma we become disconnected from the soothing and connecting impact of the ventral vagal nerve that naturally puts a brake on the revved up sympathetic nervous system. As a result of such trauma, the ability to trust, perceive safety and connect with fellow humans is often also compromised as well.

However, the good news is that for many trauma sufferers I've worked with, being in nature and with animals has often offered a corrective experience of feeling nourished and safe, helping to re-kindle the ventral vagal complex and the social engagement system to help calm down a traumatised nervous system. This then can become a bridge to learning to trust and engage with the human world.

THE IMPACT OF WESTERN CULTURE AND OUR RELATIONSHIP TO NATURE

Even without a background of significant trauma, our hyper-paced, achievement-focused and busy culture can keep us stuck in a low level of sympathetic activation which, when chronic, can flip us into dorsal vagal shutdown, numbness and disconnection. Our western culture's overemphasis on left-brain linear and logical thinking, doing and performing, materialism and consumption, indi-

vidualism, technology and industrialisation, as well as urbanisation and the emphasis on constant economic growth is another cause of human suffering and disconnection from ourselves and nature (Kanner and Gones, 1995).

As I said before, these western emphases pressure us to become stuck in low or high-grade states of stress and overwhelm that many of us now take for granted as a normal state of mind. This lifestyle of doing, rushing, performing, consuming, and technological pre-occupation tends to, in my view, re-train our brains to expect constant stimulation, and disconnects us from our sense perceptions and bodies, numbing us out to the present moment, ourselves and the beauty of the natural world. As a result of this, we stop caring for this precious planet. And as Florence Williams argues, the author of "The Nature Fix" (2017), we are suffering from an endemic dislocation from the outdoors. Interestingly enough, according to the Environmental Protection Agency, in contemporary western culture, 93% of our time is spent indoors, especially for us folks that live in cities and urban lifestyles.

Richard Louv, author of the landmark best seller, "Last Child in the Woods", coined the term Nature Deficit Disorder, to describe our pervasive disconnection from nature and the detrimental impact on our potential for creativity, mental acuity and emotional wellbeing. Researcher and writer, Chris Kresser (2018), used the term Videophilia, another term coined to point towards our increasing disconnection in the natural world, and our over access to technological devices and screens. What is the consequence of spending so much time indoors, in front of screens and technology, intruded upon by constant advertising and media, not to mention the background impact of unregulated toxins, fast food, time stressed living, COVID-19 Lockdowns, and a climate crisis to name a few problems of our day?

According to the above-mentioned writers and researchers, this is a major cause of the rising statistics in depression, anxiety, stress, and mental health issues. According to a lot of current research (Florence Williams, 2017), being disconnected from nature is not only negatively impacting on our mental health, but also reducing our empathy, sensitivity, respect, concern, and our care for this planet. This planet starts to become something that is an object that we want to take from, rather than see that we are the flesh and bones in the body of this earth and completely dependent on it.

> *Being* disconnected from nature is not only negatively impacting on our mental health, but also reducing our empathy, sensitivity, respect, concern, and our care for this planet.

WHAT NATURE OFFERS US

I wanted to say a little bit about the emerging research evidence of the benefits of being in nature. I was talking to a friend of mine the other day, who just had a week off and spent a lot of time immersed in the natural world. He said, "Nature is a natural antidepressant!" The term absolutely resonated for me. I was thinking about why nature is a natural antidepressant. We all kind of intuitively know that right!! The biophilia hypothesis, proposed by American biologist, evolutionary theorist and naturalist, Edward O. Wilson (1984), suggests humans are most at home in nature because that's where we actually evolved. We've spent less than .01% of our human history living in modern, urbanised surroundings. We've only had and lived in villages for 10,000 years. Prior to that, we were hunters and gatherers. So, for the whole history of the human race, we have spent a very small amount of time living in cities and urbanised surroundings.

This theory points to why we naturally feel good being in nature. It's because we evolved there, we were born there, and our biological non-civilised selves yearn to be re-connected in nature. Hence, we have a wired in (often unconscious) innate tendency to seek connection with nature and with other living beings, which naturally make us feel good. This innate tendency has become veiled by the impact of conditioning and the pressures of the western world that keep us in our heads and disconnected.

There are many more researchers around the world, particularly in Japan, America, and South Korea to name a few, that are exploring the positive benefits of spending time in nature. Florence Williams, author of "The Nature Fix", synthesises a lot of the research around the world on the benefits of nature. One of the big areas of exploration into nature and healing is taking place in Japan where they are doing what is known as forest bathing. In Japanese, this increasingly popular practice is called Shinrin-Yoku (Miyazaki, 2011). In fact, Shinrin-Yoku is a standard preventative medicine in Japan that is helping stressed out corporate people reconnect back to their senses and to nature, to their senses of taste, smell, sight, sound, and touch. One of the things that interested me is that being in forests allows us to smell phytoncides which are the natural aromas of the oils in forest leaves and soils (they are also antimicrobial). These oils naturally protect the leaves from insects, but they actually permeate a natural smell that has a positive impact on our well-being.

Scientists and researchers (Florence Williams, 2017: Miyazaki, 2011, Richard Louv, 2011) have found that spending time in nature reduces our blood pressure, pulse rate and cortisol levels. Hanging out with Mother Nature for a few hours relaxes the executive functioning in the frontal cortex, reduces blood glucose in diabetic patients and increases activity of natural killer cells called NK, which fight off viruses and bacteria in the body. It increases serotonin and heart rate variability which is associated with having good mental health and greater parasympathetic nervous system activity, associated with being relaxed, safe and connected. Time in nature also helps relax the frontal cortex from over-concentrating and overworking, improves cognitive performance, concentration and focus, as well as boosting the immune system. What's interesting to me is that nature not only makes us feel good, but it actually makes us physically healthier!

Research has also found that time in nature boosts positive emotions, like feelings of awe, gratitude, wonder, reverence and closeness. Even living near or in green spaces, such as grassed lawns, parks, and trees, is enough to have a positive impact on us. Ming Kuo (2009), another nature researcher in the USA, also found that just being in green spaces alone reduces crime and symptoms of ADHD, provokes pro-social and naturalistic behaviour. Ming Kuo calls it vitamin N! This is just the tip of the iceberg of the research that's now out there. It's pretty interesting and pretty clear that time in nature has an amazing benefit on us emotionally, psychologically and physically. The research shows that without doubt, the more time we spend in nature, the more we tend to feel better.

INQUIRING INTO OUR RELATIONSHIP TO THE NATURAL WORLD

One simple way I've found to start supporting my clients to connect to nature is just to start to ask questions that invite them to reflect on their relationship to nature. So just the question of *what role does nature play in your life*, can be an important question to invite people to think about their relationship to nature. Another question, like, "*What places do you go to, to resource yourself?*" Often the answer is nature! When I ask people, can you think of a place or an activity where you feel most like the self you'd like to feel, many people say, it's when they're going for a walk, or spending time in their garden, hanging with their dog, walking by a river or going to the beach. This question can then open up a whole conversation around, "*Tell me more about your relationship with nature and the natural world? What does it do for you? How does it support you? Or what does nature open up in you when you're spending time with it*"

Another way I might explore people's relationship to nature is to explore their relationship to nature growing up. For example, "*What were the influences that shaped your relationship to nature as you grew up? What was nature's impact on you as a child? How did your parents help support your relationship with nature?*"

For me, I had the good fortune of growing up opposite the famous Sherbrooke Forest in the Dandenong Ranges of Victoria, which is one of the most beautiful unlogged forests in Australia full of massive eucalyptus trees. Between the ages 7 and 12, I spent a lot of time in that forest, riding my bike in there, building cubby houses, and basically doing a lot of walking and exploring, finding lyre birds and being fascinated by the wildlife. It made me appreciate nature and all the animals that I used to see. I remember loving the birdsongs and being fascinated by the yabbies hiding under the rocks in forest creeks. Just being able to have that freedom to go out and play in nature helped me get a break from the many challenges and stressors in my childhood home environment. And it was something that my parents did support. As an early adolescent I joined Scouts, which also furthered my relationship and confidence to explore and appreciate the power and beauty of the great outdoors.

Some people I've worked with described having parents that instilled into them that nature is dangerous, and something that is scary, unfamiliar and strange — "Watch out for all the snakes and the insects that could bite you!" So, some people's relationship to nature has been shaped by their history, their parents' attitudes, and the people around them. Our early conditioning about the outdoors and being allowed to take risks and explore can get in the way of us connecting to nature, making nature become something that is daunting and to be feared, or as something to be controlled, managed, and fixed.

We can get curious about how our cultural and familial conditioning has shaped the impressions, beliefs and assumptions we carry about nature. Where did we learn some of these beliefs? This inquiry can also be furthered into our relationships with animals as well. *What was our experience with animals growing up? Did we have a connection to animals? Were there any favourite pets or were you encouraged to enjoy and to be with animals? Were you allowed to have pets? What animals or places in nature now or in the past make you feel good? Or Who and what do you spend most of your time with now? How much time do you spend indoors versus outdoors? How much time do you spend on technology compared to the time you spend with animals or nature?*

These questions open up a reflection on our lifestyle and our lifestyle habits which shape where we focus our attention, and what we spend our time doing, as well as our moods. So, I find these questions are a nice foray into starting to integrate nature into therapy. Even if we're doing indoor therapy, we can ask these questions and invite people to open up their curiosity about their relationship to nature and the animal world.

INTEGRATING NATURE INTO THERAPY

Three of the ways we can integrate nature into therapy are nature as a resource, guide and symbol.

NATURE AS A RESOURCE

Nature is a great support and a great resource for cultivating our wellbeing. But the question is how can we start to take in the nourishment that the natural world can offer us? Well, as you all know, nature is a wonderful catalyst for connecting us to our senses. Being in our senses slows us down and helps us to connect to a state of mindfulness. When we are more mindful, we naturally become more present, which as I said earlier, creates a sense of immediacy, aliveness and the simple knowing of being here and now, prior to thought and concepts. And when we are present in that sense of immediacy and awareness, we can start to feel a sense of deep interconnectedness, peace and fundamental well-being. Just like in Japan, Shinrin-Yoku and forest bathing supports people to start to connect to a sense of wellbeing. Many of the Japanese that come from the busy cities, and who are very stressed, just start to unwind and relax soon as they spend an hour or two in nature (Miyazaki, 2011).

Nature can also naturally invite us to orientate our attention to something safe, soothing and pleasurable. It gives us opportunities to shift our attention from our busy minds, or things that threaten us, to things that are pleasant to the senses. This shift in attention to pleasure or safety helps down-regulate the amygdala and the fear centres of the brain (Levine, 2011o). When nature supports us to open to our sense perceptions, we can start to not just look, but to really "see" deeply the particulars of what is around us. Instead of just automatically hearing, we can really listen deeply to the nuances of sound. My experience and I'm sure many of you would know this, is that when we

are really deeply plugged into our senses, particularly in the natural world, we start to open up to a natural sense of spacious presence, contentment and wellbeing. As this happens, the normal split between subject and object begins to dissolve, and we can begin to feel a sense of unity with all of life.

THE PRACTICE OF CONSCIOUSLY RESOURCING THROUGH NATURE

I would like to share with you a few little exercises that I do when I'm with clients out in nature. Some of them, you can even do when you're doing room-based work.

ACCESSING A MEMORY OF NATURE

The first one is for you to just take a moment to think of a place in nature that you have recently visited, or an animal that you have been with that evoked a positive feeling. I invite you now to just take a moment to remember that moment. Simply take yourself back into that memory when it comes up for you and allow yourself to relive what you were feeling and what it was like in your sense perceptions when you were with animals or in nature.

What do you remember seeing? What colours do you remember seeing? What do you remember hearing? It might have been the sound of waves, or birdsong, or wind in the trees, or a stream running by. And as you plug back into that memory of being in nature, what do you remember feeling in your body, and emotionally when you were in this place? See if you can reconnect to that felt sense. Perhaps you felt safe? Perhaps you felt connected or at peace, or a sense of stillness or expansion? And then let yourself drop into your body as you evoke that memory right now, and just notice what happens inside. When you drop down into your body in this moment, what happens to your muscle tension? What happens to your breathing? Does it deepen? Do you notice your muscles relaxing a little bit? What happens to your sense of gravity? Do you notice that you're kind of getting a little bit heavier and more grounded in the chair? What happens to your overall sense of being in your body? Do you feel more embodied after doing that little exercise?

Just take a moment to let that soak into you, this feeling that gets evoked by that memory. You can do this exercise when you're in nature, but you can also do it when you're remembering a time in the past.

CONSCIOUSLY COMMUNING WITH AN OBJECT OF NATURE

The second exercise is an exercise that I love doing, which you can really only do when you're actually in nature. And so, I would encourage you to take this exercise and go out and practice it when you get a chance. Basically, the invitation is to find a place in nature that you enjoy visiting. One of your favourite places where you can get some privacy and go and be there. It might be by a river, or in a forest, or on top of a hill, wherever this place is. When you get there, allow yourself just to start to be present and open to your senses, by becoming mindful. And if you remember the definition of mindfulness, it's paying attention on purpose without judgment to the present moment (Kabat Zinn, 2003).

As you really start to enter into your sense perceptions and become mindful, allow yourself to notice something that draws your attention. It might be a rock, an insect, it might be an animal, a tree, a pond, or a branch on a tree. And as you start to look at this object of the natural world, I invite you to really notice its particulars and what you appreciate about it. Really take your time. Is it something about the colour of it, or the texture, or the smell, or the aliveness of it? Really taking that in, what do you appreciate about this object in nature.

Then allow yourself to commune with it, letting go of being a separate self, and allowing yourself to really merge with this object. Could you imagine just letting that part of nature know what you see and appreciate about it? In expressing your appreciation, notice what it's giving you in return? Does it have a message for you? Is this part of the natural world wanting to communicate something back to you? Allow yourself to be open and receptive to any messages that are coming to you, and feel what happens in your body as you do that. Again, coming back to this present moment and what you're noticing now in your body as you complete this dialogue with nature.

I offer these little experiments when I'm out with clients doing nature therapy, such as going for a walk in the forest or out with the horses on the hill at the back of our property. These exercises open up opportunities to connect with nature.

A CASE EXAMPLE: USING NATURE AS A RESOURCE ON ZOOM!

Here's a little case example of a client that I was working with a couple of weeks ago while we were doing a Zoom session. Unfortunately, a lot of us have to do Zoom sessions these days while in lockdown or limited by COVID restrictions. My client started to get activated as he spoke about an element of his history that carried traumatic memories. I asked him to slow down and describe what he was aware of while speaking so I could track his window of tolerance and activation levels.

He described his sense perceptions as becoming quite narrow and he was losing a sense of groundedness, which is a signal that he's starting to go into dorsal vagal shutdown. Since he was showing signs of being out of his window of tolerance, I invited him to shift his attention to a resource. I invited him to look around the room and then to look out the window, and to tell me what he could see.

He took a few moments to orient to his surroundings and as he looked, he said that he could see a tree outside. I asked him what he noticed about the tree, and he said he could see new growth on the leaves. I then invited him to really look for a couple of minutes, really look at the tree and the new growth and to just take it in. After a few minutes I asked him what he was appreciating about the new growth on the leaves, and what was it about the new growth that drew his attention? He could have paid attention to anything else, but he paid attention to the new growth of the leaves, which is interesting to me. What was organising that perception?

He said that he appreciated just the sense of renewal, the trees are constantly growing and renewing themselves. There was something about that he was drawn to. I then asked him if there was anything else he noticed or appreciated about the tree. He said that he appreciated how the tree had rich soil, deep roots and a solid foundation, which he said was supporting the new growth of the leaves.

All of a sudden, his understanding of the way the tree functioned started to open up. And then I simply asked him, "What does the tree need to grow, and what supports the tree to grow?" I then asked him, "What supports you to grow?"

As he explored this parallel, he described his feet and legs being like the roots of the tree, and that they were helping him become grounded. A sense of regulation came back into his nervous system, and he described his senses opening up again. That resource of looking at the tree and seeing how it functioned then opened up the whole question of What supports his own growth? This then opened up the inquiry into the rest of the session as my client explored what gets in the way of him growing and being more regulated and what inner and outer supports facilitate his growth and regulation. Even on Zoom, this session utilised nature as a support to become more resourced.

NATURE AS A GUIDE AND TEACHER — DISCOVERING THE WISDOM OF NATURE!

Another other way nature can support us, is as a guide or teacher. I refer to this as, "tapping into nature's wisdom". So, what can nature teach us? Well, the way that I tend to do this in eco-psycho-therapy is, when a client is exploring an issue, I invite them to turn the issue into a question. With my above-mentioned client, the question was: What supports me to grow? As he saw what supports this tree to grow, he gained insight into what supports him.

I often invite clients to take their question out with the horses or into nature. To give the question to nature, surrender, and wait to see what nature offers us in response. When we spend time communing with nature, and appreciating it, we can also ask nature, "*What can you show me?*" Or, "*What can you teach me about the issue I'm grappling with?*"

A few years ago, whilst at a retreat, I spent an afternoon in a beautiful part of the bush an hour outside of Sydney pondering the question of what nature can teach me about my own lifelong struggle of self-comparison and inability to really trust and value myself unconditionally. Here are some of the things that came up for me during my own inquiry that afternoon. As I held this question in my mind, one of the things that I noticed about nature that day was that everything in nature belongs in nature, nothing is excluded. Everything has its place, from the tiniest little piece of grass to the biggest, oldest, most amazing ancient tree. I could see clearly that everything in nature has equal value; nothing has more value than something else. I could see that nothing didn't belong! It felt to me like the tiniest little flower has the same value as an ancient river or mountain. For me, I could see that all the diversity and parts of nature had equal relevance and value.

This realisation felt like a beautiful piece of wisdom that supported me to see through the fallacy of thinking other people have more value than me. As I saw this, I remember feeling a sense of peace and contentment filling me up from the inside out.

Spending time in nature can also teach us about impermanence, about the cycle of death, rebirth, and life. Nature can remind us that everything comes and goes and gets recycled back into supporting the next stirrings of life. I also think that nature can teach us a lot about natural imperfections and limitations. If you spend time looking at a tree, you'll see that it is perfect the way it is, shaped by the context in which it grows. It might have scratches, missing bark, old gnarly nodules, indentations, as well as jagged and broken branches. All of this reminds us that each tree is unique and perfect in all its imperfect glory, just the way it is. You would never expect a tree or a plant to be different from what it is. We intuitively know that a tree is growing in the angles and height it's growing into because of the environment and the quality of the soil from which it's growing. There's a sense of seeing nature as perfectly imperfect. Why is it so hard to see this about ourselves?

Nature also can show us that there is constant growth and evolution. It can show us that there is interconnection between everything. Everything is dependent on everything else in nature, which can be pretty obvious when you spend time in it. A tree will only grow because of the water and nutrients in the soil, which is supported by the decaying plant matter and animal droppings fertilising the soil. So, we can start to sense that beautiful interconnectedness when we spend time in nature, and how everything communicates with and is in harmony with each other.

The other thing that I've often got the sense of is that in nature, everything exists as it is. A tree is just a tree, a rock is a rock, or a horse is a horse. The only thing that thinks we should be different to what we are is human beings; we tend to think that we should be something other than ourselves. We can invite people to ask themselves, what would it be like if you just let yourself be where you are, without any expectation to be different just like that rock over there doesn't expect itself to be different!

Everything in nature just belongs exactly as it is and animals themselves are wonderful teachers. As those of you who are familiar with Animal Assisted Therapies will be aware, we know that animals teach us about organismic self-expression. Horses are wonderful teachers for modelling authenticity, having good boundaries, and saying no to someone. Animals teach us about unconditional love. They teach us about our own inherent value, that we don't have to earn and that we can't lose, because our value is an intrinsic part of who we are. It's like when you look at a dog or a cat or a horse, you can just see that they don't have to earn their value- it's inherent. Animals teach us about being embodied, instinctual, and grounded. They demonstrate and teach us about how to relax, how to play, and about the simplicity of just being.

So, coming back to that question, *how can nature guide you or teach you something?* I invite you to take a question into nature, surrender and let nature answer it. It can be a wonderful exercise to explore the wisdom of nature.

NATURE AS A SYMBOL

Lastly, nature can be implemented and utilised as a symbol or a metaphor. When I've spent time in nature with clients, I sometimes ask them to choose an object that represents a part of them they might be exploring. It might be a leaf, a rock, a stick, a clump of wood, or something else. So, the question that I might ask is, "*Can you find something in this forest that represents your inner critic, a young part, a disowned part of you, your anger, an imperfection, a fear, a need, your shame, something you value, or something that's triggering you?*"

Once you are asked that question and find something in nature that represents that part of you, then you can open up a dialogue with that part of nature that symbolises this part of you or a triggering situation or person. This can then open up a communication between you and a person, or you and a part, which can then deepen our understanding around what this part feels, needs and wants to communicate? If that part could speak, what would it say? And also, how do you feel towards the part that is represented by that log or that plant or that rock? That can then open up a kind of beautiful and deep inquiry into the relationship we have with these parts. We can then invite nature as a guide to see if it has something to teach us about this part. What could nature's wisdom tell us about this part of us that we've been struggling with?

So, these are the three ways I tend to bring nature into therapy and support a deepening of our relationship to nature. In summary, nature as a resource is a wonderful way to support a sense of wellbeing and regulation, often needed for people who suffer from chronic stress or dys-regulated nervous systems. Nature as a guide is a way to access the deep wisdom of nature, and what it can teach us. Nature as a metaphor and a symbol is a wonderful way to explore our inner world and start to explore our relationship with different parts of ourselves that we have disowned or been in conflict with.

CASE EXAMPLE: WORKING WITH THE INNER CRITIC

I was recently working with a client who had a very harsh inner critic, and we were out in nature, sitting in the forest, and I asked him to find an object that represented his inner critic. It ended up being this gnarly, old root that was sticking out from a tree. This in his mind, was like his critic — an old gnarly, ugly looking root! I then asked him to notice how he feels towards his inner critic, which was being represented by this gnarly old root. He said he felt fed up with how it was always undermining him and making him feel like crap.

As he expressed his anger at his inner critic, he described a feeling of satisfaction in being able to set a boundary with his Judge (another name for the inner critic) for the first time in ages. An unexpected feeling of space from the judge opened up. This then allowed him to inquire into what his critic was actually trying to achieve for him, albeit in a misguided way. The client discovered that his critic was trying to protect him from making mistakes, by making sure he was perfect and never "fucked up".

As he explored this, he was able to see that this reminded him of growing up in his family where his father was critical and had high expectations of him around anything he achieved. He learned that if he made mistakes, he would lose his parents', particularly his father's, love. The fact that the inner critic was representing this gnarly old root also reminded him that the inner critics are just part of the human condition, just like gnarly old roots are part of the tree; they belong and they have a place and purpose. And that opened up an inquiry around how his critic could work for him rather than undermine him. Could he find a healthy part of the critic that could be a support and a coach and an encourager rather than just judge his limitations?

So, there are lots of creative ways we can do those kinds of dialogues. Another little example is to ask your client what is it that they are needing at the moment, or what would support them to move forward in facing a challenge? Then we could invite them to choose an object in nature that would then represent that need (or needed support) and go out and spend time with that object and see what unfolds. That can be another way to kind of integrate nature as both a symbol and guide. These three ways of working with and integrating nature into therapy can be a great support for exploring our process, finding wisdom and accessing a sense of peace, calmness, and regulation.

Being in nature can connect us to our senses, our bodies, and a feeling of presence, which is the part of us that is most immediate and alive. When we're in connection to that sense of presence, we're not lost in thought, caught up on the hamster wheel, and worrying about the next thing that we need to achieve or avoid. When we are in that sense of presence, we're able to start to feel our interconnectedness and oneness with all of life, and a fundamental sense that everything is OK even in the face of adversity and challenge. Instead of being a separate witness, we can start to feel how we are one with our environment and one with this planet. This can help us recognise that we are cells in the body of the earth and that our psyche is as big as the earth (Theodore Roszak, 2009).

CONCLUSION

We are not living on this beautiful planet, we are of this beautiful planet, and it is something that we can actually take care of and nurture. When we can learn to reconnect to ourselves, our emotions, our bodies, and to nature, we can begin to feel a sense of wanting to care for this one and only precious planet.

More than any other moment in human history we are at a crossroads, where we need to choose to care for this planet and its resources, or let this impending climate crisis destroy our planet and all sentient beings that inhabit it. If we want to save our planet and its beautiful diversity and resources, we need to start to care for our soils, our oceans, our forests, animals and biodiversity.

How can we start to care for nature instead of treating it as an object to take from, or as a passive disconnected tourist to watch and take videos of? We need to take care of our planet, the way we take care of ourselves, our children and our families and each other. In my view, this means we need to move from a me-centred perspective to a world-centric perspective, which is big enough to include and care for everything in it. Big enough to take care of everything! And finally, we need to resurrect determination and wisdom, not just intelligence, to keep our hearts and minds open and sensitive enough to take action in caring about this exquisite home we call planet earth.

REFERENCES

Almaas, A.H (2004). *The inner journey home - Souls realization of the unity of reality*. Shambala Publications.

Chodron, Pema (2005). *Start where you are – How to accept yourself and others*. Thorsons/elemen GB.

Dana, Deb (2018). *Polyvagal theory in therapy- Engaging the Rhythm of regulation*. W.W Norton.

Kanner, Allen d. and Gomes, Mary E. (1995). Part 1. The all-consuming self. In *Ecopsychology – Restoring the earth and healing the mind*.

Kuo, Francis (2015). *Frontiers in psychology – How might contact with nature promote human health. Promising mechanisms and a possible pathway*.

Louv, Richard (2010). *Last child in the woods: Saving our children from Nature-deficit Disorder*. Atlantic PBS.

Levine, Peter (2010). *In an unspoken voice – how the body releases trauma and restores goodness*. North Atlantic books.

Miyazak, Yoshifumi (2021). *Walking in the woods, Go back to nature with the Japanese way of Shin-rin-yoki*. Octopus Publishing Group.

Williams, Florence (2018). *The nature fix: Why nature makes us happier, healthier and more creative*. WW Norton & company.

Wilson, Edward O (1984). *Biophilia: The human bond with other species*. Harvard University Press.

Roszak, Gomes and Kanner (1995). *Ecopsychology – Restoring the Earth, healing the mind*.

Tolle, Eckhart (2011). *The power of Now: a guide to spiritual enlightenment*. Hachette, Australia.

Chapter 15:

INCORPORATING NATURE-BASED CEREMONY IN THERAPY AS RESOURCE FOR TRAUMA HEALING & TRANSITION

KATIE ASMUS

ABOUT KATIE ASMUS

MA, LPC, BMP, Founder of the Somatic Wilderness Therapy Institute, Colorado, USA

Katie Asmus incorporates present-moment awareness, relationship to the natural world, body-mind connection and expressive arts practices to support people in more deeply and compassionately connecting to themselves, others, and the earth. She believes strongly in the power of spending time in nature as a way to listen deeply inward, and has a long history of creating, practicing, and facilitating personally meaningful culturally relevant ceremonies and rites of passage.

Currently, Katie directs, facilitates Rites of passage programs, sees private practice clients and trains therapists and healers through The Somatic Wilderness Therapy Institute (SWTI), a multi-dimensional therapeutic and educationally-based organisation and Body-Centered offerings in Boulder, Colorado, USA.

INTRODUCTION

Relationship with the natural world and with ceremonial practices have been a part of human existence since the beginning of time. These relationships and practices have varied greatly from culture to culture. Nature-based ceremonial practices in therapy can open the doorway to greater embodiment, processing of emotion, awareness of one's interconnectedness within the web of life, and evolution toward more whole versions of ourselves.

In this chapter, I will be discussing incorporating nature-based ceremony in therapy as a resource for trauma healing & transition. I begin with an overview of the field and practices of nature-based therapy, then discuss ceremony as a resource within therapy. From there, we'll delve further into defining ceremony and look at the stages of change within life transition. We'll then look at how ceremony can support clients in moving through transition and trauma.

Later in this chapter, I'll take you through steps for creating personally meaningful culturally relevant ceremonies, include a case example, and finish up with some important considerations as you incorporate ceremony into your work with clients.

It is important when incorporating ceremonial practices into therapeutic work that it is done in a way that recognises and respects your client's beliefs as well as honouring appropriate cultural protocols and practices. With this in mind, I believe it is important to share some of my own sociocultural identities and experiences to acknowledge the lens from which I am presenting this topic.

As a somatic (body-centered), nature-based psychotherapist and educator, I grew up as a white bodied, cisgender woman in the USA with ancestors from a myriad of western European countries with mainly Irish and German roots. I come from and grew up among generations of devout Catholics, though I have since shifted away from some of these traditional beliefs and practices. I have been a life-long seeker of meaning, self-growth, and the understanding of spirituality and human nature. This seeking has led me into global travel, study and practice within a variety of spiritual traditions, as well as being a part of short and long-term communities consciously enacting ceremonies and rituals to mark significant events and occasions.

From a young age I was steeped in the ever-evolving rituals of my own family, particularly in relation to holidays. Growing up, I also had the fortune of attending summer camps and being a part of nature-based retreat groups where we were encouraged to create our own unique ceremonies to mark special life events.

These experiences, along with 30 plus years of incorporating relationship with the natural world into my educational and therapeutic work with others, are the foundation from which I present these ideas, practices, and considerations to you.

OVERVIEW OF NATURE-BASED THERAPY

Nature-based therapy, which I define as *the conscious incorporation of the natural world into the therapeutic process* (definition adopted from Naropa University), is practiced in a wide variety of ways in North America as well as around the world. Some of the forms this takes include: incorporating adventure activities such as backpacking and rock climbing into therapy, spending months out on the land living and practicing ancestral skills, mindfulness in nature for wellness, equine and animal-assisted therapy, horticulture therapy, and nature-based ceremonial practices. I intentionally use the term *therapeutic process* in my definition above, as different cultures hold the concepts of therapy differently than others. Nature-based therapy can occur in a clinical setting, while it may alternatively take place in an educational or community-based setting.

Some additional terms and nature-based focusses of practice that are related within the psychotherapeutic paradigm include: Wilderness Therapy, Bush Therapy, Adventure Therapy, Eco-therapy, Equine and Animal Assisted Therapy, Horticulture Therapy, and Wilderness Questing. While some of these terms are overlapping or interconnected, each one points to a particular lens that influences the assessment and intervention process. These alternative therapies recognise the power of the experiential work of being embodied in relationship with some aspect of nature. Whether or not you are currently incorporating the natural world into your work with clients, know that there are a variety of accepted (and researched) nature-based modalities, paradigms, practices, and professional communities of healing professionals that exist around the world.

CEREMONY AS RESOURCE WITHIN NATURE-BASED PSYCHOTHERAPY

Nature-based therapy may be incorporated as a specific intervention or as a primary modality from which a practitioner works with clients within the context of therapy. Within either of these paradigms, nature-based ceremony can be utilised as a resource or tool for marking significant life transitions, in support of letting go of what no longer serves, in asking for greater guidance and support, in celebrating an accomplishment or completion, and overall, in honouring change. In addition, as experiences of trauma are fraught with change, ceremony can be a powerful tool in supporting clients to navigate the multi-faceted nuances of life change within psychotherapy and the healing process.

For our collective understanding, I define *Ceremony* as an intentional action or set of actions to mark a particular intention. Note that I will be further discussing ceremony and its nuances a little later in this chapter. *Resource* is a term utilised in the practice of psychotherapy to indicate anything that supports our body and minds to come into a state of greater presence, connectedness, goodness, neutrality, or ease. A resource can be many things but common types can include: supportive people, pets or spiritual allies, physical movement practices, a deep breath, a positive memory, etc. Typically, an experience that resources us helps us come more fully into the present moment and supports the conscious and unconscious mind in registering a relative sense of greater safety in the moment. It supports the parts of our brain that do not know the past trauma is over to begin reorienting us to the here and now. Connecting with that which is resourcing can help us stay grounded in the midst of life transition, especially when things feel ungrounded.

In regard to this topic, it is useful to recognise that for many, nature can be a resource in and of itself. It is also significant to note that for some, nature or being out in the natural world may be unfamiliar, may have been unsafe or may feel scarily unknown. It is helpful to inquire about your clients' relationship with nature before assuming it will be a source of resource and support for them.

Within the context of nature-based therapy, ceremony provides structure and a container to mark, honour, and support navigating the many unknowns of change. Depending on where you live in the world, you may or may not have shared familial or cultural values and celebrations with your clients. This can present an added challenge in creating ceremony that truly has personal meaning to our clients. In the USA, among other colonised nations, many people have long ago lost connection to the ceremonies within their cultural lineages as families assimilated to new lands and ways. Through industrialisation and the technological revolution, the ways of spirit, energy, and more creative right brain ways of knowing have become marginalised for the promise of science.

It is important to hold awareness of the diversity of beliefs, associations, and experiences that clients may hold around ceremonial practices as we venture to include them within the context of psychotherapy. For some, their traditional sacred ceremonial practices can only be performed by members of a particular group, or initiated facilitators.

CEREMONY DEFINED

Connection with the natural world is inherent to our experiences as humans and has forever been interwoven with our spirituality as well as our physical and emotional health and survival. Throughout time, humans have marked change with ceremony and ritual practices by dressing in specific garb for special occasions, by parading through the streets to honour or showcase a life happening, and by gathering in community to share food in remembrance of holy days, holidays, anniversaries, and life transitions. These enactments have been woven into the very fibers of our bodies, minds, and souls.

The words *Ceremony* and *Ritual* are sometimes used interchangeably, and other times differently depending on the culture, the tradition, and the literature we consult. For our purposes here, I'll be primarily utilising the term *Ceremony* which I am defining as an *intentional action or set of actions to mark a particular intention.* I am not using this word to denote any particular religious or spiritual belief or practice, but rather as a structure to honour what is meaningful in one's life. Ceremony is saying YES to what is. When we put our attention toward an intention, it is as if we are planting seeds. Through the act and our focus, our intentions take root and take on a life of their own. Of course, just as with seeds, the more we water and tend them, the more vibrant they'll become. Ceremony is a way to direct and magnetise our life energy in a particular direction.

Arnold Van Gennep (1908), European cultural anthropologist, coined the term Rite of Passage to refer to the ceremonies across time and culture that mark life transitions. Common transitions marked by many cultures have included: Birth, Coming of Age, Marriage/Partnering, and Death. Some present-day examples of coming of age ceremonies are the Quinceñera from Latin America, the Bar or Bat mitzvah in the Jewish culture, Confirmation in the Catholic tradition, Rumspringa for the Amish youth, and the Sunrise Ceremony for the Apache. In addition to the above-mentioned life transitions, other examples of life changes I have supported people to mark through ceremony include: graduating from college, moving across country, ending a relationship, and coming out of chronic illness.

STAGES OF CHANGE

In all life transitions that occur, there are three stages: a beginning, a middle, and an end. Within the Rite of Passage model, these stages are referred to as: *Severance, Liminal, and Incorporation* (note that a variety of terms are utilised for these stages within Rites of Passage literature).

Change begins with an ending, or a letting go of the old way. *Severance* constitutes a separation from, or a letting go of an aspect of our identity, role, or way of being. Whether choiceful or not, with all transitions comes loss.

The *Liminal* or the in-between stage of change is sometimes referred to as "the no-name stage". This can be an exciting time of possibility, but more often than not is a groundless, anxiety-producing time when we're not who we were before the change, and we are not yet who we'll become. There can be the experience of not being able to go back to the old way and not yet knowing how to move forward. This is a messy in-between stage likened to the soup-like state that the caterpillar disintegrates into before beginning to reform itself into the butterfly (Scientific America).

The final stage of change within the Rite of Passage model is *Incorporation* or the embodied integration of the new identity into our lives. Incorporation typically happens over time. For example, when we take on a new job or role, it often takes a while to become familiar, let alone competent within this role. This is also the time in which we begin to give our gifts away to our community from the place of clarity and confidence around our values and what we have to offer.

It is not uncommon to find ourselves simultaneously in more than one of these stages within different aspects of life. For example, I might at once be in the incorporation stage of my work teaching all the things that I've been doing for the last 10 years, in the liminal stage around a state of health, whereas I could be in the severance stage in a significant relationship.

CEREMONY FOR TRAUMA AND TRANSITION IN PSYCHOTHERAPY

People typically come into therapy or therapeutic work when something is no longer working in their lives, when they desire to make a change, or when they are ready to learn more about themselves. We will look here at the role of ceremony in psychotherapy, considerations for incorporating it into that healing context, as well as structure and steps for creating personally meaningful and culturally relevant ceremonies for our clients. I will also offer an example of a ceremony that I co-created and facilitated.

With all transitions comes loss. Sometimes the loss is welcome, while other times it is not. We have choice around some of the changes that occur in life, while others are not what we are wanting. With loss comes grief. Grief is a complex emotion that typically takes a while to feel and work through. As the process of letting go is multi-faceted, non-linear, and not predictable, ceremony can be a valuable tool to give structure to transition. Considering the stages of change in creating ceremony can normalise the complexity of transition and create space to acknowledge both the challenges as well as the possibilities. Ceremony is something to do when it feels like there is nothing we can do as we ride the many waves within change. It gives us a container to channel the emotions and energy moving through us in the midst of our own evolution.

Even with seemingly positive change there can be grief. I recently facilitated a ceremony for someone who graduated from college. While relieved for the completion and excited for what was next, they shared, "Even though I'm so happy to be done with the papers and deadlines, I'm going to miss my friends and having access to my community right outside my door at any moment." So, whether the transition is choiceful or not, it's important to acknowledge the ending and make space to feel all of the feelings in relationship to the losses.

The psychotherapy process can be looked at as a rite of passage in and of itself. Typically, clients are in an identity crisis, a life change, a stuck point in life, or wanting something more. The therapy container is intentional, ritualistic, personal, and meaningful. It offers a structure that assists people in moving through phases or aspect of their lives.

TRAUMA AS A TRANSITION AND RITE OF PASSAGE

If the transition that we've gone through was traumatic, and there wasn't a choice, there's typically an even greater need for support in grieving and moving through the impact on one's life circumstances, identity, and experience of the world. We can be thrown into new ways of being with previous perceptions of safety taken away. There are often abrupt endings or losses involved and we are left asking the question, "Who am I now?" For instance, when one experiences a serious car accident, they may deal with physical or mental impairment or fear of driving. When one experiences loss of a loved one there can be significant grief and feeling of being lost.

Ceremonies can serve as structure and container to hold our experiences and to help us channel the energies, questions, and emotions into reflection and action. They can provide something to do when there is nothing to do. Ceremonies help us gain clarity on our intentions- that which we are letting go of and asking for support around, completing or claiming in our lives. They provide a sense of honouring the challenges of change. They may provide an opportunity to call together our communities or help us feel our place in the bigger web of life. Ceremonies help to ground us, to keep us in our bodies and on the earth, and to remain aware of our resources while we navigate the ungrounded moments that exist within change.

Examples of reasons to do ceremonies to support healing from trauma:

- Grieving ceremony for loss of a loved one

- Return from illness to health (mental or physical) ceremony

- Ceremony honouring life change due to COVID, such as giving up an identity as a professional, to home-school children

- Ceremony marking and exploring the question "who am I now?" after I have lost. . . (a child, a parent, a significant job or role in life, etc.)

There is a body of work called *post-traumatic growth* (PTG) (Tedeschi and Calhoon) that looks at some people's experiences of going through a traumatic event, getting to the other side of their healing, and identifying the gifts in the struggle. If and when someone reaches this place in their process, it is not uncommon to hear spoken sentiments such as, "I never would have chosen to go through that, though I don't know that I'd change it now, because I wouldn't be the person I am today. I wouldn't know the things that I know now, and I wouldn't have the same wisdom and gifts to give if I hadn't been through that." Note that not everyone who experiences trauma can or does get to this perspective, as PTG is influenced by a myriad of personal, social, cultural, situational and genetic circumstances.

CREATING PERSONALLY MEANINGFUL, CULTURALLY RELEVANT CEREMONIES

Given all that I have shared so far, how do we begin to create personally meaningful, culturally relevant ceremonies for ourselves and our clients? We do this by first looking at our own beliefs, cultural symbols, and practices. I suggest beginning by doing ceremonies for yourself to become familiar with creating intentional space, shifting out of ordinary consciousness, enacting symbolic gestures, and trusting what is flowing through you in the moment. Ceremony can be very simple or full of big energy and fanfare. It can be spontaneous, or it can be intricately planned. It can be as simple as lighting a candle in your room and saying a prayer, or speaking out loud to the fire. In the next section I will share some of the steps I consider and follow when creating ceremony.

STEPS FOR CREATING CEREMONY

1. Get clear on the intention for the Ceremony

2. Decide when and where the Ceremony will take place

3. Determine how you will open and close the Intentional/Sacred space

4. Decide what symbols and symbolic actions you will include in the Ceremony

5. Consider incorporating additional meaningful, ceremonial elements based on client's belief system

6. Identify *who* will witness the Ceremony (*humans, the earth, spiritual beings, or other*), and *how* you will weave in the presence of community (*in person or from afar*)

Let's explore these in more detail.

1. GET CLEAR ON THE INTENTION

The intention is the compass that guides the direction and energy flow of the Ceremony. It impacts the building of the ceremonial components. The intention will influence everything about the ceremony and beyond. It guides what you do, what you create, the seeds you are planting, and the trajectory of the energy you put into motion.

2. DECIDE WHEN AND WHERE THE CEREMONY WILL TAKE PLACE

Once we commit to doing a ceremony, it begins. The Universe and energies begin aligning in response to our intention. Our being starts quickening as we orient toward the ceremony, because if we're doing the ceremony right, typically we're stretching a bit beyond our edges, stretching beyond our identity, to something bigger, something greater, something more expansive, something else or something more focused. I've heard many stories wherein people have shared some version of "I set the intention, went home and *this thing* happened. . ." (a friend called, a gift showed up, ultimately something in relation to the intention presented itself). A friend of mine recently said, "I set the intention for Ceremony: I'm going to be retiring this year. I came home the next day and I had an email that I was getting laid off." This sort of thing is not uncommon when we align our energy in service of an intention.

3. DETERMINE HOW YOU WILL OPEN AND CLOSE THE INTENTIONAL/ SACRED SPACE

Decide how you will open and close intentional space to mark that something special is happening outside of the norm or the usual day-to-day. In beginning, you may choose an action or practice to call attention to the present moment and signal this change in focus, presence, and consciousness. For instance, often sensory experiences are practiced: the singing of a song, playing of music, burning of incense, saying prayers, lighting a candle, etc. A part of opening the intentional space may include calling on spiritual support, a ceremonial entrance, or a crossing of a physical threshold. There are many ways to create space and bring attention to that which is about to be honoured.

Similarly, to creating a conscious beginning, it is helpful to delineate a clear ending to the Ceremony in order to close the container of the Sacred intentional space. Although the integration and fruits of the Ceremony will continue to unfold, the focused time of honouring should end as intentionally as it began. You may want to end similarly to how you began such as: by crossing back over the threshold you entered, by blowing out the candle you lit to begin, or by offering prayers of gratitude to that which supported you within the Ceremonial process. These intentional actions in the beginning and ending of Ceremony support the shift in consciousness and alignment of our body, mind, and soul, and ultimately the creating of Sacred space.

4. DECIDE WHAT SYMBOLS AND/OR SYMBOLIC ACTIONS YOU WILL INCLUDE IN THE CEREMONY

Symbolic actions: Guided by the *Intention* of the Ceremony, determine what actions you want to take or what meaning to enact as a symbol of what you're marking. If your intention is to let go of something, you may want to burn or bury something. If you are marking the middle phase of a transition, a symbolic action may be to ask a question out loud to the natural world and listen for some guidance. In marking a completion, celebration, or new way of being in the world, you might receive an award, don a new piece of clothing, receive a gift, or explicitly give your gifts to the world. Essentially, consider symbolic actions to enact the energetics of the *Intention* in the physical realm.

Symbols: Consider what *symbolic items* you want to include within the Ceremony. These symbols might signify such things as comfort, support, familiarity, or old ways in light of your Ceremonial intention. This might include a shawl from your wise grandmother, a spiritual icon that has meaning, or flowers to mark the specialness of the situation. Additionally, you may include symbols that represent your intention such as an old letter or photo to be burned, a staff that symbolises claiming your power, or a ring symbolising commitment to yourself or another. Symbolic items can serve a variety of functions.

5. CONSIDER INCORPORATING ADDITIONAL MEANINGFUL, CEREMONIAL ELEMENTS BASED ON CLIENT'S BELIEF SYSTEM

Depending on your own and your client's belief systems, there are many other paradigms that can serve to support the creation of the Ceremony. Some of these include: sensory experiences, the natural elements, the 7 directions, or any other maps, beliefs or practices that you already engage within your spirituality, rituals, beliefs or practices. Including the senses can help bring us into the present moment, can be utilised to signify a stepping out of ordinary consciousness for the Ceremonial time, and can also be woven into symbolic actions.

The natural elements, incorporated differently in different cultures include, earth, air, fire, water, metal, and sometimes others. The elements each have their own wisdom and transformational properties and associations which can be utilised as a symbol or in conjunction with a symbolic action such as burning something or using water for cleansing. Similarly, to the elements, cultures throughout time have had diverse functional and spiritual relationships to the directions of the South, West, North, East, Below, Above, and Centre. Depending on one's physical location on the earth and on one's lifestyle and connection to earth, these directions will have different associations for different people.

It is important to evoke these unique personal associations, to honour making the ceremony personally meaningful. I like to think about the directions as a mirror of our wholeness as they represent and hold diverse universal energies and qualities that can be found within each one of us.

6. IDENTIFY WHO WILL WITNESS THE CEREMONY AND HOW YOU WILL WEAVE IN COMMUNITY

We live within a larger web of life and all our actions have ripple effects throughout the greater ecosystem. It is often said in Ceremonial circles that we do Ceremony not for ourselves, but for our human and more than human community. We do it in order to see our own strengths and challenges more clearly and to openly and fully offer our gifts and services to the world. When creating Ceremony, at the most basic level, knowing and feeling this embeddedness is central. From there we can consider the following questions: Who or what will witness the Ceremony? Will there be human beings, earth beings, spirit beings or others there in real time to support the Ceremonial intention? If not in-person, are there ways to inform those others in order for them to hold support from afar (for example, we might ask a loved one to light a candle for us, say a prayer, or send a letter of support). Will there be a facilitator or will it be a self-led ceremony? Do you bring symbols or photos that remind you of those that you are woven among?

What we put our attention on grows. When we are witnessed, it ups the ante, the power and the accountability to live out our intention. When our human community is involved, we can ask them to remind us of who we are or to ask us how our intention continues to unfold and incorporate throughout time.

THERE ARE SO MANY DIFFERENT WAYS TO DO CEREMONIES

Ultimately, Ceremony is saying "YES" to what is: what is unfolding, what is ending, what is emerging, or simply to being present within the unknown. Ceremony can look many different ways. Along with the above considerations, it is important to note that Ceremony can be planned and prepared for a year or more in advance, or it can be spontaneous. It can be very simple or it can be grand and regal. It can be enacted alone or with witnesses. Malidoma Some, teacher of Ceremony and Ritual, speaks about the importance of being open to the structure or planned aspect of Ceremony while leaving space for the Spirit to move, or in other words, to listen and be in active conversation with our intention, synchronicity and the wisdom that moves through the collective in the moment (Some, 1994).

CASE STUDY

I want to go back through the considerations for Ceremony creation and offer an example of a Ceremony that I supported, created, and facilitated for a client. For purposes of this example, I will refer to the client as "Sarah". I had been seeing Sarah for 4 years. She originally came to me when she was diagnosed with a severe and mysterious chronic illness that eventually had her effectively house bound for two and half years. During that time, she had to let go of her job, of spending time in person with most people, and of going out to do many of the things that she enjoyed. Through a great deal of inner resource, drive and impeccable self-care, many medical and health experiments, along with personal and professional support from many humans, she found herself gaining more and more energy as well as capacity to be in the world.

One day during our session I was struck by Sarah's energy, optimism, health, and realisation that many of the capacities she'd lost were back on board. She was out in the world working again, socialising, while continuing to take excellent care of herself. I paused her as she was talking to reflect this back to her. She welled up with tears at the acknowledgement of all she had experienced and come through. I said out loud, "You survived. Not only did you survive, but you've come out the other side alive and thriving."

She has a particular connection to the mythopoetic realms and likened her journey to Persephone's of having been kidnapped into the underworld and not knowing if she'd ever return. As the immensity of her journey and reemergence became apparent, I asked her if she would like to do a ceremony to *let all of her* know that she had made it out, and to allow her community to welcome her back. Tears flowed with both grief and gratitude and her answer was a resounding "Yes!".

The Ceremony Creation: We co-created the Ceremony as she welcomed guidance, ideas, direction, and facilitation, while also having many ideas and desires of her own. She is someone who already had a personal relationship with Self-created Ceremony. Following is a description of how the Ceremony considerations came into play.

The Intention: *Welcome all of her- body, mind, and spirit, back from the underworld journey of chronic illness.* Acknowledging the intensity of that time and the hardships she navigated and being witnessed in this experience allowed both her conscious and unconscious mind to recognise she had come through allowing the grief, relief, and gratitude to be more fully felt and expressed.

When and Where the Ceremony Will Take Place: Sarah decided to plan the Ceremony for about 4 weeks out so that she could secure a location, invite loved ones, consider the additional design, and be with her intention. In the end she decided to do it outside on private land owned by one of her friends near where she resides in a place with a beautiful view of the mountains.

Identify Who Will Witness the Ceremony or How You Will Weave in Community: Sarah invited approximately 12 people to be present, represented by both family members and friends and by me, who facilitated the Ceremony. We were all people who had known her through her time experiencing debilitating chronic illness and witnessed her journey throughout. She also called in the 7 Directions, Spirit guides, Ancestors and the Earth as support and witness.

Opening & Closing Intentional/Sacred Space: Sarah began with a few hours of solo time out on the land reflecting on her journey. At an agreed upon time of day, her community gathered around a fire and began playing rhythm as a way to call her back home to herself, her health, and her community. She entered the circle being welcomed back by her people with spontaneous words of welcome. I gave her a smoke blessing. Once in the circle around the fire, as a community we called on the support and wisdom of the 7 directions, and Sarah called on her Spirit guides, Ancestors, and the Earth to be present as witness and support for the Ceremony. All of this was a part of beginning and creating the Sacred/Intentional space for the celebration.

To end the Ceremony, we gave gratitude for the unseen support we had called on in the beginning and released them from our gathering. The community once again played rhythm as Sarah walked out and away from the circle to spend a few moments on her own with the natural world, soaking in the impact of all that the Ceremony represented. When she was ready, she came back, and we all shared food together.

Symbols and/or Symbolic Actions: So, what actually took place in the Ceremony? Sarah brought some items from her alter at home that had helped her hold hope and keep moving through her journey one day at a time. She brought those to symbolise some of her inner and outer support. She also brought a piece of artwork she had made during that time to let go of and burn in the fire to symbolise that this time of illness was over. She intentionally entered the ceremonial space by being welcomed back by her community. She was witnessed and reflected so that she could acknowledge and feel the reality of her underworld journey as well as the reality of being in a different place in her life now.

During the Ceremony she spoke spontaneously about what the journey had been like for her, as well as the learnings and gifts she has taken from it. Some of her community spontaneously spoke as well, bearing witness to what they experienced of her on this journey, as well as some sharing some of their own experiences, feelings, relief, and love for her. After these words were spoken, Sarah symbolically placed the art piece in the fire acknowledging the aspects of her identity from the ill-

ness that she was letting go of, and then she spoke words of recognition of what is possible for her now with more health, energy, capacity, and new perspectives. There was spontaneous celebration, cheering, tears and hugs.

When the ceremony felt complete, we ended similarly to how we began by giving gratitude for the support that had been called in for the ceremony and by playing rhythm, which was much more celebratory and lighter as Sarah walked out to take moments to feel and integrate the impact of this ceremonial experience.

Inclusion of Additional Ceremonial Elements: As described previously, due to Sarah's personal practices with Ceremony, she included acknowledging the 7 directions, calling in unseen support, incorporating the element of Fire as a part of the ceremony, as well as rhythm and the burning of herbs.

Symbols or Symbolic Actions: In terms of symbolic items, one of the things Sarah included was a piece of art she had made while she was sick. To her this represented that long time of not knowing what was going to happen and the long time of the liminal. She also had a statue of a goddess that had been in her meditation room during the time of her illness. She felt this had supported her in staying connected to strength and hope in her time going through this experience of severe illness. Finally, Sarah also had asked friends and loved ones who couldn't be at the ceremony if they would write words of support for her to read afterwards.

NOTES FOR PRACTITIONERS FOR CREATING CEREMONY WITH CLIENTS WITHIN THERAPY

If you are supporting clients in creating ceremony to mark meaningful life transitions or move through traumatic experiences, the following are some considerations for developing your skills and incorporating this practice into your healing work with others. To begin, as shared earlier in this chapter, if this is something that is newer for you it is a helpful to enact and develop relationship with ceremony for yourself first. There is a comfortability that develops over time around trusting yourself and trusting the process as well as around trusting the unfolding balance within the ceremony between the planned and the spontaneous. As you engage in this process, you may want to start by keeping it simple.

Consider your own personal, cultural or spiritual beliefs, as well as how these might be similar or different to those of your clients. The more familiar you are with the basic components of creating ceremony, the more you will understand how to evoke personal meaning and identify symbols and symbolic actions relevant for your client while not arbitrarily placing your beliefs or practices on the process. That said, if clients don't have clear spiritual or cultural identities and have not participated much in ceremony, they may look to you to offer or suggest ways of opening or closing, creating intentional space, or identifying symbolic actions to support their intentions.

When you are inspired to incorporate ceremony into your work with a client, some questions you might ask to assess for interest, comfortability, and need for guidance include:

- Are you interested in doing a ceremony for (whatever it is they are in transition around)?

- What are your experiences and/or associations with ceremony?

- Have you created your own ceremony before?

- If you have created your own ceremonies: How comfortable are you with this process?

- How much guidance would you like from me in the creation and/or facilitation of it?

After an initial conversation about this, making the decision to do ceremony, and briefly discussing the considerations and steps, have them journal about all aspects of the ceremony as outlined previously in this chapter. After considering and journaling on these aspects, have them come back and share their thoughts and ideas with you. At this point, you can ask clarifying questions, ask if they would like suggestions, and offer overall support for them to create a clear plan for the: what, where, when, how, and who factors.

Included in the structure and details, I suggest supporting them to clarify if and how they would like you to be involved in the ceremony itself. Do they want you to facilitate it just with them or with another loved one's present? Do they want to enact it with you as witness? Will they do the ceremony solo or with other friends or family and ask you to hold space from afar?

FINAL WORDS

In closing this chapter, I want to circle back to where we began. Connection with Nature and Ceremony is in our blood and in our bones. If you open up the doorway to include nature-based ceremony into your healing work, you invite in additional guidance, support, healing forces, and other ways of knowing and perceiving in support of life transition. Allow your own and your clients' desires, intuition and knowing to lead the way. Remember and trust that when enacting Ceremony, while allowing the intention to guide, more than any pre-planned structure, be in the moment, allow for spontaneity, and listen to allow for what is moving through to move. Ultimately, know and honour that you are truly saying YES to what already is.

REFERENCES

Jabr, F. (2012). https://www.scientificamerican.com/article/caterpillar-butterfly-metamorphosis-explainer/, Scientific America.

Some, M. (1994). *Of Water and the Spirit: Ritual, Magic, and Initiation in the Life of an African Shaman.* Penguin Group, New York.

Tedeschi, R., Shakespeare-Finch, J., Taku K., Calhoun, L. (2018). Rutledge, New York.

Van Gennep, A. (1908, 1960). *The rites of passage.* Trans. Monika B. Vizedom and Gabrielle L. Caffee. University of Chicago Press, Chicago.

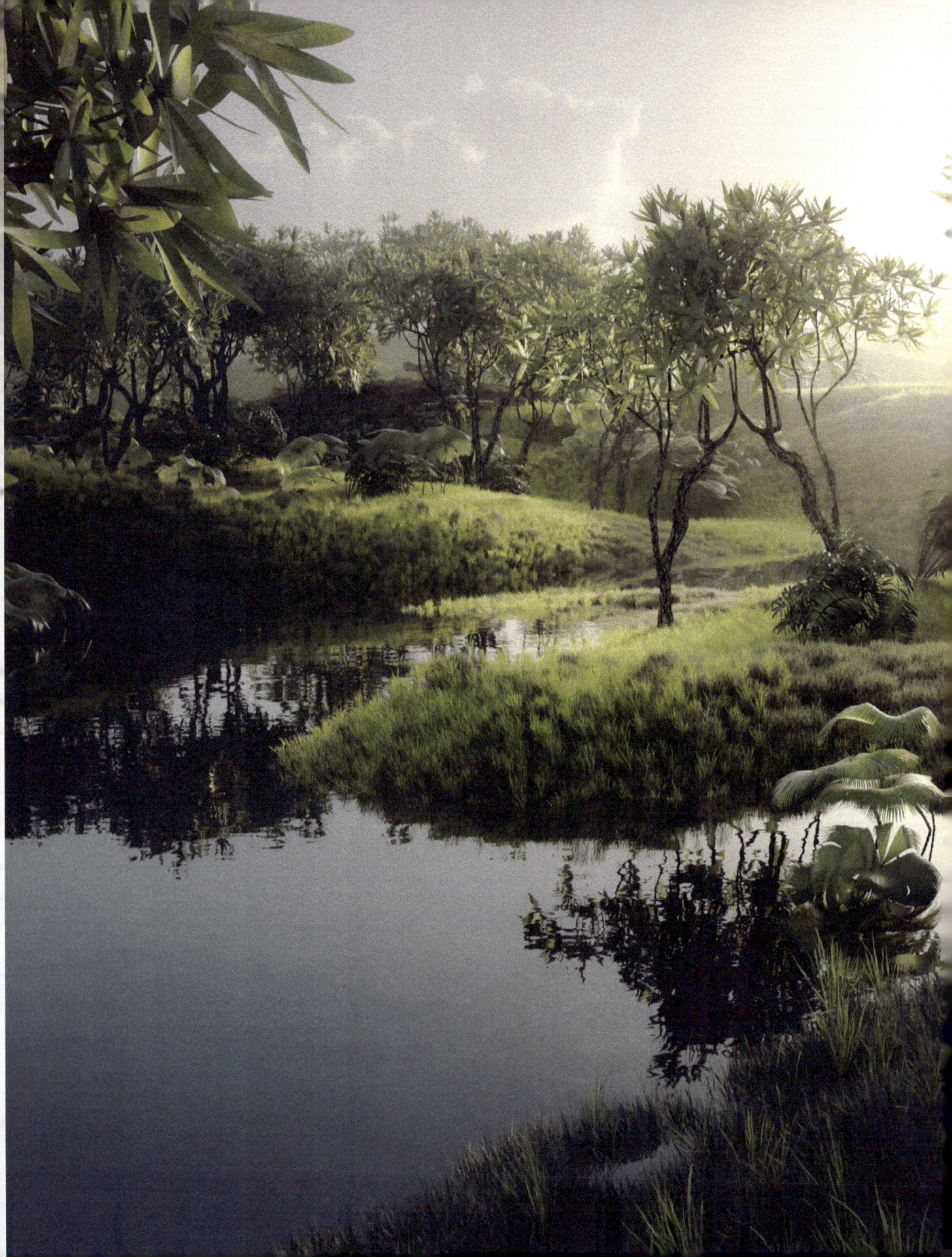

Chapter 16:

UN-DOMESTICATING THERAPY

COMING HOME TO THE NATURE OF OUR BEING

KIMBERLY ROSE

ABOUT KIMBERLY ROSE

BA. M.Ed., CC, Founder of Un-domesticating Therapy™ and Relational Rewilding Nature Guiding, Colorado, USA

As a naturalist, nature-based therapist, herbalist, and educator, Kimberly considers herself to be living her childhood dreams. She is owner and operator of Colorado Ecotherapy Institute and Relational Rewilding Nature Guiding where she facilitates nature therapy, ecotherapy trainings, nature education, and nature connection for Colorado communities and organisations. Kimberly is also faculty and coordinator for the Gestalt Equine Institute of the Rockies.

She holds a Master's degree in Counselling, a Bachelor's degree in Outdoor Education & Plant Biology, and blends Gestalt, herbalism, ecology, survival and animal tracking into her work. Kimberly believes the health of people is absolutely intertwined with the health of our ecosystems and values helping others improve their health, confidence, relationships and sense of belonging in the world by restoring the original kinship we humans share with nature. She lives in the wooded foothills of Golden, Colorado, USA, in the traditional territory of the Arapaho, Cheyenne, and Ute nations with her partner, 3 horses, and a diversity of wild beings.

INTRODUCTION

Therapy is wild by nature, yet it has become rather tame in the face of increasing healthcare regulations, controlled protocols, and psychology's ongoing avoidance of our inter-connectedness with the living world. Immersed in society's paradigm of control — land, people, and the field of therapy itself have become domesticated. Luckily, growing research and interest in the therapeutic potential of nature on mental and emotional health has some practitioners taking their clients into wilder spaces. But un-domesticated, nature-based therapy is more than simply relocating sessions. It is about actively and relationally collaborating with the natural rhythms and richness of one's local bioregion.

To optimise this active engagement with dynamic ecosystems between client, nature, and therapist requires more than loving animals and nature. Un-domesticated, nature-based therapy requires the therapist to expand their conceptualisation to include human's historical relationship with ecology. It asks the practitioner to remember their roots by attuning to landscape patterns and learning the wild beings of their environment. It also compels helpers to think outside the box of symptom amelioration and adjustment to colonial civilisation, and instead step into a shared journey of discovery and an embodied remembering that we are relational, earth beings. In essence, it requires a process of un-domesticating ourselves and our therapeutic work. The following provides stories, rationale, and a framework of nature engagement to spark your own creativity for nature-based, therapeutic openings.

COLLEEN

It was a beautiful, spring, Colorado day when I met Colleen (name changed to protect client confidentiality) at a local city park for our 4th session together. I was working with many young women struggling with eating disorders and attachment difficulties during this particular time and Colleen was no exception. We sat near a river running through the park, underneath old and wise cottonwood trees that seemed to envelope us with their hanging branches above and nest-like roots below. Due to spring run-off, the river was full, flowing, and vibrant. It was also fledgling season, meaning the young songbirds were just starting to try on their wings in flight and experiment with independence.

Upon my initial assessment with Colleen a month prior, I asked a variety of ecological identity questions as I do all my clients. She revealed a love for animals and nature, despite not always taking the time she wanted to engage this passion. We collaboratively decided to progress with nature therapy as this approach generated curiosity within her and seemed hopeful compared to the traditional eating disorder methodologies she had tried.

On that spring day, we began our session with a few minutes of sensory engagement with the nourishing, natural stimuli surrounding us, and then did a check-in. Colleen shared successes and challenges from the past week, which included apathy feelings and a frequent desire to give up. Suddenly, we were interrupted by the sound of a small splash up-river. Coming towards us, flailing desperately in the rivers flow, was a fledgling bird that had dropped from a nest on a cottonwood branch. Without hesitation, Colleen and I looked at one another, scanned the environment for a quick safety assessment, nodded our heads, and got in the river. She headed toward the river's centre in front of me, taking my hand for balance. We navigated in far and quick enough for Colleen to scoop the young songbird up into her hands. She then handed him to me as she wobbled back to shore holding onto my shoulder. As we crawled back onto land, we placed the drenched young sparrow at the base of the tree he fell from, and we watched him shake and re-orient.

After a minute of catching our breath, I invited both of us to shake like the bird in order to move and dissipate the adrenaline energy running through our bodies. Then we sat back down on the river's bank, and I turned to Colleen and spoke, "When you saw the sparrow coming down river, what did you notice about him?"

"I noticed he was flapping his wings hard and fast and trying to keep his head above the water."

She responded, "Yes."

I said softly and slowly, "That bird was doing his best to fight for his life. My inquiry to you is, how are you going to fight for your life?"

Colleen sat stunned for a moment and tears welled in her eyes. "I have never thought of my recovery in that way before. I guess I am an animal too."

"Yes, you are," I replied, "which means you have animal instincts for survival. Just as you were there to help the sparrow, I am here to help you when you fall; you are not alone."

The statement of "fighting for your life" became a recurring theme in our ongoing nature-based work together, with much of our time watching wildlife as they reliably model this instinctual, life-preserving response to crisis. In order to optimise our wildlife watching, we would practice delicate stalking movements and blending in with our environment, which aided Colleen in reinhabiting her body in fun and playful ways.

In a hundred years, I could never have crafted such an impactful experiment or intervention as the river and bird did that day. Something shifted in Collen the moment we looked into each other's eyes and nodded before jumping in the river. The spontaneity, presence, equitable cooperation, and a little bit of mystery contributed to this shift in her therapeutic and personal goals. When driving to this session, I had no plans for jumping into a river, or of saving a life with my client. I had no agenda for relating nature's drive for life to my client's instinct for saving her own. What I did walk in with is this: competent knowledge of and relationship with this particular environment; trust in our species long history of awareness and participation with the living world; an attitude of collaboration with nature as my co-therapist; and trust in spontaneity and trust in my client. None of this would have occurred without these ingredients, nor had I let myself be limited by the constraints of controlled, protocol-driven, domesticated therapy.

THE 4 DS

Most clients enter my private therapy practice dysregulated, disconnected, distracted, and domesticated, or what I call the "4 D's". They are uncertain how to participate in their mammalian nervous system's responses to stress. They have little to no relationship with their wild mind or wild surroundings. Clients struggle in making true contact amidst life's commotion. Lifestyles run counter to their biological design, wreaking havoc on body and psyche.

The 4 D's are expressed through endless combinations of symptoms, complex diagnoses, and heart-breaking stories common to the modern, human condition. As a psychotherapist, I am humbled to attend to their trials with my professional training as a mental health counsellor and as a fellow human on her own healing journey. Yet as a nature-based psychotherapist, I also take in the long view of who we are as Homo sapiens. This means I consider the context of our ancient, but not forgotten, un-domesticated selves and I allow this perspective to inform my approach to supporting health.

Over 97% of Homo sapien history has been spent living as un-domesticated beings — wild, free, aware, embodied, self-reliant, egalitarian, and strong due to natural diets and movements. Mary Midgley (2002) said, 'we are not like animals, we are animals', and therefore we are nature. Shaped by the elemental, biological world for nearly 300,000 years, humans lived in sync with nature's and the body's innate rhythms and intelligence. As a result, our species developed physical and relational needs that can only be met by the natural world and by safe, authentic human connection.

Author, environmental philosopher, and human ecology professor Paul Shepard alludes to the complex integration between people and the living world:

"The shape of all otherness grows out of the maternal relationship. And this relationship is formed within the backdrop of the environment that exists for both infant and mother. In the evolution of humankind this setting took the form of living plants, wild birds, rain, wind, mud, the taste and texture of earth and bark, the sounds of animals and insects. These surroundings were swallowed, internalised and incorporated as the self." (1995)

Our mammalian bodies and sensory systems require nature for ultimate health, and so does our sense of self. Attachment and trust in the world, foundational to self-development, emerge from the matrix of all our relations — the human and more-than-human together. From a Gestalt perspective, the self is co-created in the process of making contact with the environment, and it is between I and other

that we form. Important in attachment theory is the idea of a "secure base" (Bowlby 1969; Ainsworth 1978). Natural environments and animals, in addition to caregivers, are seen as representing this base that provides consistency and comfort in relationships.

Psychiatrist Harold Searles (1960) sees our relatedness to the non-human environment as one of the transcendentally important facts of human living. Nature is often considered a transitional object between infant and mother (and later client and therapist) helping to create a vibrant and steady emotional space for the self to evolve (Winnicott, 1951). This biological blending between self and the world grew out of our ancestral history with nature.

Today, most humans live in artificial environments and social systems that are in stark contrast to those experienced by people prior to domestication. In the move from hunter-gatherer communities to agricultural societies, there was a shift that crippled our human-nature relationship. In exercising control over plants, animals, ecologies, and each other, we split ourselves off from the living world and her inhabitants which includes our own sensuous bodies, authentic feelings, and our wise, instinctual selves. The whole of nature became other, and therefore dangerous, which in turn required more control.

Industrialisation, land development, and the technological revolution further increased human dislocation from nature, other species, and seasonal cycles. Living deeper into artificial environments, primarily full of human artefacts, contributes to the indoor, sedentary, and disembodied lifestyles of modern, westernised cultures. The growing movement of ecopsychology posits that human psychopathology increases the more we find ourselves in this dislocated state. The paradigm of individualism and a materialistic value system leaves people with an increasing sense of anxiety, loneliness, and depression, all worldwide public health concerns (D. Kidner). I agree with eco-psychologist Theodore Roszak when he says that a psychological theory that does not address alienation between people and the natural environment is deeply flawed.

Psychology emerged as a separate discipline in the late 1800's with its roots in the scientific methodologies of the 17th century. The scientific revolution that defined this time created drastic changes in human perception and thought, including viewing nature and humans as machine rather than living organisms. Collateral to this new worldview was a growth in the quantitative value of nature and outcomes over the qualitative. Prominent Jungian psychologist, James Hillman (1995), spoke of this scientific influence in psychology:

> "The traditional argument of psychology says: maintain the closed vessel of the consulting room, of the behavioural lab, of the field itself, for this tradition is born from nineteenth century science, which continues to define psychology as the scientific study of subjectivity. And science works best in controllable situations, in vitro, under the bell jar, where it can carefully observe, predict and thereby perhaps alter the minutiae of the subject."

The modern-day, medical model, managed care push for evidence-based therapy that occurs in controlled, indoor, and predictable spaces is an outcome of this history. Such approaches prioritise the rational which further divides mind and body, and are data driven versus relationship driven. They focus on fixing rather than discovering. Interventions are often planned rather than spontaneous. They approach the body as machine instead of miracle. They work from the neck up versus the ground up, omitting conceptualisation of our human ecology; they risk not attending to clients as their own empowered agents of change. While such approaches are indeed helpful for some people and contexts, to many therapists and clients alike this domesticated approach limits creativity, individuality, and often excludes a relational, nature-based, systemic perspective.

HOW DOES A PRACTITIONER UN-DOMESTICATE THEIR OUT-PATIENT THERAPY?

This "rewilding" of conventional therapy may have as many paths as there are therapists. Challenging societal conditioning and norms, exposing familial and somatic introjects, integrating plant medicine, engaging somatic approaches, and partnering with "wilder" animals such as horses are but a few of the ways professionals are stretching the psychotherapy status quo.

Another popular route toward un-domesticating mental health is through nature-based therapy. Drawing on their own love for nature and the increasing evidence of the effectiveness of nature on health and well-being, many private-practice clinicians and some mental health agencies are beginning to engage appropriate clients in yards, parks, on greenways and at trailheads. Relocating sessions to outdoor spaces exposes clients to "active ingredients" in nature that contribute to positive mental and emotional health effects. Some active ingredients include balanced and diverse levels of sensory stimuli, biodiversity, enriched oxygen, exposure to phytoncides, and the 'big 3' relaxing sounds: bird song, trees in the breeze, and water (Ming Kuo). These and other para-sympathetic activating ingredients can be found in many urban, suburban, and front-country settings around the globe.

That said, un-domesticated, nature-based therapy is about more than moving sessions outdoors. It is about considering humans' historical relationship with nature in client conceptualisation, and actively collaborating with one's local bioregion from a place of competence.

The first part emphasises holding a general understanding of human ecology, or humans' place in nature, which can offer therapists a level of trust in nature-based work that extends beyond one's theoretical orientation. As a fallible practitioner myself, I may be uncertain of my own therapeutic ability or intervention choices at times, yet my trust in the evolutionary truth that humans are part of and interdependent with ecosystems reinforces a sense of "coming home" to body and earth, even in imperfect therapy.

The second part encourages creativity over control, and competency versus ignorance in local outdoor settings. Active, nature therapy does not follow a protocol, formula, or method. The therapist

embodies the mindset of an artist instead of a technician and creates interventions in the vibrant interface between their clients and nature. Such creativity is enhanced when the therapist has ecological knowledge of and deep relationship with the landscapes they collaborate with. This competency also supports ethical practice since physical safety becomes an added responsibility in this approach. What is your level eco-literacy and connection?

Here are a few questions to reflect on about your bioregion and her cycles:

- Who are the first-nations people native to your region?

- What is something natural in your yard or neighbourhood you are aware of today that you were not aware of yesterday?

- Name 3 year-round songbirds in your area, and 3 potential predators of songbirds.

- From where you are right now, point to and name the river nearest to your home. Where does it begin and end?

- What weather patterns specific to your region do you need to remain aware of as a nature-based therapist? What signs, in nature or your body, might indicate these patterns are approaching?

- Were stars out last night? What is the phase of the moon today?

- Name 3 edible, 3 medicinal, and the 5 most poisonous plants in your bioregion. Could you identify them in the field?

- At what time of the year or in what setting does your animal body feel most alive and connected to nature? How do you know?

Working as a master naturalist, native plant master, herbalist, and nature-connection facilitator for over 20 years prior to becoming a psychotherapist has significantly contributed to my therapeutic work. While mental health professionals do not need to have degrees in wildlife biology or ecology, I do believe practitioners have an opportunity and a responsibility to be nature-connected and ecologically literate.

Integrating this awareness and relationship with nature into our lives and work promotes a quality of power all people deserve to remember and embody. When I say "power", I do not mean the conventional definition of "power over" that is commonly spoken. That version of "power" is control, which is the root of domestication, colonialism, and ecocide. What I am referring to is a relational definition of "power" that psychotherapist Duey Freeman has identified and teaches:

Power is the ability to influence and be influenced in contact and relationship.

This reciprocal dynamic more accurately reflects human's evolutionary relationship with nature as well as a healthier interpersonal perspective.

4 PART NATURE MODEL

OK, so you are on your way to becoming more educated about your ecology, which alone will generate more creativity in outdoor work with clients, but what else? How else can embracing nature connection and eco-literacy support your therapeutic process with clients?

An organisation I have trained with in nature education and nature connection is 8 Shields Institute. They often refer to a four-part model (see below) when discussing how people do and can engage with nature. When I began blending nature and psychotherapy at the beginning of my counselling career, I borrowed this framework and started to see how activities in each category could be facilitated in such a way that they provide therapeutic openings and experiments in my client work. The following are brief descriptions and client examples that hopefully will inspire your creativity outdoors.

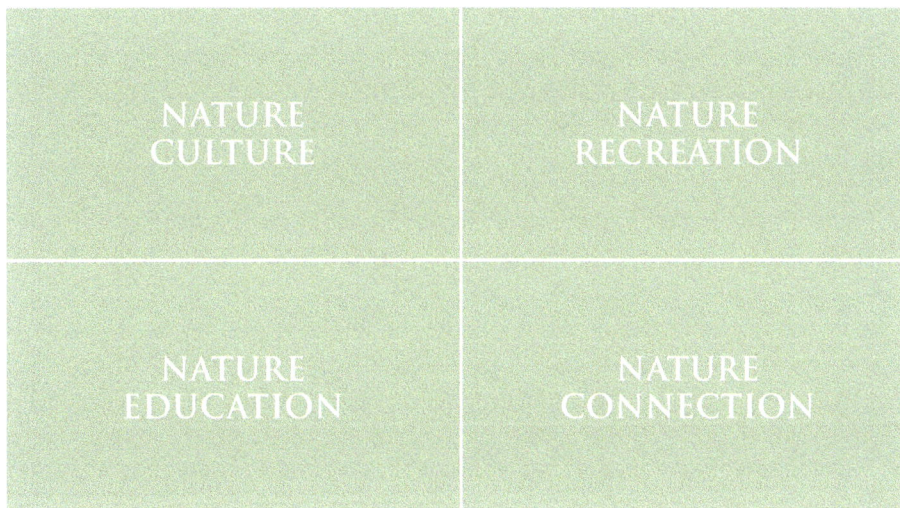

NATURE CULTURE	NATURE RECREATION
NATURE EDUCATION	NATURE CONNECTION

NATURE CULTURE

The first quadrant in the four-part model is Nature Culture. This is the foundation and container for the other forms of engagement. Establishing a nature culture is about creating regular practices in your work that connect clients to their environment and that normalise the inherent value of nature. It is about norming nature. Norming nature communicates that this focus is not just reflective of your personal interest or hobby. It conveys your acknowledgment that we are a member of nature's community and that we are designed for relationship with our surroundings.

What are some ways to cultivate a nature culture? One of the most significant ways is through our language. What pronouns do you use when referring to beings in the natural world? The societal language of objectification through the pronoun "it" creates distance between us and plants and animals, making it easier to minimise, exploit and extinguish them. The common way people speak of birds, squirrels and other life is by saying something like "it went across the field" or "it flew that way". This is a learned form of objectification.

One day a client and I were walking up our hill when two female mule deer and three baby deer came into the yard. The young teen pointed and said, "Look, it's eating a raspberry!" I responded simply by saying, "She is, isn't she?" If we are uncertain of an animal's gender such as a hawk or a rabbit, it takes only an extra second of time to say "he or she" instead of "it" when speaking about them. I will even refer to plants as "they", "he", "she", or their given name as they too are botanically male and/or female. If we are going to be outdoors with others engaging with the living world, this is a great way to model what theologian Martin Buber refers to as an "I/Thou" relationship with others. And as author, botanist, and member of the Potawatomi Nation Robin Wall Kimmerer says, "we can save the word 'it' for bulldozers, not our kin".

An additional way we can use language to normalise nature is by bringing nature and non-human beings back into ordinary conversations. Jim (name changed to protect confidentiality), a young adult client that I have worked with for a year, arrives to our sessions and organically reports new nature sightings. "The tree on my property is blooming pink flowers and smells amazing, and the humming-birds have returned!" The unsolicited observations are new in our relationship and grew out of our time together.

The lives and language of western society citizens are extremely human-centric and are virtually devoid of dialogue with or about other species. This is especially true in psychotherapeutic dialogues unless the therapist specifically partners with animals. Nature, animals and elements are commonly referred to in my sessions and may enter in through grounding/supporting experientials, metaphors, sensory exercises, relational experiments, and through ordinary conversation. My clients expect me to ask them about their struggles. They also anticipate questions about which birds and plants they observed since our last session.

A second way of creating nature culture in your practice is through your formal and informal assessments with clients. While they may know that you offer outdoor sessions, you communicate a greater set of values when asking them about their personal rhythms and cycles, and about their historical and unique relationship with nature in your information gathering.

Next has to do with how you collaborate with the natural world. Is your engagement primarily passive or do you regularly invite encounters and sensory experiences into your interventions? Session length is another way to collaborate with nature, though it can be more complicated for a variety of reasons. All my clinical sessions are minimum of an hour and a half long and sometimes may be scheduled for two or three hours. The diversity of life, stimuli, and dynamics outdoors translates to increased relational interactions and therefore more opportunities for engagement. Clients often "drop in" in a different way in natural settings than they do in indoor spaces, and the 50-minute hour can be very limiting in my experience. If a client is not financially able to extend their sessions, I offer financial flexibility. We may have longer sessions less frequently, or they pay what is personally workable. It is important to me that this form of therapy is accessible to everyone.

A fourth way of creating a nature culture in your practice is through rituals. A ritual is an act, set of actions, or words performed regularly. They may be intentional and part of a ceremony, may be a stand-alone act, or may be unconscious and habitual. There are many forms of rituals and it is likely that you already perform them as part of your practice, such as a simple daily clearing of your workspace.

An example of a nature culture ritual in my work is how clients and I transition from human artefact spaces, such as parking lots, to more natural spaces where the bulk of our session takes place. There is a pause at such a threshold. In this pause exists an acknowledgement of the physical, energetic and life/species differences between the two areas. There are invitations for intentional breaths and more blended, natural movement through the changing landscape. Another simple ritual is regularly practicing gratitude in sessions. This may be done as we open or close our work together. These few, simple rituals serve the philosophy of reciprocity in our work and serve to ground the clients in their bodies and in the surroundings during session. This is often new to clients initially, but after a few sessions they expect these simple and honouring rituals and eventually even begin initiating them on their own.

The above nature culture creations are core and foundational to active nature-based work. They can all be applied regardless of you working in a cityscape, a suburban-scape, or a more natural landscape. They can also be created and developed in partnership with your clients.

NATURE RECREATION

The second quadrant in the nature engagement model is Nature Recreation. Weaving nature recreation into therapeutic work will depend on your location, the terrain, your experience and ability level, appropriateness for a particular client, the interests of you and your client, and/or accessibility. A few general examples include hiking, snowshoeing, rock climbing and canoeing. These activities are commonly thought of in the realm of intervention-based wilderness therapy for groups, yet with some planning, may also become a part of individual or small group, out-patient therapy.

My primary recreational activity of choice in therapy sessions is archery. While not everyone is an archer, archery is not difficult or too expensive to learn and set up so it may be worth looking into as an option. The following is a client example.

I was working with a young woman, Jasmine (name changed for privacy), who had just completed a 6-week in-patient therapeutic program for her eating disorder. Entering out-patient therapy with me, she was still significantly struggling with body image, low self-esteem, and disordered eating. I did nature therapy with her solely. On just our second session together, I had Jasmine sit along a creek quietly for a few minutes, observing and taking in the environment. I invited her to close her eyes. I then placed my bow in Jasmine's lap and asked her to feel the bow with her hands. As Jasmine slowly explored the length, curved shape, and natural wooden texture of this ancient tool, she began tearing up.

After some time, she opened her eyes and I invited her to make a statement about her experience when she was ready. She stated that she "felt something old" in her. The young woman was referring to

a primal and strong feeling deep within and stated that it felt familiar. We stayed with that feeling for a while prior to engaging with the bow on the range.

I worked with Jasmine for a few years, and she enjoyed archery so much that it became the foundation of our work together. When we met, she was walking through the world in a hunched down posture that reflected her esteem. There was minimal ability for her to make true contact with herself, her body, me, or her surroundings. With each session she learned to handle the bow firmly yet softly, she would stand tall and straight, pull the arrow back through the tension of the string, take a breath, imagine her goal as she aimed, and released with an exhale. Her archery experience lent itself easily to many metaphors and lessons applicable to the trust, attachment, and insecurity she struggled with.

Jasmine learned to stand tall, to make contact with the moment, to feel energy and vitality once again flow through her exhausted body and activate a strength that had been dormant. To witness this was magical. In fact, Jasmine eventually decided that she wanted a bow of her own and so one of our sessions took place at a sporting goods store. In her default states of protection, she was timid and wanted support in her communication with the staff. A few weeks later Jasmine purchased her own archery set, and after my work with her ended she would regularly send me photographs of her standing tall and strong at our favourite outdoor archery range.

NATURE EDUCATION

The third quadrant is Nature Education. I regularly and appropriately weave nature education into sessions and clients love it. People become excited and interested in learning the natural life in their bioregion yet often remain ignorant due to a conditioned focus on alternate, human-centred societal values. Walking through a local ponderosa pine forest, each of my clients reveal their level of awareness of the sensate, living world around us. Regardless of where they are in their awareness, learning bits of ecology about plants, animals, and natural patterns contributes to an upregulation of positive emotions and a sense of curiosity that often becomes paralysed in trauma. It also offers a set of metaphors that can be a powerful engine for change.

Danny (name changed for privacy), a 14-year-old female client that entered therapy for interpersonal struggles, spontaneously became interested in a nearby plant that was particularly hairy. Wanting to take her curiosity to the next level, I squatted down next to the plant and joined in her interest. As a plant teacher and fanatic, I frequently carry a loupe with me outdoors, which is a small magnifying glass with which to explore small plant features and I handed it to her. As she explored the trichome texture with the loupe and her fingers, I shared the many ways that plants protect themselves. As if the surrounding botanicals wished to contribute to the conversation, we looked around to find an array of other plants displaying hairs, spines, and thorns. We also tasted the bitter and spicy flavours of a few leaves and discussed how various organic compounds in plants contribute to protection from herbivory.

At some point, we organically transitioned to examining her unique protection strategies and how they link to the frequent arguments with family and friends that brought her to therapy. While sitting in the calming presence of the plants, she grew in acceptance and understanding for her own armouring, without judgement. This metaphor was re-visited in our work together as we further un-packed the origin of her strategies and the mindful skill of discernment in applying them. The brief lesson about native plants provided an opening for exploring her own parallel process.

NATURE CONNECTION

The last quadrant in the nature engagement model is Nature Connection. Learning from nature rather than learning about nature, contact through the heart sense and 5 senses, and moving more deeply toward an I/Thou relationship with other beings constitutes nature connection processes. Some examples of activities that promote this quality of relationship include outdoor sit spots, animal tracking, nature journaling, listening for bird language, and nature caretaking. Each of these find their way into my therapeutic work.

Various animals participate in my nature therapy practice such as horses, dogs, birds, insects and other local wildlife. Animals provide many opportunities for self and relational reflection including the awareness of projections. All people take in stimuli through the senses, run it through personal filters and make meaning out of it. The meaning is usually a projection until we check it out. Sara (named changed to protect privacy), 32-year-old client, and I were walking on a trail near a pond when a shorebird stepped out from between the swampy grasses and onto the trail. After a few moments, the bird suddenly noticed our presence and then began moving away. Sara immediately stated, "I must be scary, I am always chasing others away."

Projections can and do destroy relationships so when they arise between a client and a person or animal, I interrupt them. Depending on the context I may do a variety of experiments to help the client open to the experience of another, and to own their projection. On this day I asked Sara if she was willing to ask the bird what his experience was. She said yes, so I invited her into a process of inquiry that dog trainer Suzanne Clothier calls the "6 Elemental Questions".

The 6 Elemental Questions were originally designed for human/animal therapy teams. Guardians of dogs, horses or other animals that participate in animal therapy or animal-assisted activities are encouraged to ask these questions of their partners, to listen deeply, and to respond ethically. I frequently invite clients to engage these questions with the various animals we come into contact with during therapy. On this day, I introduced Sara to the first 3 questions as they were most relevant to the situation, then she took a breath and asked them of the shorebird.

The simple questions are:

1. Hello? (Asking for permission to engage)

2. Who are you? (As a species and as an individual, what is your worldview?)

3. What is this like for you? (How might this exact moment or interaction be for you as an individual?)

4. Can you? (Are you physically, mentally, behaviourally able to do what I am asking?)

5. Can I? (Can I lead you, groom you, touch you, work with you, etc...)
6. Can we? (Can we do this together?)

Sara listened deeply and opened herself to any feeling, image or impression in response. After a few minutes of this quiet contact between herself and the shorebird, she spoke. "I am uncertain if what I feel is truly the bird communicating, but I sense he's willing to engage with me." "What else?", I said. "He says he is small, vulnerable, needs to protect himself. And that he was surprised by us." By asking the few questions to the bird, Sara came to understand that it was not her personally that is "scary" to the bird, nor that he was even scared of us. He was a prey animal caught off guard.

In this brief, empathetic exchange, Sara made noticeably improved contact with herself and another being. She tuned into her body and intuition, recognising that her frequent reactive thoughts and projections go un-checked, robbing sovereignty from others as well as herself. She began understanding how this process inhibits contact, presence, and intimacy in her relationships. On this day, Sara learned from the bird, not about the bird.

Considering the four models of engaging with nature, what are some interventions you could create with your unique clients and bioregion? Naturally, these will vary depending on your terrain, population, access, cultural norms, skill, and interest levels. Additional opportunities for your collaboration with the natural world that are not specifically spoken here but that could be considered include mindfulness in nature, dreamwork, myth and storytelling, primitive skills, nature art, deep somatic therapies, earthing, and practices specific to cultural traditions such as drumming or ceremonies. Hopefully, this engagement model and the stories within will expand your sense of what is possible for you and generate ideas for relational and therapeutic experientials.

CONCLUSION

Relationship with nature is an essential part of a healthy, balanced life for Homo sapiens. Deepening understanding of human ecology and embracing new levels of eco-literacy enhance therapeutic creativity and supports alignment with our natural functioning and intelligence. Amidst epidemic-levels of mental health disorders and increasing global ecological crises, therapists willing to un-domesticate their therapy can be powerful catalysts in the healing of both people and the planet. I hope professionals across the human service fields will be inspired trust in the generative powers of nature and ethically implement active, nature-based approaches in their work.

SUGGESTED READING

As an addendum, I would like to briefly acknowledge additional, ethical considerations in nature therapy practices. Important topics not addressed in this essay include but are not limited to: confidentiality; ableism; cultural appropriation; collective, intergenerational trauma of indigenous people;

the meaning of nuanced terms such as "nature" and "wild" to different ethnicities and populations; the colonial position of "using" nature for the benefit of humans often found in research language; and a possible perception that this approach is a romantic panacea in light of my western, privileged viewpoint. To fill in such gaps, I encourage further reading on these ethical subjects prior to engaging in nature-based therapies. Some reading suggestions include:

I. Hooley (2016). "Ethical Considerations for Psychotherapy in Natural Settings." *Ecopsychology*, 8(4), 215-221.

A.T. Jones and D.S. Segal (2018). "Unsettling Ecopsychology: Addressing Settler Colonialism in Ecopsychology Practice." *Ecopsychology*, 10(3), 127-136.

D. Mitten (1994). "Ethical Considerations in Adventure Therapy: A Feminist Critique." *Women & Therapy*, 15(3-4), 55-84.

A.C. Anthony (1995). Ecopsychology and the Deconstruction of Whiteness." In T.E. Roszak, M.E. Gomes, and A.D. Kanner. *Ecopsychology: Restoring the Earth, Healing the Mind.* San Francisco: Sierra Club Books, p. 264.

REFERENCES

Ainsworth, M. (1978). *Patterns of Attachment: A Psychological Study of the Strange Situation.* Lawrence Erlbaum Associates, Hillsdale, NJ.

Hillman, J. (1995). A Psyche the Size of the Earth. In T. Roszak, A. Kanner and M. Gomes (eds) *Ecopsychology: Restoring the Earth and Healing the Mind.* Sierra Club Books, London.

Kidner, D. (2007). Depression and the Natural World: Towards a critical ecology of distress. *Critical Psychology* 19, 123-146.

Searles, H. (1960). *The Nonhuman Environment: In Normal Development and in Schizophrenia.* International Universities Press, New York.

Seltenrich, N. (2015). *Just What the Doctor Ordered: Using Parks to Improve Children's Health.* Environmental Health Perspectives Vol. 123, No. 10.

Shepard, P. (1995). Nature and Madness. In T. Roszak, A. Kanner and M. Gomes (eds) *Ecopsychology: Restoring the Earth and Healing the Mind.* Sierra Club Books, London.

Winnicott, D. (1951). Transitional objects and transitional phenomena. In D. Winnicott (1958) *Collected Papers: Through Pediatrics to Psycho-Analysis.* Tavistock, London.

Chapter 17:
CONCLUSION

MEG KIRBY

CONCLUSION

I trust that you have been Nourished as you have journeyed through this book.

I am hopeful you have experienced some sparks of excitement, inspiration, resonance, and hope.

This book is my gift to you.

My heart's desire was to bring together diverse international education experts and passionate voices in the fields of equine assisted psychotherapy, animal assisted therapy, and nature-based therapy, to teach, demonstrate and showcase a way forward. A Way towards New Awareness, Relationship, Healing, and Deep Connection.

I truly hope this book lights a fire inside you.

Together, let's cultivate our aliveness, connection and capacity to thrive, and invite the wisdom of all animals and the natural world to guide us Home. You are Animal. You are Nature. You have the innate capacity to contribute in profoundly healing ways to the future of our humanity and planet.

Let's do this together.

Meg Kirby

www.ingramcontent.com/pod-product-compliance
Lightning Source LLC
Chambersburg PA
CBHW051616030426
42334CB00030B/3215